Remembering the Modoc War

REMEMBERING THE

Modoc War

*Redemptive Violence and the Making of
American Innocence*

Boyd Cothran

The University of North Carolina Press / Chapel Hill

*First Peoples
New Directions in Indigenous Studies*

PUBLICATION OF THIS BOOK WAS MADE POSSIBLE, IN PART, BY A
GRANT FROM THE ANDREW W. MELLON FOUNDATION.

Manufactured in the United States of America
Set in Miller types by codeMantra
The paper in this book meets the guidelines for permanence and durability
of the Committee on Production Guidelines for Book Longevity of the Council on
Library Resources. The University of North Carolina Press has been a member
of the Green Press Initiative since 2003.

Library of Congress Cataloging-in-Publication Data
Cothran, Boyd.
Remembering the Modoc War : redemptive violence and the making of American
innocence / Boyd Cothran. — 1st edition.
pages cm. — (First peoples: new directions in indigenous studies)
Includes bibliographical references and index.
ISBN 978-1-4696-1860-9 (cloth : alk. paper)
ISBN 978-1-4696-3334-3 (pbk. : alk. paper)
ISBN 978-1-4696-1861-6 (ebook)
1. Modoc Indians—Wars, 1873. I. Title.
E83.87.c67 2014
979.4004'974122—dc23   2014009209

Part of this book has been reprinted in revised form from "Exchanging Gifts
with the Dead: Lava Beds National Monument and Narratives of the Modoc War,"
International Journal of Critical Indigenous Studies 4, no. 1 (2011): 30–40.

To Tanya

Contents

PROLOGUE / A Tour of the Lava Beds, 1

INTRODUCTION / Marketplaces of Remembering, 8

PART I: REPORTING

1 / The Sensational Press, 29

2 / The Red Judas, 50

CODA / American Innocence in My Inbox, 76

PART II: PERFORMING

3 / Pocahontas of the Lava Beds, 81

CODA / A Drive through Settler Colonial History, 106

PART III: COMMEMORATING

4 / The Angels of Peace and Progress, 113

5 / Faithful Americans, 141

6 / Redemptive Landscapes, 162

CODA / An Outlaw to All Mankind, 184

EPILOGUE / Exchanging Gifts with the Dead, 187

Notes, 199

Bibliography, 221

Acknowledgments, 235

Index, 239

Figures

1 / Canby's Cross, Lava Beds National Monument, 5

2 / "Signature of the Modoc Chief the Evening before His Execution," 11

3 / Photograph of Captain Jack by Louis H. Heller, 12

4 / Wood engravings of the Modoc prisoners based on Louis H. Heller's photographs, 13

5 / The Klamath Basin in the nineteenth century, 17

6 / "The Modocs—Murder of General Canby," 51

7 / "Oregon—The Modoc War—Captain Jack and His Followers Checking the Advance of Union Troops in the Lava-Beds," 54

8 / "The Modocs in Their Stronghold," 55

9 / "The Head of the Nation's Nightmare," 58

10 / "Modocs Scalping and Torturing Prisoners," 60

11 / "The Two Vultures," 61

12 / "Uncle Sam Hunting for the Modoc Flea in His Lava Bed," 62

13 / "Alfred B. Meacham Lecture Company," 89

14 / "Winema and Her Son Jeff," 91

15 / Title Page of Alfred B. Meacham, *Wi-ne-ma (The Woman-Chief) and Her People*, 94

16 / "Opening a New Empire," 123

17 / The Klamath Basin Project, 1904–1970, 129

18 / "The Old and the New Way," 133

19 / "The Author and Wife, Jeff C. Riddle & Manda," 138

20 / Dedication of the Golden Bear Monument by the Native Daughters of the Golden West, Lava Beds Monument, June 13, 1926, 163

21 / "Trip to the Lava Beds: Ivan and Alice Applegate at Canby's Cross at Lava Beds," 167

22 / "Grave of Warm Springs Scouts," 180

Remembering the Modoc War

Prologue

A TOUR OF THE LAVA BEDS

It smelled of wet dirt and sage. I was standing in the blacktopped parking lot of Captain Jack's Stronghold, a popular historic site in Lava Beds National Monument, just a few miles south of the border between California and Oregon. It was the summer of 2008. It was nine o'clock. And I was waiting for Modoc historian Cheewa James. Two weeks earlier, I had arrived in nearby Klamath Falls, hoping to learn more about the Modoc War, California's so-called last Indian war. My plan was to poke around some local libraries, get the lay of the land, meet with the Klamath Tribes' culture and heritage and public information managers, and, with any luck, speak to a few Klamath tribal historians and elders. But things were moving slowly. Meetings were missed, and the library was open only a few hours a day. So when Todd Kepple, manager of the Klamath County Museum, invited me to a join him and a few others on a guided history tour of the region with a Modoc historian and some of her family members, I jumped at the opportunity. We agreed to meet in the Lava Beds.

Encompassing some forty-six thousand acres in far northeastern California, Lava Beds National Monument is the federally administered name for the ancestral home of the Modocs. For thousands of years, they used every inch of what is now the park for some purpose, to the extent that one simply cannot discuss Modoc history without the Lava Beds. But though they were central to the Modocs' conception of an ancestral, managed territoriality, that relationship was profoundly altered by the five-month-long peace negotiation turned campaign of extermination known today as the Modoc War. The conflict began on November 29, 1872, when soldiers of the U.S. Army attempted to arrest the Modoc headman Kintpuash, or Captain Jack, as he was more often known, and his followers and return them

1

to the Klamath Reservation in southern Oregon. The Modocs, together with the Klamaths and the Yahooskin Paiutes, had been party to the Treaty of 1864, which reserved more than one million acres of land from their original claim of more than twenty million acres in the Klamath Basin. In exchange, they were to receive thousands of dollars in supplies over the next fifteen years and the government's protection from Euro-American settlers. When the promised supplies failed to arrive and conditions on the cold, rocky Klamath Reservation proved intolerable, Jack and some three hundred other Klamath Basin Indians left the reservation and repudiated the treaty. In the fall of 1872, the federal government sent soldiers to the Indian villages on the banks of K̲óketat,[1] or the Lost River, as settlers called it, and the Modocs resisted. In the fight that ensued, several soldiers were killed or wounded, as were at least fourteen Euro-American settlers in the surrounding countryside. Escaping with only a handful of casualties, the Modocs took shelter in a series of highly defensible caves along the south shore of Móatokni É-ush—the center of the Modoc universe, where Gmu-kamps, the Creator, shaped the world out of mud from the bottom of the lake. Known today as Tule Lake, the ancient shores of Móatokni É-ush were where our guided tour was to begin.

The first to arrive, I didn't have to wait long before a line of cars appeared over the still-green sagebrush-and-pumice horizon. And as the caravan pulled up, I saw Cheewa James emerge from a black sedan. James is an energetic and animated storyteller. A keynote speaker and corporate trainer, she exudes the kind of confidence that can fill any space. She had come to the Klamath Basin from Sacramento to celebrate the publication of her recent book, a history of the Modocs and their experiences during the war and subsequent exile in Oklahoma. For many of her friends and family, this was their first visit to the Lava Beds. But for James, it was a kind of homecoming. She had spent two years working in the park as a National Park Service ranger-interpreter in the mid-1980s—the first and only Modoc, she says, to don a ranger hat and wear a park service badge.[2] And for those two years, she had led tours through the park, recounting the history of the Modoc War, three times a week.

"What most people don't recognize is that this was their home," James explained as we entered the rugged complex of caves and lava flows known as the Stronghold to survey the battlegrounds. "When we get inside, realize that 150 men, women, and children lived in there. It wasn't just 53 warriors who faced nearly a thousand soldiers of the U.S. Army, but their families too."[3] And for James, like most other Klamath Basin Indians, the Modoc War is very much a family history and one that still matters today. James's great-grandfather, Shkeitko, or Shacknasty Jim—so named, it is believed, because his mother was a poor housekeeper—fought in the war and her grandfather, Clark James, was born in a cave during the war. As a child, she had also learned stories of the war from one of its last survivors, Jennie Clinton. For Klamath Basin Indians, the Modoc War is an exceptional conflict that marks each of their lives. But for all Americans, it remains a pivotal moment, too, whether they know it or not.

Long overshadowed in the nation's historical memory by events such as the Sand Creek Massacre, the death of Lieutenant Colonel George Armstrong Custer at the Battle of Greasy Grass, and the Massacre at Wounded Knee, the Modoc War was in fact one of the most important conflicts of nineteenth-century American expansion. In 1888, historian Hubert Howe Bancroft called it "the most remarkable [war] that ever occurred in the history of aboriginal extermination," while anthropologist Jeremiah Curtin signaled its enduring significance when he wrote in 1912, "The majority of Americans know who the Modocs are and where they live, for on a time their bravery and so-called treachery gave them widespread notoriety."[4] Remarkable and notorious, the Modoc War was unlike many episodes of nineteenth-century U.S.-Indian violence. It wasn't over in a day or a week but consumed the nation's attention for months, and as a result, it was characterized by intractable negotiations between the federal government and the Modocs and by intense newspaper coverage with only periodic if nonetheless profound incidents of violence. At issue were the Modocs' desire to remain in the Lost River area and their refusal to return to the Klamath Reservation. But Euro-American settlers also desired the land and so pressured the state and federal governments to insist that the Modocs had violated the treaty, which, the settlers maintained, had extinguished the tribe's right to the land. Moreover, a grand jury in Jacksonville, Oregon, had indicted several Modocs for "murdering" the fourteen settlers during the attempted arrest. Following another crushing defeat of the military by the Modocs in January, the government appointed a peace commission to negotiate a settlement. For a little over two months, the commission, chaired by Alfred Meacham, Oregon's former superintendent of Indian affairs, and advised by Major General Edward R. S. Canby, commander of the Department of the Columbia, met with Jack and members of his tribe to discuss terms. Ostensibly under a flag of truce, the U.S. Army nonetheless continued to build its forces and to surround the Modocs' position, moving troops closer with each passing week.

Touring the Stronghold in 2008, it was easy to see why the Modocs chose this spot for their defense and how they had forced the federal government to negotiate. Razor-sharp rocks and jagged pillars surround it, hidden drops and confusing trails dead-end most approaches to the higher ground of the Stronghold. As we wound our way through the place, James recounted stories of the Modocs' valor. She showed us where they built fortifications, marked their escape routes, cooked their meals, slept, and told stories like how Gmukamps created the Klamath Basin Indians out of bones taken from the house of spirits. This story, as told to Jeremiah Curtin by Koalakaka in 1884, probably sustained the beleaguered defenders through its jingoistic message. Gmukamps named each people as he threw the bones, calling the Shasta "good fighters," the Pitt River and Warm Springs Indians "brave warriors"; but to the Klamath Indians, who during the Modoc War aided the U.S. Army to some extent and lost several battles alongside them, Gmukamps said, "You will be like women, easy to frighten." And to the Modocs, whom he created last, he said, "You will eat what I eat, you will keep my place when I am gone, you will be bravest of all. Though you may be few, even if many and many people come against you, you will kill them."[5] Stories, then, nourished the Modocs throughout the war, but so, too, did dance. Indeed, during the war, they built a ceremonial circle in the Stronghold where they could dance at night in the sight of the major sacred peaks of the Modoc world: Schonchin Butte, Horse Mountain, Medicine Lake Highlands, Sheepy Ridge, and the great Mount Shasta. Standing there 135 years later, I could still sense the power of the place and of those revered sites.

But as our group emerged from the Stronghold and moved across the road through a short expanse of sagebrush and gravel, we entered a very different kind of space. In a clearing about half a mile from the Stronghold there stands, towering overhead, a large white cross held in place by a cairn of lava rocks with the inscription "Gen Canby USA was Murdered Here by the Modocs April 11, 1873" in black, hand painted lettering (figure 1). And indeed, it was here that the Modoc War became a national and international sensation when the Modocs attacked the peace commission during negotiations, killing two of its members, General Canby and the Reverend Eleazer Thomas, and wounding a third, Alfred Meacham. Decried by the press and government officials as "murder" and "base treachery," the attack on the peace commissioners resulted in government officials' calls for the Modocs' "utter extermination." On April 15, the army attacked the Modocs' encampment and forced them from the shores of Tule Lake. The Modoc War ended six weeks later when Jack and a handful of followers

Figure 1. Canby's Cross, Lava Beds National Monument. Photo by author.

surrendered on the banks of Willow Creek, a site our tour group had visited before coming to the Lava Beds.

From Canby's Cross, we proceeded up a slight incline toward Gillem's Bluff, a site of rich oral tradition and ritual importance known as Sheepy Ridge to the Modocs. During the siege of the Stronghold, the ridge served as a strategic location for U.S. troops, who established their headquarters at its base with gun placements above for their howitzers and a burial ground to the south. These uses by the military, it was said, destroyed the sanctity of the place; many Modoc families who once used the area for ritual and ceremony never returned after the war.[6] James led the tour through these sites, explaining how the Army's strategy had been thrown off by the terrain and by their Civil War–era tactics. But I lost interest in this part of the story and fell back to take a second look at that cross.

Contemplating Canby's Cross alone, I was surprised that such a memorial to the Modoc War had persisted. Freighted with the victimization imagery of Christian martyrdom and clear in its accusatory language, the memorial left little room for alternative readings. Canby was the true victim of the Modoc War. He was the country's innocent Christian martyr, and the Modocs had murdered him. They were the criminals, the aggressors, the Judases. It struck me as a throwback to an earlier, less culturally enlightened and sensitive era. "Why had this been permitted to remain?"

I asked myself. A helpful National Park Service sign nearby sought to explain:

> Although the inscription on the cross may elicit strong emotions in some modern visitors, it illuminates the point that people see events through the lens of their own culture and time. In 1873, what some Modocs considered a justifiable war tactic, the U.S. Army considered murder. No monument commemorates the places where Modocs may have felt their attempts to live peaceably were betrayed.
>
> More than any other Modoc War site, Canby's Cross represents the vast gulf between the perceptions of the two sides during wartime, and challenges us to look beyond history to the assumptions of our own cultures. As in all wars, there were no innocent parties in this conflict.

These historical explanations for the enduring presence of this memorial got me thinking about the nature of innocence and the meaning of the past.

Our interpretations of history change over time, sometimes because new information emerges, new documents are discovered, new artifacts are unearthed, but more often because our sensibilities have changed and because when we look to the past from the vantage point of the present, we see things differently. "The past is a screen upon which each generation projects its vision of the future," wrote Carl Becker, a prolific writer, historian, and polymath who always considered his investigation into the meaning of history his greatest achievement.[7] "History is the memory of things said and done," he further explained in his 1931 presidential address to the American Historical Association. But there are always two histories, he said, "the actual series of events that once occurred; and the ideal series that we affirm and hold in memory. The first is absolute and unchanged. . . . The second is relative, always changing."[8] Historical facts (that which happened) and historical interpretations (the meanings, values, and associations we assign to those occurrences) cannot be reconciled.

This book investigates the gulf that necessarily exists between these two kinds of histories. It is a history of the Modoc War of 1872–73, one of the most costly Indian wars ever fought by the United States in both lives and resources.[9] It is a history of violence in northern California and southern Oregon's Klamath Basin, and as such it tells a familiar story of military conquest, economic incorporation, cultural suppression, domestic upheaval, and political betrayal. But it is also a history of the history of the Modoc War. It is a story about how generations of Klamath, Modoc, Paiute, and Warm Springs Indian men and women, along with their

Euro-American settler neighbors, have remembered episodes such as the Modoc War since the nineteenth century. This book, then, is concerned with both the past and the present, with what actually happened and with the "foreshortened and incomplete representations,"[10] which have given meaning to the past in the present.

"People see events through the lens of their own time," the National Park Service reminds visitors to the Lava Beds who might be shocked by the message of Canby's Cross. This sentiment underscores a central theme of this book, which challenges us all to look beyond history to the assumptions that structure Americans' understandings of their own past. But as to the interpretative sign's last point: "As in all wars, there were no innocent parties in this conflict": that is a much more complicated and complex assertion. Indeed, one of the fundamental objectives of this book is to interrogate the nature of innocence and its uses as well as its persistence and prevalence in American history and, in particular, in the history of nineteenth-century U.S.-Indian violence. Because if one thing was abundantly clear to all Americans following Jack's surrender in 1873, it was who was innocent and who was guilty, who was a criminal and whose laws were just, who was civilized and who was savage.

Our tour though Lava Beds National Monument had left me wanting to know more about the Modoc War and the people who told and retold its history. I wanted to know more about this place, the people involved, and how this often-overlooked conflict fits into Americans' understandings of their history. I wanted more time to consider the nature of history and of memory and of innocence. But by the time I had finished contemplating Canby's Cross, Cheewa James and the rest of the group were on their way to the visitor center for some lunch. And I had to hurry to catch up.

MARKETPLACES OF
REMEMBERING

The sun rose bright and early on the morning of Friday, October 3, 1873. The clear, cool night had left a dusting of autumn frost on the ponderosa and lodgepole pines around Fort Klamath, a remote military outpost some fifty miles north of the California border in southern Oregon's Klamath Basin. The smell of bacon grease and coffee filled the morning air as the soldiers prepared the duties of the garrison half an hour earlier than usual. Lieutenant George W. Kingsbury, post adjutant, expected a large crowd for the day's spectacle.

Propelled by curiosity and a desire to witness the final act of the Modoc War, a drama that had captivated the nation for nearly a year, visitors had been arriving for more than a week. Many were farmers and ranchers from the surrounding valleys or merchants, lawyers, and craftsmen from the nearby towns of Ashland, Medford, and Yreka. Others had come from much farther afield. Tourists from across the country had made the difficult journey to the Northwest. Leonard Case Jr., a Cleveland philanthropist and future benefactor of Case Western Reserve University, had undertaken the arduous journey along with his assistant, Henry Abbey, as did at least three prominent businessmen from Pittsburgh. Special correspondents representing the *New York Herald, Chicago Inter Ocean, New York Times, San Francisco Chronicle, San Francisco Evening Bulletin, San Francisco Call-Bulletin,* and the Associated Press had also been dispatched to cover the day's events in minute detail. Based on media coverage alone, it was one of the most anticipated public executions of the 1870s.[1] In all, about 200 soldiers, 150 other Euro-Americans, and more

8

than 500 Klamath Basin Indians had assembled to witness the hanging of Modoc headman Captain Jack and his five alleged coconspirators. They were to die for the "murders, in violation of the laws of war," of General Edward R. S. Canby, commander of the Department of the Columbia, and the Reverend Eleazer Thomas.[2]

At approximately nine o'clock in the morning, Fort Klamath's soldiers assembled on the parade ground. Once the artillery and cavalry mounted, they all proceeded to the guardhouse. Loading the alleged criminals onto a wagon, the troops escorted the condemned men to a scaffold some four hundred yards south of the stockade while the band played the "Dead March" on muffled drums. The scaffold was an impressive structure. Thirty feet long and made of dressed pine logs each a foot in diameter, it was capable of hanging all of the condemned at once. The previous day, Captain George B. Hoge, the officer of the day, had demonstrated the gibbet's trapdoors and the strength of its ropes and beams for the benefit of the garrison's guests.[3] Arriving at the scaffold, Lieutenant Colonel Frank Wheaton, commanding officer of Fort Klamath, ordered Captain Jack, Schonchin John, Black Jim, and Boston Charley to mount the platform. But the colonel told the two remaining prisoners, Barncho and Slolux, to stay on the ground in front of the stockade. The soldiers had dug six graves and prepared six coffins, but only four men would die that day. Three weeks earlier, Wheaton had received word that President Ulysses S. Grant had commuted the two younger men's sentences to imprisonment for life on Alcatraz Island. As President Abraham Lincoln had commuted the death sentences of 264 of the 303 Sioux prisoners following the Dakota War of 1862 to appear merciful, Grant's commutations were meant to demonstrate the state's judicious application of justice. But Wheaton had kept this information from the prisoners until the day of the execution.[4]

With this act of clemency completed, the remaining Modoc prisoners sat on chairs above the scaffold's trapdoors before the audience as Lieutenant Kingsbury read their sentences aloud. Then the chaplain of Fort Klamath offered a prayer for the condemned men's souls as the executioner and his assistants placed the nooses around their necks and the black hoods over their heads. At approximately 10:20 A.M., a captain made a signal with his handkerchief, the executioner cut the rope holding the trapdoors closed, and, in the words of one observer, "the bodies swung round and round, Jack and Jim apparently dying easily, but Boston and Schonchin suffering terrible convulsions."[5] From their cells behind the stockade, the wives and children of the condemned broke into anguished wails as a stifled cry of horror rose forth from many of the Indians in attendance.[6] A quarter of an hour later, the condemned men's bodies swung lifelessly in the air.

■ The army had carefully choreographed the execution of Captain Jack and the other Modocs from start to finish. A gruesome commerce in mementos followed. For several days, visitors to the stockade had bartered with the prisoners for various trinkets, including hats, moccasins, necklaces, and other kinds of jewelry.[7] Robert Nixon, the editor of the *Yreka Journal*, bought Schonchin John's hat and a pistol belonging to another Modoc and sent them to the California Society of Pioneers as "valuable mementoes" to be "preserved as curiosities of the history of California."[8] The night before the execution, an entrepreneurial officer visited Captain Jack and procured a dozen autographs, which he later sold. These souvenirs circulated for years among private collectors and institutions, accruing symbolic and pecuniary significance: in 2005, the Klamath County Museum paid $5,449 at auction for one of Jack's autographs (figure 2).[9]

After the execution, the mementos became more grotesque. Captain Hoge sold lengths of the hangman's ropes and locks of the dead men's hair for five dollars apiece, the proceeds to be shared among the officer corps. These souvenirs, too, proved quite popular, and their dissemination suggests just how many U.S. museums and archives were born out of the violence of Indian subjugation and removal in the West. Thomas Cabaniss, a surgeon in Yreka, purchased segments of the ropes that hanged Captain Jack and Schonchin John as gifts for a friend, Dr. Flemming G. Hearn, a dentist and prominent gold prospector in the Yreka area. The State of California later purchased Hearn's extensive cabinet of so-called Indian curiosities for twenty-five hundred dollars and exhibited the ropes at Sutter's Fort in Sacramento, where they remained until the 1970s when the museum removed the artifacts from display after receiving complaints.[10] Daniel Ream, a former sheriff, a tax collector, and a future state representative, bought Captain Jack's personal effects, including his coat and a pair of gloves. R. W. Hanna, a Standard Oil executive, later acquired these items and in 1929 donated them to the University of California's Museum of Anthropology collection.[11] Together with the nooses, these souvenirs are today part of the California Indian Heritage Center's permanent collection.

Few items escaped the grasp of the determined souvenir hunters. Several claimed bits and pieces of the gallows itself. One spectator refashioned his white-pine souvenir into a gavel, a grisly relic he wielded for

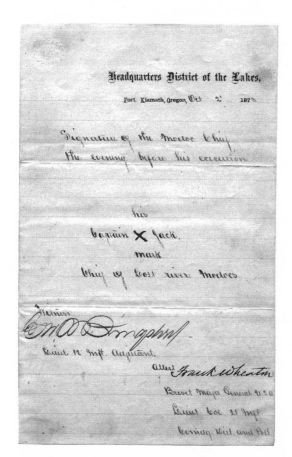

many years as the commander of the Oregon Department of the Grand Army of the Republic.[12] Even the condemned men's physical remains became commodities. Sheriff McKenzie of Jefferson County reportedly offered Colonel Wheaton as much as ten thousand dollars for Captain Jack's body to display as a warning to neighboring Indigenous communities that might consider armed resistance in the future.[13] But the sheriff was frustrated in his efforts, for the remains had become the property of the U.S. government. The condemned men's heads were removed after the hanging, placed in a barrel of spirits, and shipped to the Army Medical Museum in Washington, D.C. Preserved for scientific study, they became part of the Smithsonian Institute's "People of the United States" archaeological collection in 1904 and remained there for eight decades.[14]

The commerce in mementos extended beyond the physical remnants of the condemned to include visual reproductions of their bodies. In the decades after the Civil War, photography combined with public acts of

I certify that L. HELLER has this day taken the Photographs of the above Modoc Indians, prisoners under my charge.
Capt. C. B. THROCKMORTON, 4th U. S. Artillery, Officer of the Day.
I am cognizant of the above fact.   GEN. JEFF. C. DAVIS, U. S. A.
Published by WATKINS, Yosemite Art Gallery, 22 & 26 Montgomery St., opp. Lick House

Figure 3. Photograph of Captain Jack by Louis H. Heller, 1873. WA Photos 2; courtesy of Klamath County Museum, Klamath Falls, Ore.

vigilante violence to produce an exceptional brand of American terrorism we most often associate with the Ku Klux Klan. But lynching photography was not limited to the South. It was also prevalent in the West. And perhaps that is why the most popular mementos from the execution of Jack and the other Modocs were Louis H. Heller's postcard-sized souvenir cabinet cards. A photographer based in Yreka, Heller visited the Modocs in their jail cell and transformed their images into miniature portraits (figure 3). Sold for four dollars a dozen and widely available in San Francisco, Yreka, and Portland, the images included a statement from the officer overseeing the Modocs' imprisonment certifying their authenticity. These mementos, like their Jim Crow–era counterparts, often were later displayed in household parlor collections as well as alongside lurid accounts of the execution in popular periodicals such as *Frank Leslie's Illustrated Newspaper* and *Harper's Weekly* (figure 4).[15]

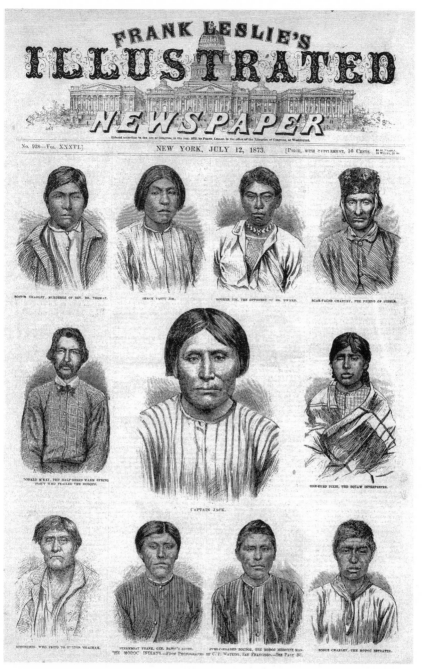

Figure 4. Wood engravings of the Modoc prisoners based on Louis H. Heller's photographs. From Frank Leslie's Illustrated Newspaper, *July 12, 1873.*

Produced with the intention of preserving the condemned men's like-nesses, these ersatz trophies appropriated and rearticulated their bodies, transforming their images into objects of display. But these souvenirs and mementos constituted more than mere curios. While it is tempting to read the buying and selling of these objects as a grotesque by-product of vigilante justice in some figurative Wild West, the effect these exchanges have had on how events like the Modoc War were remembered is far more dense and thorny than such a reading allows.

A noose, a lock of hair, a dead man's jacket, his photograph: this book contends that historical remembrances of nineteenth-century U.S.-Indian violence have been made and remade through the circulation of such cul-tural and memorial objects in commercial marketplaces. These patterns of circulation and commodification transformed horrific objects from suitable souvenirs to trophies for display and finally to historical artifacts of considerable cultural and material value. In this way, the supposedly invisible hand of the marketplace amplified the economic and cultural logics embedded within the spectacle of a public execution, in the process transforming traces of brutal violence into commodity goods.[16]

The marketplace of macabre memorabilia and the mnemonic and com-mercial dynamics put into play by the execution of Captain Jack and the other Modocs represent an important point of departure for this book. But my interests here are not limited to the realm of souvenir goods alone. Indeed, my examination extends beyond the physical immediacy of ex-ecution memorabilia. The production and consumption of more mun-dane and ephemeral traces of remembering such as newspaper accounts, traveling Indian shows, dime novels, promotional literature, petitions for veterans' benefits, commemorative reenactments, memorial celebra-tions, and even scholarly texts are all part of the networks of exchange and commodification—what I term the marketplaces of remembering—through which we access the past. These processes of commercializa-tion have occurred, of course, within various marketplaces or spaces in which markets operate. These marketplaces have at times been actual, literal places; at other times they have been metaphorical. Either way, they have been sites of negotiation, trade, exchange, accumulation, estimation, agreement, conflict, and deception. These marketplaces of remembering, moreover, were part of the commercialization of everyday life. Born out of the rapid industrialization of the postbellum era, new transportation and communication networks spread across the continent, transform-ing Gilded Age America. Economic changes produced new marketplaces through which people experienced their recent present and formed their perception of the past. And today, these marketplaces continue to shape our understanding of the era. Indeed, separating historical remembrances from the marketplaces within which they circulate and for which they were made is not only counterproductive but also obfuscatory, because it fails to acknowledge the economic pressures these markets have exerted on how we access and use the past in the present. But that is not usually part of the story.

This understanding of historical knowledge production or simply the making of history emerged from my research into the historiography of the Modoc War. This book explores the complex and often-overlooked relationship between how Indigenous and Euro-Americans alike have remembered incidents of U.S.-Indian violence and the marketplaces—the systems, institutions, procedures, social relations, and arenas of trade—within which those remembrances have circulated. In exploring these cultural and commercial associations, I delve into the question of how they have been directly related to the widespread belief that the Modoc War and other incidents of U.S.-Indian violence were justified and to the tendency to view the westward expansion of the United States within the framework of inevitability. Ultimately, I argue that individuals have shaped historical remembrances of the conflict, transforming an episode of Reconstruction-era violence and ethnic cleansing into a redemptive narrative of American innocence as they sought to negotiate these marketplaces. To tell that story, however, we must first consider the history of violence and settler colonialism in the Klamath Basin of southern Oregon and northern California.

▓ The public execution of Captain Jack, Schonchin John, Black Jim, and Boston Charley may have marked the titular end of the Modoc War, but the trajectories of settler colonialism, empire, and violence that gave it shape and poignancy stretched back decades. Indeed, throughout the eighteenth and nineteenth centuries, European and later North American nations expanded and competed over the American West. The expansion, establishment, and exploitation of colonies—a process known as colonization—wreaked havoc on Indigenous populations. Epidemic diseases, ecological devastation, social upheaval, systemic violence, and exploitive labor practices ensued as European and North American settler nations claimed sovereignty over property owned, used, and governed by Indigenous nations. As a result, by the mid-nineteenth century, most North American Indigenous communities were engulfed in processes of settler colonialism, a specific colonial formation involving the elimination of Native populations, the large-scale immigration of settler populations, and the imposition of settler social and cultural conventions, governmental and legal structures, and economic systems of relations.[17] Settler colonialism, then, is the logic that gives meaning to the history of North America and the American West, including the Klamath Basin.

Essentially a linguistically homogenous region, the Klamath Basin was home to three semiautonomous though culturally similar groups of people: the É-ukskni (Klamath people), the Móatokni máklaks (Modoc people), and by the mid-nineteenth century at least one community of Yahooskins and Walpapis (Northern Paiutes). At the beginning of the nineteenth century, the people who would come to be known as the Klamaths lived in four or five semiautonomous political groupings along the rivers, streams, lakes, and marshes of the heavily timbered parts of the Klamath Basin's western edge, while those who would be known as the Modocs lived in three major communities around Móatokni É-ush and the lava beds to the south (figure 5). All communities within the Klamath Basin were bound together by marriage, political alliances, and a shared sense of peoplehood. They all saw themselves as máklaks.[18]

The nineteenth century brought swift changes to the political, economic, and social world of the Klamath Basin. Beginning in the 1770s successive waves of epidemic diseases such as smallpox changed the demographic landscape of southern Oregon and northern California. The adaptation of horses in the 1820s and increases in the Klamaths' slave trade with northern tribes in the 1830s engulfed the region in a period of endemic violence that stratified Klamath Basin society as military leaders supplanted religious leaders, gaining a greater proportion of the region's wealth.[19] The arrival of American colonial settlers in the 1840s further exacerbated these changes. Covered wagons loaded with valuable trade goods lumbering through the sagebrush of the Klamath Basin proved opportune targets, and Klamath and Modoc warriors terrorized American colonists as they traversed the region. Increased militarism between settlers and Klamath Basin Indians produced waves of violence, which in turn altered social structures that further enabled warfare.

The establishment of U.S. settlements in the Klamath Basin corresponded with an escalation of violence throughout California and Oregon in the late 1840s and early 1850s. The killing of Marcus and Narcissa Whitman and the destruction of their Presbyterian mission at Waiilutpa on November 29, 1847, enraged American settler-colonists and became the rationale for years of government-backed vigilante justice and militia offensives against Natives throughout Oregon. The retributive campaign

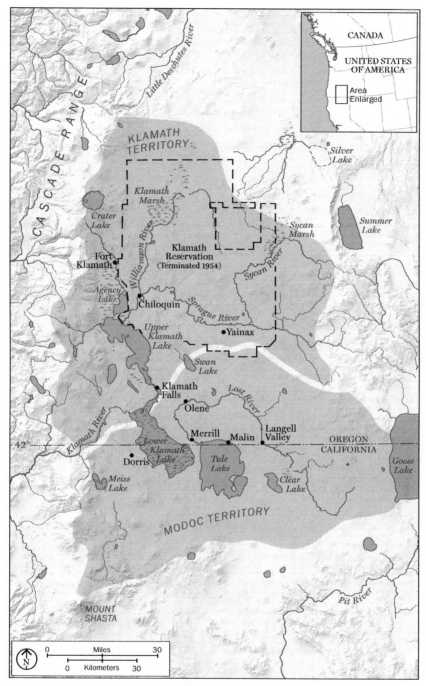

Figure 5. The Klamath Basin in the nineteenth century

known today as the Cayuse War fueled numerous calls for the extermination of Indians throughout the Pacific Northwest. Armed with genocidal
rhetoric and a determination to kill Indigenous people, many Oregonians
brought their destructive views to the goldfields of northern California
after 1848. Murdering Natives in the mining towns of Mariposa, Siskiyou,
and Lake Counties, the settlers repaid a thousandfold any violence perpe-
trated by Indigenous peoples.[20]

Acts of violence against Indians inspired a surge of annihilationist bru-
tality that swept through all of northern California and southern Oregon.
Between 1854 and 1861, the Klamath Basin in particular witnessed a con-
flagration of state-sponsored Indian killing, including the notorious Ben
Wright Massacre and the murderous 1856 Crosby or Modoc Expedition,
which resulted in the deaths of scores if not hundreds of Klamath Basin
Indians and may have been the most lethal California militia expedition in
a very bloody era. The massive demographic decline of American Indians
in California—the Indigenous population plunged from around 150,000
to fewer than 30,000—ended with the Modoc War, a fact that contributed to its dubious distinction as California's so-called last Indian war. Indeed, the death of General Canby triggered what one historian has called
"a final, genocidal phase" of U.S.-Indian violence in the region, a strategy
President Ulysses S. Grant endorsed when he called for the Modocs' "utter
extermination."[21]

Colonial violence reshaped the Klamath Basin in the nineteenth century. It altered community life in the region and pitted Indigenous people
against one another. But was American settler colonialism strictly limited to the physical realm of death and dying? The answer is an emphatic
no. Rather, in the aftermath of the Modoc War, dramatic representations,
novelistic adaptations, personal reminiscences, and academic and antiquarian histories of these colonial conflicts continued the violent reorder-
ing of the world begun by people such as Ben Wright and Ben Crosby.
Encoding U.S.-Indian relations within supposedly self-evident categories
such as the frontier, savagery, development, and progress, these cultural
productions structured Americans' understanding of and relationship to
the past.[22]

History is part of settler colonialism, for history is not just written by the
winners; history helps to create the winners by serving as a tool of colonial
oppression. And only in labeling the writing and circulation of history as
violent can we connect the long-recognized violence of conquest with the
unnamed and normalized violence of writing histories of conquest.[23] In
the context of the Modoc War, settler colonial histories have emphasized

the fundamental innocence of the American character, contributing to the self-image of the United States as neither an expansionist nor a colonial power. Americans have strewn their history with claims to innocence.

But what is innocence? Simply put, innocence is the absence of guilt. An innocent person has performed no crime, committed no sin, participated in no wrongdoings. The notions of individual innocence can be traced back to Greek mythology and early Hebraic writings, if not earlier. But it is associated most often with Judeo-Christian symbols such as the martyr, the lamb, the child, the virgin, and the victim. The innocent, then, are most often portrayed as existing in states before sin, of divine providence, or of righteous victimhood. But innocence does not require inactivity or a state of perpetual loss. Indeed, actions that might otherwise be deemed sinful or wrong may be judged innocent if they are done for reasons of moral outrage, self-preservation, or naïveté or paradoxically to maintain one's innocence. In other words, innocence is both a state of being and a contextual description. And while these conceptions of innocence originated with the individual, they have often become attached to political and social institutions as well. The Puritans, for example, believed that they were establishing a City on the Hill, a beacon to the world of a divinely inspired and innocent new beginning. They deemed the horrendous violence, genocide, and ethnic cleansing they unleashed on colonial North America justified because it was seen as preserving the fundamental innocence of their endeavor.

The myth of American innocence may have originated with the Puritans, but nineteenth-century Americans further developed it as they adopted a theory of the United States as an empire of innocence. Organized under the banner of Manifest Destiny and founded on republican ideas of political freedom stemming from economic freedom, they rationalized a version of history in which the endless—or seemingly endless—expansion of the nation was necessary for the success of their republican experiment. The United States, they insisted, had to expand to maintain its freedom through a culture of broad-based white, male landownership. The inevitable violence resulting from this expansion was thereby justified as innocent, for theirs was, in the words of Thomas Jefferson, an "empire of liberty."[24] If the freedom of the republic depended on the westering impulses of a virtuous yeomanry, any obstacle to that movement or any attack on that citizenry became a threat to the nation itself. Americans, then, were innocent, and their wars of aggression were justified. They were, after all, the victims of frontier violence. And in this context, Indians were the irrational aggressors and violators of a civilized nation's just laws.[25]

Developed in the nineteenth century to justify and enable the conquest of Indigenous peoples and the colonization of the American West, innocence soon became an enduring script in American history, not limited to the Indian wars. Indeed, in the twentieth and twenty-first centuries, narratives of American innocence proved to be highly communicable concepts. From the explosion of the *Maine* in Havana Harbor (1898) and the sinking of the *Lusitania* by a German U-boat (1915), to the Balangiga Massacre in the Philippines (1901), the bombing of the Pacific fleet in Pearl Harbor (1941), the Gulf of Tonkin incident in Vietnam (1964), and the destruction of the World Trade Center on September 11, 2001, allegedly unprovoked assaults on supposedly innocent American citizens or service personnel have been used to justify belligerent policies and wars of aggression throughout the long twentieth century. The perseverance of these historic and nationalistic narratives, then, can be observed in the tendency of Americans to view their wars as defensive conflicts.

Persistent claims to innocence have permitted the United States to pursue its domestic and foreign policies as well as enabled its citizens to live in a state of touristic indifference. "The tourist is a figure who embodies a detached and seemingly innocent pose," writes cultural critic Marita Sturken. The tourist's subjectivity is that of an observer, with an experience of the past mediated through consumerism and popular culture. History, for the tourist, is something to be consumed and experienced through site visits, images, souvenirs, and other commodities. By assuming a touristic subjectivity, Sturken contends, Americans inscribe narratives of exceptionalism onto traumatic events and then reduce complex historical narratives to consumable objects, which enable naive political responses.[26]

This retreat to aloof voyeurism can be observed in the consumer culture of the Indian wars. Through the depiction of Indians in the Gilded Age popular press or on the lyceum lecture stage, newspapermen as well as performers such as P. T. Barnum and his famous traveling museum of so-called freaks and William "Buffalo Bill" Cody's Wild West Show blended history with discourses of American innocence and Indian savagery to convince white Americans that they were the victims of the Indian wars and not in fact the victorious aggressors.[27] Books, photographs, paintings, films, reenactments, and commemorations likewise reduced the complex and political nature of the Indian wars to consumable objects. Through the consumption of history, Americans have made and remade their self-identity as fundamentally innocent through remembering past episodes of violence.

Memory, American innocence, and the marketplace, then, are intricately linked. Indeed, the act of remembering is by its nature performative and deeply imbricated within networks of production, exchange, and commodification. In using the term "marketplaces of remembering," I am describing a particular mode of historical knowledge production in which individuals manipulate the narratives they tell to conform to the markets in which they come to circulate. Rather than dwelling on the social and cultural implications of remembering alone, I am concerned principally with tracing the substantive influences these markets have had in shaping how individuals articulate their understandings of the past. Historical narratives are always social, political, and cultural constructions, but by investigating the fundamentally materialistic nature of remembering the past, I seek to uncover the too-often disregarded influence of capitalism on what we call history.

A materialist understanding of historical knowledge production, however, must first acknowledge the psychological, social, and cultural uses of the past. In the late nineteenth century, postbellum commemorations combined with urbanization and industrialization to fuel Americans' expanding desires for the historical and memorial. From popular art and public commemorations to the proliferation of published works of reminiscence, antiquarianism, and regional and ethnic historical societies, Americans compulsively evoked the past in a self-conscious effort to invent tradition. Indeed, as historian Michael Kammen has observed, "Anyone who probes historical sources for this period will be figuratively assaulted by the nation's arsenal of memory devices and by the astonishing diversity of its stockpile."[28]

The American West provided a fruitful ground for this invention of tradition. Although belief in the uniqueness of the North American frontier had long given meaning and structure to the moral landscape of American history and identity, white Americans around the turn of the twentieth century brought greater intensity to their embrace of the idea of the West, finding in the proliferation of mass culture and historiography a palimpsest on which to inscribe their contemporary political, social, cultural, and economic anxieties.[29] Transforming memories of the violent conquest of American Indians into the "red-blooded realism" of Theodore Roosevelt, Jack London, and Stewart Edward White, Americans celebrated the open spaces, autonomous individualism, personal sacrifice, and masculine heroism endemic to narratives of the American West.[30] Frederick Jackson Turner, Buffalo Bill, and the cult of Custer also spring to mind, but countless other artists, novelists, memoirists, and historians found the American West an alluring wellspring of material for remembrances.[31]

Yet the social, cultural, and political focus of most memory scholarship concerned with the turn-of-the-twentieth-century United States has led historians to overlook the commercialization of the past and to neglect the importance of locating cultural productions within markets. This phenomenon is particularly surprising in the context of Indigenous history. Indeed, no culture in American history has experienced commodification to the degree American Indian cultures have. From Land O'Lakes butter and tobacconist statuaries to Disney films, Halloween costumes, and professional football teams, commoditized representations of American Indian culture and identity suffuse the American consumer landscape.[32] This economic circulation of things Indian has been part of American settler colonialism. And some observers have argued that the commercialization of Indian culture by non-Natives ought to be viewed as an extension of American imperialism and analogous to the wholesale theft of Indigenous lands, resources, and sovereignty.[33]

But the commodification of American Indian cultures has not been a one-way street. Indigenous artisans, writers, actors, guides, motivational speakers, and historians have participated in the commercialization of Indian cultures.[34] And their involvement in these processes of production, distribution, and consumption often brings issues of authenticity and modernity to bear on their role in the marketplace.[35] Many non-Indigenous consumers have imagined Indian cultures as premodern, timeless, natural, traditional, and free of the corrupting market, but Indigenous producers often have cocreated these narratives to protect or enhance the marketability of their goods and services while simultaneously romanticizing and mystifying their own labor.[36] The process by which Natives and Euro-Americans alike have transformed Indian identity, histories, and cultures into marketable goods, in other words, remains a vital and important site for historical investigation.

This book, then, contributes to our understanding of American settler colonialism by exploring the various marketplaces in which both Natives and Euro-Americans have commodified their remembrances of nineteenth-century U.S.-Indian violence. But they have not done so under conditions of their own choosing. Karl Marx's oft-quoted statement that "Men make their own history, but they do not make it as they please . . . but under circumstances existing already" suggests how we might write a history of American settler colonialism that views the production of historical knowledge as itself a category of transformative labor.[37] The literature on memory studies is full of "collective memories," "tangled memories," "chords of memory," and "memory boxes."[38] Memory is said to "sit in places," "reside in objects," and even to create "sites" in which to live.[39] In these formulations, the act of remembering is transformed from a performative representation of the past to an interpretive object, and the analytic thrust is toward reading that object rather than understanding the lives of those who produced it. And we can even see this reflected in our word choice and scholarly discourse: memory is a noun, it is a thing; remembering is a verb, it is an action, a kind of labor in the production of a version of the past.[40]

By examining the material circumstances surrounding the production, distribution, and exchange of individual and collective remembrances, this book explores how historical memories of the Modoc War have been made and remade over the past century and a half. The circulation of historical remembrances within discrete markets has intertwined the conflict and notions of American innocence. And it has provided Americans with an enduring script for understanding their role in global histories of empire and colonialism. But this volume also pays particular attention to the participation of individuals within these marketplaces of remembering and seeks to understand the conditions that have structured the historiography of the Modoc War. By tracing the origins and contours of these various marketplaces of remembering, it makes sense of how Natives have sometimes resisted and sometimes participated in the construction of the ideological and historiographical systems that have maintained and sustained their political and economic marginalization. And in the process, the book offers us a new way of thinking about memory, colonialism, and the American West by focusing our attention on the influence of marketplaces in transforming an episode of ethnic cleansing into a redemptive narrative of American innocence.

■ American innocence is negotiated in what I term the marketplace of remembering. Proceeding chronologically and thematically, the parts of the book explore how different marketplaces have commoditized remembrances of U.S.-Indian violence in the Klamath Basin to sustain and reproduce the myth of American innocence on a grand scale. As a result, remembrances that have circulated widely and between Natives and settler communities often receive greater attention than more intimate memories shared among families or within specific communities. This is not because these cherished stories are trivial. They are important. And they have been essential to my understanding of and relationship with the history of the Klamath Basin. But the story I am telling here focuses on the circulation of historical remembrances within specific marketplaces and the continuation of those memorial practices into the present as a means of critiquing Americans' belief in their fundamental innocence in the face of settler colonial legacies of violence. To that end, I conclude each of the book's three parts with a coda in which I reflect on the presence of the past, connecting the dots among history, the marketplaces of remembering, and American innocence today.

Part I considers the Gilded Age newspaper industry and its coverage of the Modoc War. Throughout the conflict, the media explained this episode of interethnic violence to their readers. Early on, the conflict became enmeshed with the partisan politics of post–Civil War Reconstruction, revealing deep fissures within American society regarding the future of American Indians within the body politic. Newspaper coverage of the conflict shifted following the death of General Canby and others, as the press represented the attack on the peace commissioners through the prism of Christian martyrdom and white victimhood on the frontier. Indeed, by the spring of 1873, the press combined arguments for Indigenous savagery and criminality in their reporting to transform the Modoc War into a spectacle of racial violence that suffused the conflict with a narrative of American innocence.

Part II investigates the immediate aftermath of the war and performances of its history on stage and in books. Indeed, if newspaper coverage of the Modoc War laid the foundation for future historical interpretations, the era's vibrant entertainment industries afforded some of the most enduring embodiments of that narrative. Throughout the 1870s and 1880s, traveling Indian shows, itinerant public lectures, rodeos, circus acts, and patent medicine shows provided popular entertainment for many Americans. Acting out recent historical events with melodramatic license, the symbolic and commercial semiotics of these performances imbued the Modoc War with romantic and reconciliatory overtones. In examining this marketplace of remembering, Part II considers in particular the stage career of Toby Riddle, a Modoc woman who served as a U.S. interpreter during the war, considering how one woman used existing narratives of violence and gendered tropes of savagery and civilization to become an international star, earn a federal pension, and grow to be a local legend. Her prominence in public representations of the Modoc War since the 1870s points to Americans' desire to view episodes of nineteenth-century U.S.-Indian violence as the tragic result of cultural misunderstandings.

Part III moves our story into the twentieth century by tracing three separate threads: property, pensions, and tourism. The Modoc War put the Klamath Basin on the map, but for the next three decades, it remained on the margins of American colonial settlement. Geographically isolated, the advent of the railroad around the turn of the twentieth century coupled with the expansion of the nation's timber industry into the region after 1909 led many residents of the Klamath Basin to embrace the rhetoric of modernization. Expectations of a profound transformation in the Klamath Basin's regional economy from one dominated by small-scale agriculture and ranching to one focused on industrialized timber production, moreover, resulted in competing understandings of the region's history. For Euro-American land promoters and boosters, the Modoc War represented a rupture in the region's history, the beginning of the Klamath Basin's transformation from savagery to civilization, its incorporation into the nation-state, and its embracing of modernity. But for the region's Native peoples, the Modoc War marked their violent suppression and political subjugation. I explore these contradictory understandings of the Modoc War by analyzing the stories people told about the conflict in the midst of dramatic economic and technological change. In so doing, many Euro-Americans clung to a vision of American settler colonialism as benign, benevolent, and beneficial despite protestations to the contrary by Klamath Basin Indian political leaders and tribal historians.

Native leaders may have opposed narratives of reconciliation, especially after promises of economic inclusion proved false, but, as Part III explains, not all Klamath Basin Indians rejected such stories. Indeed, between 1910 and 1940, dozens of Klamath Basin Indians applied for and received veterans' benefits for their service as scouts for the U.S. Army by telling stories that emphasized their service to civilization. Adopting strategies similar to those used by fraternal societies and associations such as the National Indian War Veterans, these Native veterans of the Modoc War, like their non-Native counterparts, sought to produce heroic narratives of progress that reconciled the violence of colonization with notions of inevitability. Yet Native veterans encountered great difficulty in navigating the bureaucratic requirements of the veterans' benefits system. Couching their narratives in the rhetoric of citizenship and service, they reproduced narratives of individual valor in the service of civilization as they sought to monetize their experience within a system dedicated to the myth of American innocence.

The turn of the twentieth century saw dramatic economic change in the Klamath Basin as well as the proliferation of fraternal and sororal societies. Together, these twin impulses found expression in the rise of automobile tourism and Indian war memorialization, which is the subject of the final chapter. Nineteenth-century Americans maintained their claims to innocence by reifying the death of General Canby as a quintessential moment of white victimization at the hands of unlawful Indian violence. The rise of automobile tourism in the 1910s and 1920s expanded this cult of victimhood to include all Euro-American soldiers and settlers. This commemorative work was done by heritage groups, local business leaders and entrepreneurs, and outside investors who surrounded themselves with domesticated representations of modern-day Modoc Indians who had supposedly forgotten the violence of the past. Disentangling the history of memorials and tourism in the Klamath Basin, I argue that monuments and memorials to the Modoc War have reproduced claims to American innocence through the commercialization of white victimhood and Indian outlawry even as they purport to revise historical interpretation through shifting categories of victimhood.

The epilogue extends this critique by exploring the legacy of nineteenth-century U.S.-Indian violence in the late twentieth century through an analysis of a 1988 Indian-inclusive memorial to the casualties of the Modoc War. Using as a starting point a National Park Service–sponsored Symposium on the Modoc War in which all participants were purportedly treated the same, I argue that multiculturalism has in recent decades perpetuated narratives of American innocence while masquerading as a vehicle for reconciliation. By exploring the anthropological and sociological concept of the gift to critique the possibility of historical justice through such commemorative gestures, I suggest that such acts of reparations actually obscure the continuing power imbalances inherent in American settler colonialism while enforcing the obligation to forget ongoing inequalities as the price of inclusion in reconciliatory national narratives. In the end, this book contends that by imagining the Indian wars as cultural rather than political conflicts and that by insisting that atrocities were committed on both sides, multiculturalism has perpetuated the persistent belief in American innocence.

Part One

Reporting

Chapter One

THE SENSATIONAL PRESS

Shortly after three o'clock in the morning on January 20, 1873, the telegraph wires out of Yreka came alive with alarming news for the American public. A courier had arrived to report that Lieutenant Colonel Frank Wheaton and his four hundred soldiers and volunteers had been defeated by perhaps as few as fifty Modoc fighters armed with muskets and revolvers. Wheaton, supported by howitzers, had intended his attack to dislodge the Modocs from their makeshift village along the southern shore of Móatokni É-ush, or Tule Lake, where they had been based since the army's failed attempt to arrest them in November. But dense fog rendered the artillery useless and hindered communications. And the Modocs' intimate knowledge of the perplexing lava beds, their ancestral home, had allowed them to fend off their attackers without suffering a single casualty. A local correspondent for the *San Francisco Chronicle* broke the story: "A Disastrous Assault on Capt. Jack's Camp. The Troops Repulsed With Great Loss ... No Indians Reported Killed ... Long and Bloody Campaign Predicted."[1] Within a week, newspapers throughout the country published similar accounts. By the end of the month, multiple reporters were en route to this remote corner of northern California to cover what would become one of the most deadly and costly Indian wars ever fought by the United States.[2]

"Who are the Modocs, and what is the Modoc war?," asked the *Boston Evening Journal* after publishing reports of fighting in the Klamath Basin.[3] When violence erupted in the region, few Americans had heard of either the Modocs or the Klamath Basin. Between January 1873, when the war became a national story, and April, when the death of General Edward R. S. Canby transformed it into an international sensation, intense newspaper coverage familiarized readers throughout the country with the region's history and informed them about the current state of Indian affairs there. Publishers, editors, journalists, and commentators debated the causes and origins of the conflict. Journalists covered it in great detail. But the changing nature of the Gilded Age newspaper industry meant that political muckraking and shameless self-promotion dominated early coverage, while Indigenous perspectives and more nuanced explanations were marginalized.

The economics of political partisanship defined the newspaper industry in many ways throughout the nineteenth century. Prior to the Civil War, the vast majority of American newspapers were firmly aligned with political parties. Indeed, parties often subsidized the operations of newspapers by providing lucrative government printing contracts as part of the spoils system or even directly paying publishers, editors, and reporters for their loyalty. And politicians got what they paid for. Editors and journalists shaped news stories, features, and editorial commentary to appeal to partisan audiences and unabashedly spread the party's creed to readers. As one nineteenth-century journalist explained, "The power of the press consists not in its logic or eloquence, but in its ability to *manufacture* facts, or to give coloring to facts that have occurred."[4]

In the 1830s and 1840s, the penny press revolution of James Gordon Bennett's *New York Herald* and Horace Greeley's *New York Tribune* began to change the marketplace for news. Partisanship remained strong, especially in smaller markets and in some weeklies. But in larger cities, the difficult aftermath of the Civil War and the grim realities of southern Reconstruction led to the rise of sensationalism and scandal in daily reporting. Indeed, the 1860s and 1870s were a period of greater journalistic independence as newspapers increased their circulation and outgrew their financial dependence on political parties. They replaced partisan sloganeering with boasts about their ideological independence and their editorial reach. As they professionalized, the number of newspapers increased. By 1875, the northern states alone had an estimated six thousand independent journals.[5] Partisanship remained an important aspect of the Gilded Age press, but the industry was undergoing significant change.

Even as this process was still under way, the shift away from political patronage left publishers more dependent on circulation revenue, and the competition for readers was fierce. Publishers and editors drove their reporters to pursue sensational stories with greater intensity. And they boasted about every scoop and every scandal they could claim to have uncovered. The *New York Times*, for example, became famous for its 1870–71 campaign against William "Boss" Tweed and his Tammany Hall political machine. The *New York Herald* similarly garnered wide publicity in 1872 when James Gordon Bennett Jr. sent reporter Henry Morton Stanley to Africa to find Scottish missionary David Livingstone. Fed on a steady diet of political brinkmanship, cowboy adventures, railroad scandals, and salacious Indian wars, the increasing sensationalism of the era's newspaper industry combined with the fierce partisanship of many papers to shape coverage of events such as the Modoc War.

My aim here is to explore how the dynamics of the Gilded Age newspaper industry shaped and influenced historical understandings of the Modoc War as the conflict unfolded. But it cannot be a straightforward and objective account of historical events. Embedded within my analysis is a critique of the era's media marketplace and its relationship to historical memory. Indeed, though clichéd, the axiom that "journalists write the first draft of history" should not be forgotten. Journalists, after all, report on history in the making. They influence how a given community relates to its past or whether it remembers certain events at all. This was especially true in the mid-nineteenth-century United States, when the primary locus of American mythmaking shifted from popular novels to popular journalism.[6] This process changed how historical events were remembered. Indeed, the press became a kind of historical memory sausage factory in which, according to Richard Slotkin, "the raw material of history was immediately processed, conflated with ideology and legendry, and transformed into myth."[7] In other words, newspapers created, represented, transmitted, preserved, and promoted collective constructions of historical events as they unfolded, informing the American populace and influencing policy decisions.

This chapter and the next tell the story of the Modoc War through the lens of the Gilded Age newspaper industry to understand how, from the very beginning, the conflict became embedded with narratives of American innocence. It did so in three overlapping phases that at times blended together. In the first, partisanship combined with the federal government's contentious Indian policy after the Civil War to expose the violence inherent in the Grant administration's approach to Indian affairs. Competing explanations emphasized the social, cultural, and economic origins of the conflict but in each case reinforced notions of American innocence. The second phase of coverage corresponded with the arrival of journalists from across the country and the establishment of the Modoc peace commission in early February. Finding little to cover and stymied by the commission's secrecy, journalists turned to self-promotional stunts and exaggerated or fabricated sensationalism. These methods of report-ing the news had their costs and consequences. By focusing on political scandals and masculine feats of journalistic prowess, the press advanced arguments for American innocence that marginalized the Modocs' moti-vations and obscured Native perspectives even as they complicated and undermined efforts at peace. The third phase of coverage, marked by a spectacle of extreme racial violence, erupted following Canby's death on April 11, 1873 and is considered in greater detail in the next chapter. But first we must consider how the war started and how partisan newspapers exacerbated an already volatile situation.

■ On the morning of November 29, 1872, according to subsequent news-paper accounts, Captain James Jackson, with about thirty-five soldiers from Fort Klamath and a troop of around forty citizens from the nearby town of Yulalóna[8] (Linkville) arrived at the complex of Modoc villages along the banks of Kóketat (Lost River). Captain Jack's Modoc village was located on the south side, along a sharp bend in the river. About half a mile downstream, a second, smaller village was located on the opposite side of the river. Farther downstream was a cluster of cabins occupied by recently arrived Euro-American settlers. Relations between the Modocs and their non-Indigenous neighbors were tenuous, to say the least. In 1864, Jack and the other Modocs had relocated onto the Klamath Reservation. But when the federal government failed to deliver the promised supplies, the Modocs had left the reservation and repudiated the treaty.[9] Returning to live near their traditional winter villages along the Lost River, many found jobs working for local farmers and ranchers. But some Euro-American set-tlers wanted the fertile land along the Lost River. By January 1872, these settlers were pressuring the federal government to arrest Jack and force him and his followers to return to the Klamath Reservation, insisting that the Modocs uphold the requirements of the treaty.[10] In late November, Thomas B. Odeneal, the newly appointed superintendent of Indian affairs in Oregon, requested the assistance of the military. And shortly thereaf-ter, Captain Jackson received his orders: "You are directed to remove the Modoc Indians to Camp Yainax on Klamath Reservation, peaceably if you can but forcibly if you must."[11]

Captain Jackson arrived in Jack's village and caught the Modoc head-man unprepared. With winter approaching and no real desire to fight, Jack initially agreed to return to the reservation. He understood how to negotiate these tense situations. Jack had spent years working with Euro-American settlers, and many of his female relatives had married those settlers. Jack and the other Modocs often visited the town of Yreka, where they worked, traded, and socialized. They even attended holiday celebrations there and joined in saving the settlement when a major fire broke out on the Fourth of July 1871. Like many Klamath Basin Indians, Jack wore American-made shirts and trousers, and like many of the Modocs, he spoke English.[12]

Jack and the other Modocs were prepared to cooperate to some degree. But the situation at Jack's Lost River village turned violent when a scuffle broke out between Lieutenant Frazier A. Boutelle and Chĭkclĭkam-Lupalkuelátko, a Modoc Indian more commonly known by the colorful nickname Scarface Charley. Shots were fired, though accounts differ about who fired first. And in the ensuing battle, the Modocs escaped their villages, seeking refuge among the Lava Beds south of Móatakni É-ush. Although Jack and most of his followers made off with minimal fighting, a group of Modocs from the second village fled downriver, attacking homesteads along the northern and eastern shores of Móatakni É-ush and killing at least fourteen settlers.[13] By evening, news of the botched arrest and deadly aftermath had reached Yreka.

Eager to report any incident of Indian violence, newspapers published their stories before confirming rumors. As a result, confusing and contradictory accounts characterized early reports of what exactly had happened. In page 1 stories, the *Daily Alta California* claimed that the soldiers had killed eighteen Indians, while the *Sacramento Daily Union* reported the number of casualties at fifteen. The fight was described as a "desperate one" in which "nearly all the women and children and some of the warriors and a number of horses were captured." Other newspapers reported that U.S. soldiers had killed Captain Jack.[14] But if the narrative initially portrayed the Lost River fight as an early morning raid on an Indian village, the story shifted as additional details emerged. When news of the settlers' deaths reached the newspapers, various reporters and editors revised their previous assessments. "The Red-Skins Taking Vengeance on White Settlers," announced the *Hartford Daily Courant*, which also declared, "News from the scene of war between the United States troops and the camp of the Modocs shows the trouble is much more serious than at first indicated."[15]

News of the killings spread and tensions escalated as journalists reported on or editors reproduced in full stories that appeared in other publications. Within a few days, newspapers from New York to San Francisco were decrying the "Modoc Massacre" as a "Reign of Terror."[16] Many commentators called for a military response: "The people of Oregon are becoming apprehensive of a general outbreak of the Indians," reported the *New York Times*, which added, "Under these circumstances it behooves the people of Oregon and Washington Territory to be on their guard, and the Government should at once increase the military garrisons throughout the threatened district."[17] Those nearer the Klamath Basin tended to criticize the army for its inaction. "The Modoc war, in the northern part of California, has continued for a longer time than Germany took to overrun France," grumbled the *Gold Hill News* in an early January reference to the Franco-Prussian War. "There is something ludicrous," asserted the southern Oregon paper, "in a small band of sixty or seventy warriors thus setting the United States at defiance."[18]

Public outcry and calls for military action in the press were consistent with the contradictory and contentious nature of federal Indian policy in the 1870s. Following the Civil War and the end of slavery, erstwhile abolitionists such as Lucretia Mott and Wendell Phillips turned their attention to the plight of American Indians and the U.S. Army's strategy of warfare against Indigenous communities in the American West. They advocated a more benign approach to the "Indian question" that sought to remove control of federal Indian policy from the hands of corruptible bureaucrats in favor of the presumably incorruptible oversight of Christian missionaries. Under the pretense of pursuing more peaceful relations with the continent's Indigenous peoples, Congress adopted an approach that favored the establishment of reservations where Indian wards would be far removed from white settlement and under the guidance of Christian missionaries, at least in theory. In this way, Indians might eventually assimilate into the American Christian-capitalist system. Popularly referred to as the "Peace Policy" or "Quaker Policy," the federal government's approach to Indian affairs after Ulysses Grant's inauguration as U.S. president in 1869 sought to balance limited recognition of Indigenous sovereignty with a kind of law-and-order federalism that emphasized separating and isolating Natives from white settlers.[19]

Contested and criticized from the beginning, the Grant administration's Indian policy shifted in the 1870s following the ouster of Ely S. Parker, the first Native American commissioner of Indian affairs, amid accusations of corruption. The results were anything but peaceful. In January 1870, the U.S. Army in Montana slaughtered more than 200 Piegans in the Marias Massacre. Fifteen months later, at Camp Grant in Arizona, a group of Euro-Americans, Mexicans, and Papago Indians killed 144 Apaches in a cold-blooded early morning attack.[20] These episodes of U.S.-Indian violence revealed to many what historian Karl Jacoby terms the "germ of violence" in the logic of the Grant administration's Indian policy. "Those who do not accept this policy will find the new administration ready for a sharp and severe war policy," Grant declared. The government, in other words, would be justified in pursuing total war against any Indians who refused to live "peaceably" within the boundaries of a reservation.[21]

The violence inherent in the logic of the Grant administration's Indian policy had manifested itself before the Modoc War. But the Modoc War differed in important ways. Its protracted nature permitted journalists to cover the conflict as it unfolded. And the public outcry and the direct involvement of the Gilded Age press in promulgating calls for violent retaliation revealed the extent to which the so-called Peace Policy came by 1873 to depend on a severe war policy.

Federal Indian policy aside, the prospect of an Indian war in the Klamath Basin soon became a partisan issue that played out on the pages of the nation's newspapers. California's Republican governor, Newton Booth, for one, refused to provide state funds to raise a company of volunteers to assist the army. "The United States forces are quite strong enough to cope with Captain Jack without any aid from the States," he believed.[22] Instead, the governor, observing that the Commerce Clause of the Constitution placed Indians under federal jurisdiction, proposed that the federal government provide Jack and his Modocs with a separate and smaller reservation in Oregon's Lost River Valley.[23]

But many Oregonians, including LaFayette Grover, the state's Democratic governor, did not favor Booth's solution. Grover fired back in the pages of the *Daily Oregon Herald*, accusing the California governor of endangering Oregon residents by allowing the Modocs "to rove at will, dictating to settlers where they shall locate their future homes on unoccupied lands, and by a system of threatening and intimidation, prevent the progress and settlement of the country." He expressed concern that federal government negotiations with the Modocs would serve as a precedent for future Indian "misbehavior" throughout the region and across the continent. "If this course should be adopted, what is to prevent every Indian on any reservation from leaving, then raising the war whoop, and dancing the scalp dance in every exposed settlement?" In a crescendo of vitriol, Grover concluded by declaring, "Justice, sharp and bloody, ought to be executed against these remorseless scoundrels. . . . We believe that any white man's life, however humble he may be, is worth all the murdering vagabonish [*sic*] Indians now roving over the continent. . . . We trust, and we know it is the general wish, that by this time every cutthroat Modoc who has aided and abetted these murderers has expiated his crimes by his worthless life. All we regret is that any white man should be hurt in the struggle. Then we are willing that the government should donate to each one of them a Reservation—of six feet of unoccupied land."[24]

Suffused with overt racial hatred, Grover's statement not only ignored the Indigenous perspective on the conflict but also represented a concerted effort to promote notions of American innocence in the evolving conflict. By representing the Modocs as violent, criminal, and disrespectful of property while portraying Euro-Americans as noninvading, noninterfering, blameless property holders, Grover and the Democratic-leaning press ignored alternative explanations for Indigenous resistance and inscribed the conflict with a narrative of white victimhood. But Democrats were not the only ones to advance narratives of American innocence.

While Democratic-leaning papers stoked racial animosities and fears, the Republican-leaning press sought to defuse the situation by accusing local non-Indigenous settlers of exploiting the Natives. "The whites have encroached upon their country and appropriated their lands for agricultural and grazing purposes," explained the *San Francisco Chronicle*. "The Modocs have once been driven upon a Government reservation, a cold and dreary spot, where, neglected by the authorities, swindled by the traders, insulted and outraged by vagabond whites, they felt that they were unjustly dealt with."[25] Samuel A. Clarke, a prominent Portland businessman and politician and the former editor of the *Oregon Statesmen*, tended to agree. In a letter to the editor of the *New York Times*, he wrote, "Having read several notices of the Indian troubles in Southern Oregon, in the New-York papers, none of which show accurate knowledge of the circumstances, I have worked up the facts." The Modocs, he asserted, were convinced to leave their reservation by "a certain class of whites who are decidedly 'of the baser sort,' and who have persuaded them that they are under no obligation to carry out their treaty."[26]

Appearing sympathetic toward the Modocs, the Republican press nonetheless manipulated the Indigenous perspective to further the party's national political goals. Indeed, commentators on both sides of the partisan divide were advancing both subtle and not-so-subtle political and ideological arguments that reveal the complex racial and class dynamics of many reform movements after the Civil War. The Democratic press, for example, was exploiting a populist and antifederalist sentiment that opposed the government's postbellum racial reforms. This manifested itself in a hard-line posture toward Indian affairs that emphasized the Natives' racial inferiority and viewed reservations as so-called donations and evidence of illegitimate governmental largesse. But race and class also colored Republican understandings of the conflict, reflecting a managerial impulse on the part of bourgeois eastern reformers. Among the predominantly conservative, middle-class readers of the Republican-leaning *New York Times*, for example, oblique references to "vagabonds" and "the baser sorts" of whites would have reinforced suspicions of working-class immigrants and the dangers they represented.[27] As the Republican-leaning *New York Tribune* asked, the local government "wants to hang a few Modoc; but who will hang the whites?"[28]

Partisanship dominated the early coverage of the Modoc War. But occasional revelatory glimpses into a Modoc perspective did emerge. And from this reporting, careful readers would have learned of the conflict's deeper political and economic origins, aspects often lost in the partisan clamor. Elijah Steele, the former agent of Indian affairs for the Northern District of California, gave an interview to the *San Francisco Chronicle* that subsequently was widely circulated. A respected judge in Yreka, Steele was a former legislator in the California State Assembly and an ardent Republican who had campaigned for presidential candidate Abraham Lincoln in 1860. Steele had also negotiated an earlier though unratified treaty with Captain Jack in February 1864. Known as the St. Valentine Day's Treaty, the agreement would have reserved Jack's individual claim to the Lost River Valley for fishing and hunting but obligated him to allow settlers to graze their cattle in the area.[29] In an interview with the *Chronicle*'s Robert D. Bogart, Steele explained what he believed was the root cause of the Modoc War: the Indians' right to property and Indian agency graft. Employing his own interpretation of the Fifteenth Amendment, Steele said that he had advised Jack that he could "pre-empt eighty acres of the land . . . , live upon it, cultivate it, pay taxes, and in short live like white people."[30] According to Steele, the Modocs were attempting to protect their land and exercise their rights as U.S. citizens. And Steele accused the Indian agent on the Klamath Reservation, Oliver Knapp, of having established a shadow business to supply beef and other provisions to the reservation. He allegedly charged twice the market rate for beef and then supplied half the contracted amount of meat.[31]

True or not, Steele's allegations were never substantiated by members of the media. But maybe they were never intended to be. Allegations of corruption were as much a political tool in the postbellum era as was actual corruption and were part of the marketplace of the Gilded Age press.[32] Scandals sold newspapers and had the added benefit of sustaining the innocence of the American colonial project. Indeed, by suggesting that Klamath Basin Indians were the victims of corruption within the Office of Indian Affairs, Steele perhaps unintentionally contained responsibility for the conflict. From his perspective, the abrogation of federal treaties with Indian nations was not the logical consequence of American colonialism but the regrettable failing of corrupt individuals. A corrupt system was not to blame. Within this explanatory framework, American colonialism was fundamentally innocent, albeit threatened by the avarice of fallible individuals. The solution, Steele and others suggested, was to vigorously enforce existing treaties, not to reexamine their justice. In other words, even when a Modoc perspective emerged from time to time, the political motivations and incentives of the Gilded Age press framed its presentation and shaped its content.

The Gilded Age newspaper industry's penchant for political scandal turned the Modoc War into a partisan issue that advanced notions of American innocence in the conquest and colonization of Indigenous peoples. It excused the violence inherent in the logic of American colonialism and instead insisted that individual corruption was to blame. Accusations of corruption would persist, providing glimpses into the economic and political origins of the conflict. But even as reporting on the war veered toward the sensational, coverage of the conflict preserved notions of American innocence in the face of colonial violence.

▧ Throughout February and March 1873, newspapers from across the country dispatched special correspondents to the Klamath Basin to cover the conflict. But they found little of substance to report. What had appeared to be a promising source for sensational accounts of Indian massacres and military defeats devolved into a protracted and secretive negotiation and a soporific cease-fire. To meet their publishers' and editors' demands, some reporters relied on a tried and true genre: the political crusade. And the first political crusade they waged was against the newly appointed Modoc peace commission.

The Modoc peace commission was both the product and the victim of the politically poisonous policy environment of the postbellum era. Peace commissions originated in the 1860s as a way of bringing together military, civilian, and religious officials to engage directly with Native nations and negotiate settlements. In 1865, Congress appointed a commission to investigate the condition of Indian nations and their treatment by civil and military authorities. Its report, released in 1867, detailed the poor and declining condition of tribal populations and concluded that warfare on the Great Plains had been preventable if the government had strictly enforced existing treaties. In response to these findings, Congress established the Board of Indian Commissioners (BIC) in 1869 to advise the government on policy and supervise the fulfillment of federal treaty obligations. But the BIC and in particular, its first chair, William Welsh, soon became obsessed with controlling the Office of Indian Affairs, using accusations of corruption to discredit their political opponents and stifling policy alternatives. Indeed, as historian C. Joseph Genetin-Pilawa explains as way of postmortem, "The BIC could have provided transparency and public oversight. . . . Instead, it sought to limit public access to Indian policy, while placing it in the hands of a small circle of respected white elites who shared similar religious, business, and social interests."[33]

Appointed on January 25 by Columbus Delano, the secretary of the interior, the peace commission charged with negotiating with Jack and the other Modocs originally consisted of three Oregonians. The chair was Alfred B. Meacham, a passionate advocate for Indian rights and the former Oregon superintendent of Indian affairs. Samuel Case, the agent at the Alsea Indian Reservation on Oregon's western coast, was to represent the interests of the Office of Indian Affairs. The interests of local non-Indigenous settlers were overseen by Jesse Applegate, who though living in California was the head of a prominent family of Oregon settlers and cofounder of the famous Applegate Cut-Off, the primary route by which settlers migrated to the region. General Edward R. S. Canby, commander of U.S. Army forces in the Pacific Northwest, was appointed to serve as an adviser to the commission.[34]

The commission soon became embroiled in journalistic scandal, with politicians and the media calling on members to answer charges of illegitimacy. At their initial meeting on February 19, the first order of business was to respond to a blistering open letter from Governor Grover. Newspapers in Oregon, California, New York, and beyond had published Grover's letter even before he delivered it to the commissioners. Using the language of Indigenous criminality and American innocence, the governor insisted that the Modocs were "murderers" and that "the massacre of eighteen citizens . . . in cold blood at their homes and in their fields" was committed "without provocation and without notice." He asserted that the trial and punishment of the Modoc "murderers" fell under the jurisdiction of local civilian authorities, not the military or the federal government. Finally, Grover insisted that in the interest of "future peace," no reservation could be established in the Lost River Valley.[35]

The commission's reply was cool. In an open letter to Grover, Applegate chastised the governor for showing "undue haste" in addressing a letter to a board not yet constituted. And he reminded "his excellency" that although the Modoc War had begun in Oregon and was being conducted in California, it was nevertheless being prosecuted under the direction of the U.S. Army, and the commissioners derived their authority from the federal government.[36]

But Grover was not alone in questioning the legitimacy of the peace commission. Many journalists—in particular, Robert Bogart of the *San Francisco Chronicle*—criticized the commission for its composition and spread rumors of Applegate's involvement in defrauding the Klamath Reservation. "It is generally believed that no one had more to do with getting up the Modoc war than the numerous tribe of Applegates," complained Bogart in a dispatch to the *Chronicle*. "They wanted the Indians driven into the reservation that the Applegate pocket might be more plethoric with the plunder to be obtained from Uncle Sam, on the one hand, and the Modoc on the other." Instead of Jesse Applegate, Bogart and others proposed that the government appoint Steele and Alexander M. Rosborough, a judge in California's Eighth Judicial District and a vocal advocate for fair treatment of the Modocs.[37]

Bogart's efforts worked well for the Modocs, who were also keen to replace Applegate with an ally such as Rosborough or Steele. Indeed, during the Modocs' initial meeting with the commissioners, Jack had refused to negotiate at all until more "impartial arbitrators" were appointed.[38] Jack would discuss surrender, he said, only if Steele and Rosborough replaced Applegate on the commission.[39] Unknown to the Modocs as well as to the media, General Canby had weeks earlier recommended that Rosborough be appointed to the commission to represent the interests of California settlers. With the Modocs on record and with Meacham and Canby's tacit support, Rosborough was added to the commission in late February. In response, Applegate resigned, citing a conflict of interest if the commissioners were to further investigate charges of fraud on the Klamath Reservation.[40] This small victory for the Modocs would not last.

Spirited debate regarding the causes and origins of the conflict and the media's pursuit of accusations about political corruption were emblematic of the nature of journalism in the mid-nineteenth century. The crusade against Applegate was sincere. The Modocs supported his ouster, and the limelight did bring to public attention serious accusations of corruption in the Office of Indian Affairs. But it also represented a sensationalist mentality that would continue into the next stage of the war. As the newly appointed peace commission convened to begin negotiations with Jack and the other Modocs, the media stood poised to unleash a flood of information from the Indigenous point of view. But while journalists reported on the accusations of corruption, violence, and exploitation, they only further marginalized the Modocs' concerns in favor of print sensationalism.

■ Edward Fox, a reporter on assignment for the *New York Herald*, could see the horse tracks in the fresh snow. The tracks were those of animals ridden by John Fairchild, a local rancher, and Robert Whittle, who operated the ferry across the Klamath River with his Modoc wife, Sokegs Matilda Whittle. The peace commissioners had sent them as emissaries to negotiate with Captain Jack. A half hour earlier, the two had turned Fox away, insisting that Meacham, chair of the peace commission, had forbidden reporters from accompanying them. But Fox would not be deterred. He had been sent to the remote battlefields of the Modoc War by the *Herald*'s famous publisher, James Gordon Bennett Jr., to get an exclusive interview with Jack. After giving the emissaries a head start, Fox doubled back and followed their trail, overtaking the party just before it arrived at Jack's village on the south shore of Tule Lake.[41]

Writing later of his exploits in a series of extensive front-page stories, Fox employed the sensational style of an adventurer-correspondent. He placed himself at the center of these narratives, writing in the first person and datelining his accounts "in Captain Jack's cave" or from "Herald Headquarters." And he trumpeted the historical importance of what he reported. "The history of this country has recorded many celebrated Indian fights," he wrote, "but during the past ten years, there has not been a battle with the red men of the forest which created a greater sensation throughout the United Sates than the recent fight with Captain Jack and his band of Modoc Indians."[42]

Fox, an Englishman who had served in the British Army before becoming the yachting editor of the *New York Herald*, had been in the Klamath Basin since early February. In previous articles, he had reported on the causes of the Modoc War. Based in part on interviews with settlers from both California and Oregon, his stories nonetheless tended toward sympathy with the Modocs.[43] But in reporting on his interview with Jack and the other Modocs, Fox exchanged sympathy for sensationalism. For example, he provided grisly descriptions of the Modocs. "They were all painted pretty much alike," he wrote. "The entire lower part of the face was smeared with a brownish or black composition of a greasy nature [that] gave them a very hideous appearance." He did not inform his readers that this paint meant they were in mourning for the women, children, and other members of their community who had died. He described a "strange scene and a fit subject for some figure artists, for certainly no troop of Italian bandits could have made a wilder or more picturesque picture." Throughout his reports, Fox affected the jovial aplomb of Stanley, who just the previous year had riveted the *Herald*'s readership with tales of his heroic pursuit of the elusive Dr. Livingstone.[44]

But if his tone was lighthearted, Fox's interviews nonetheless conveyed the root causes and origins of the conflict from the Modocs' perspective. According to Schonchin John, the eldest headman in the Lava Beds, the Modocs had accommodated American settlers' economic and property demands, but the soldiers persecuted them anyway: "Tell your people white men shoot first," he admonished the reporter. "I gave away all my country [and] ke[pt] a little piece on Lost River, yet they shoot me. I don't know what for. I thought I gave them all my land, water, grass, everything. I don't charge nothing for my country; give away all, yet they shoot me." The Modocs had integrated themselves into the expanding Euro-American economy, he insisted. They had allowed settlers to establish farms in the region, collecting only modest rents in kind during times of need. They had also established working relationships and entered the cash economy by taking positions as ranch hands or agricultural laborers when the opportunities arose. But despite these efforts to coexist and to create a shared Klamath Basin society, the U.S. Army and settlers had attacked. All he wanted, Jack said, was to have peace and to return to working and trading with settlers in the region. "I go as white man; money in pockets; go to store; buy what I want. I make more friends with whites."[45]

Beyond the economic causes, Schonchin explained how American settler colonial politics exacerbated the situation. The Modocs would not come to the soldiers' camp to talk, he insisted, because they "remembered the Ben Wright treachery." In 1852, Wright, a federal Indian agent and a Quaker, had invited the Modocs to a "peace feast" to negotiate a lasting agreement between Klamath Basin Indians and the newly arrived settlers. But when the Modocs had gathered, Schonchin explained, Wright and his men opened fire and killed forty or fifty of them. The history of treachery in earlier negotiations between the Modocs and the United States, symbolized by Ben Wright's attack, was a crucial aspect of the Modocs' collective memory, making them distrustful of the peace commission and rendering future negotiations impossible. And even today, after 140 years, many Klamath Basin Indians still point to the Ben Wright Massacre as the only precedent the Modocs knew for what "peace talks" meant.[46]

Economic marginalization and political distrust contributed to the conflict, but Fox's reporting also captured the complexity of the Indigenous perspective and provided the Modocs with an opportunity to articulate their more immediate grievances. Earlier journalists had reported that widespread corruption on the Klamath Reservation had forced Jack and the other Modocs to return to their villages along the Lost River. Fox's reporting confirmed these allegations. But the Modocs also provided additional details of mistreatment. According to one Modoc man, they had been "moved three times from place to place" in the middle of winter and "only given half a blanket"—if they got blankets at all. Others complained to Fox that they had received no food and had to "kill their horses for meat," which made them despise the place.[47] Fox's interviews, then, confirmed that the Modocs held a diversity of positions: some believed the conflict resulted from their mistreatment on the Klamath Reservation; others suggested that its roots lay in a much longer and more complex history of colonization, violence, and exploitation. Some sought peace, others did not.

But in transmitting and commenting on Fox's account, newspapers editors and publishers across the country ignored the diversity of opinions among the Modocs and the longer historical context they highlighted. Indeed, many excerpted the interviews or summarized them inaccurately. And they minimized the substance of the interviews by transforming the event into a spectacle of masculine journalistic prowess, to readers' delight. The *New York Herald* dedicated an entire first page to the story and confirmed reports that the telegraph fees alone cost the paper five hundred or six hundred dollars.[48] "This feat of Fox has placed the *Herald* in the van, and distanced all competitors in the race for news!," declared the *Yreka Union*. The *Trenton Gazette* praised Fox for his gumption and courage: "It reads more like some knight's tale, related at King Arthur's Round Table, than a mere matter-of-fact piece of modern newspaper enterprise. . . . What sagacity and courage was needed to conceive and so successfully to execute the mission . . . to the Modoc chief among the almost inaccessible wilds of Northern California."[49] Several papers compared Fox's success and style to that of Stanley.[50]

The Gilded Age popular press, then, with its fondness for sensationalizing encounters with racialized Others, portrayed the first exclusive interview with Captain Jack not as a substantive statement on the causes and origins of the Modoc War from the Indigenous perspective but rather as evidence of the bravery of the white adventurer-journalist, suggesting the degree to which the marketplace of memory transformed stories of

U.S.-Indian violence into consumable objects for eastern, cosmopolitan audiences. By minimizing the political and economic origins of the conflict and blaming a "few Oregonians," moreover, the press maintained the notion that in general Americans were innocent, despite the fact that the conflicts resulted from expansion and the ideology of Manifest Destiny. Although other correspondents emulated Fox's success and published their own interviews with the Modocs, Fox's performance and fame persisted, and for many years he maintained the sobriquet "Modoc Fox."[51]

■ While the *New York Herald* and other national papers marveled at their own capacity for delivering spectacle to the masses, events continued to unfold in the Klamath Basin. The arrival of Rosborough and Steele to join the peace commission seemed at first to yield results. On February 27, the commissioners met and agreed on the terms they would offer the Modocs: first, they were to surrender to the U.S. Army and military authority; second, they were to agree to move to a new reservation in Arizona, Oklahoma Indian Territory, or southern California.[52] The following day, Steele and Fairchild, with a Kentucky-born settler, Frank Riddle, and his Modoc wife, Toby, as translators, brought these terms to Jack. But the Modocs were uncertain. "I do not want to leave my country," Jack responded when told he would have to leave his cherished Lost River Valley. "Not to any other country that I know of to live in. My father, mother, and brother also, are buried here. I desire to live and die in my own country."[53] The Lost River Valley, Tule Lake, and the Lava Beds were the Modocs' home, and above all else, they did not want to leave it.

The following day, the two parties met again. After several more hours of discussion, the Modocs had agreed to nothing. But the emissaries left with Steele convinced that the Modocs would agree to the terms. This was a huge mistake and a complete misunderstanding on Steele's part. Upon returning to the Army's camp, Steele's rosy assessment of the Modocs' willingness to settle created a cavalcade of reactions that echoed across the media landscape. Meacham sent a hasty telegraph to Washington, D.C.: "Modocs to surrender as prisoners of war, to be removed to a southern and warmer climate and provided for. They accept the terms and have sent a delegation of eight to talk over details but not to conclude them. . . . Everything looks favorable for peace."[54] The popular press picked up on the story and celebrated the news with banner headlines: "Captain Jack Abdicates!" and "Burying the Hatchet, Smoking the Pipe of Peace with the Modocs," declared the *New York Herald* and *San Francisco Chronicle*, respectively.[55]

The euphoria was short-lived. When Steele and the others returned to the Modocs' camp to resume negotiations, they were apprehensive and distrustful. The Modocs knew that Steele had misrepresented them to the soldiers and became suspicious of his motives. In the end, they had decided to reject the commissioners' proposal requiring them to leave the Klamath Basin.

In rebuffing the commissioners, the Modocs reiterated the importance of the land and reaffirmed their resolve to remain there. "Captain Jack don't know anything about another country—don't want to go there," Schonchin told the *New York Herald*, adding, "I want a good country to live in." As an alternative, Jack suggested that if a reservation in the Lost River Valley would cause too many problems, the Modocs might remain in the Lava Beds and allow the Oregonians to have the rest. "I am not like the Oregonians," he said, "I have been staying around here and am willing to stay here; let them have that side of the lake and I will keep this side; I don't know of any other country; don't want any but this, and have nothing to say about another country. . . . This is my home; I was born here, always lived here and I don't want to leave here."[56]

Although Jack's proposal struck Steele and Fairchild as absurd because the area seemed so inhospitable to them, it made a great deal of sense to the Modocs. Located on the shores of Móatakni É-ush, the Lava Beds were the center of the Modoc world. Many of the Modocs' most productive fishing sites were located along the shores of Tule Lake, and the Modocs believed that Gmukamps had created the world there by stacking handfuls of mud onto the lakeshore. Jack's willingness to accept a reservation in the Lava Beds, then, might have been acceptable to both sides. Steele and Fairchild, however, rejected the idea as certain to invite future conflict, ending the meeting with vague promises of another in the future.[57]

This failure at compromise marked the end of the first stage of peace negotiations. "So ends the first chapter of the Peace Commission, which has been fraught with dangers, blunders and serious mistakes," wrote H. Wallace Atwell in the *San Francisco Chronicle*.[58] It also corresponded with yet another reconfiguration of the peace commission. On March 2, Samuel Case resigned, pleading urgent business on his reservation. Two weeks later, Delano appointed to the commission the Reverend Eleazer Thomas, a Methodist minister from Petaluma, California, and Leroy S. Dyar, the newly arrived Indian agent on the Klamath Reservation—the third in six years. Beyond the fact that the commissioners combined inexperience with unfamiliarity, relations between the Modocs and the commissioners were further exacerbated by the departures of Steele, who returned to

Yreka, and Rosborough, who technically remained a member of the commission but left in early March to attend to his judicial duties. Without the support of those allies, the Modocs soon found themselves with few options.[59]

From the Modocs' perspective, they had sought to avoid conflict at all costs. They had accommodated the newly arrived Euro-American settlers. Even after being betrayed and massacred by representatives such as Ben Wright, they had still tried to reach an agreement with the newcomers. Meeting at Council Grove in 1864, the Modocs had agreed to a treaty that would force them to move from the Lost River Valley to the Williamson River and Klamath Marsh area, a major concession. But the Americans had yet again betrayed the Modocs and failed to meet obligations. When the Modocs left the Klamath Reservation to find food, the Americans called them criminals, renegades, and oath breakers. When the soldiers had come to their village, the Modocs had tried to talk. But when shots were fired, they fought back. When the soldiers again attacked, the Indians did not try to talk. They fought. And once again, they won. Despite misgivings and internal dissent, Jack had steered his fellow Modocs toward a more accommodating approach. In council, he had convinced his followers to meet with the peace commissioners to find a resolution. But the Americans had insisted that the Modocs who fought were criminals and murderers, demanding that they be handed over to face American justice. To add insult, they now insisted the Modocs had to leave their beloved homeland, this time forever. And many of the Modocs began to insist it was time to fight before they were betrayed again. The talks had failed.

Even as negotiations deteriorated, the press continued to follow every development for eager readers. In March 1873, Odeneal, Oregon's superintendent of Indian affairs and the editor of the *Portland Daily Bulletin*, published a fifty-six-page pamphlet in which he chided the "sensational press of the country—especially that of California" for promulgating "erroneous impressions" and "false accounts" of the origins of the Modoc War. The end of the Franco-Prussian War, Odeneal explained, and the resolution of a sensational presidential race between Grant and newspaperman Horace Greeley "had left the newspapers of the land almost without material to work upon." When news of the Modoc War "broke the monotonious [*sic*] quiet of the times," Yankee humanitarians and prejudicial Californians kept "up the wail for a weekly stipend about the abuses, frauds, and injustice of the authorities against this band of Modocs" until "the sound was heard in every nook and corner of the nation." Fortunately, the "press of enlightened Oregon" had been spared this "flood of misrepresentations." In defense of the people of Oregon, Odeneal intended "to furnish for publication a brief history" and "to dissipate the cloudy fancies of roman[ti]cists."[60]

The stalemate in negotiations, according to Odeneal, was a product of lenient federal policy that allowed the Modocs to ignore their treaty obligations and persist in an illegal and belligerent occupation of the Lost River Valley. Grant's Peace Policy was "the source of more trouble with Indians than anything else," for too much "pow-wowing" had "emboldened" Jack into believing that a peaceful settlement might be reached through negotiation. Immediate and decisive military action, Odeneal insisted, would have "accomplished the desired object."[61]

In addition, Odeneal held firm to his belief in the fundamental legitimacy of American settlement in the region. Indeed, the historical and legalistic explanations he presented drew on a rich tradition of justifying interracial violence through appeals to American innocence and indigenous criminality. Settlers in the Lost River area had "vested rights in the land," and by agreeing to the treaty of 1864, the Modocs had "divested themselves" of all claims to the region. Thus, in Odeneal's estimation, allowing Jack to remain in the Lost River Valley would have been "a violation of equity and justice." Odeneal concluded his explanation with a familiar warning: "Let Captain Jack dictate his own terms, and it may not be long before the Klamaths, the Snakes, some of the Umatillas, and others may feign to be aggrieved, and follow Jack's precedent."[62]

Of course, Odeneal's perspectives ignored the Modocs' claim to land rights in the region and their understanding of the conflict's causes and origins. But such arguments played well among Oregon voters and readers and may have stemmed from Odeneal's ambitions for state office. They also had the added benefit of portraying American settlers as the aggrieved party whose expansive property rights were not being protected by the government. But in emphasizing the supremacy of Euro-American jurisprudence, Odeneal ignored Oregon's sordid history of contested land claims. The Donation Land Claim Act of 1850 had granted settlers moving west to Oregon huge tracts of land. Congress, however, had granted those lands without first negotiating treaties with the Indigenous nations already residing there. When violence erupted, settlers had argued that their property rights were being infringed upon. Although the situation differed in the Klamath Basin, where treaties had been negotiated but imperfectly enforced, the rhetorical retreat to white victimhood to defend Euro-Americans' right to property had by the 1870s become a familiar motif in calls for violence against Native communities. These notions of innocence suffused Odeneal's diatribe.[63]

Calls for aggressive military action resulted in a further deterioration of negotiations. By the second week of March, the peace talks had all but ended, and General Canby began a policy of "gradual compression." A variation on the classical double-envelopment strategy, Canby tightened the perimeter around the Stronghold and moved his headquarters closer. The Modocs became alarmed by these developments and began to make plans of their own. After several weeks, detachments of troops were patrolling the area south of Tule Lake on a regular basis, drawing occasional fire from concerned Modocs. On April 1, Canby relocated his headquarters to a bluff within three miles of the Stronghold. Shortly thereafter, the Modocs sent a courier to the peace commission in hopes of arranging another meeting.[64]

The final stage of negotiations proceeded rapidly. On April 2, Jack met with the commissioners halfway between the army's new encampment and the Stronghold. He demanded a full pardon for all the Modocs, the immediate withdrawal of all troops, and a reservation in the Lost River Valley. Canby and the commissioners balked at these proposals and insisted on the earlier terms. Two days later, the two sides met again, this time in a tent because of the weather. But they adjourned without coming to terms. After the meeting, General Canby informed the Modocs that his troops would move closer to the Stronghold unless the Indians responsible for killing the Lost River settlers were handed over. The Modocs responded by requesting another meeting.[65]

On April 11, 1873—Good Friday—the Modocs and the commissioners met for the last time. Two days later, a telegram from Dyar arrived in Washington, D.C.: "I have to report that . . . while this commission was holding a council with the Modocs, by an act of unparalle[le]d and premeditated treachery on their [the Modocs'] part, General Canby and Dr. Thomas were brutally murdered, Meacham left for dead."[66] News of the attack precipitated a national outcry as political leaders, military officials, and the press waved the bloody shirt and called for vengeance. "The President now sanctions the most severe punishment of the Modocs and I hope to hear that they have met the doom they so richly have earned by their insolence and perfidy," declared William Tecumseh Sherman in a letter to John McAlister Schofield, commanding general of the Division of the Pacific. In a second telegram that asserted a claim to American innocence in the face of these genocidal tendencies, Sherman added, "You will be fully justified in their utter extermination."[67] Published in newspapers across the country, such official declarations were accompanied by battle-field reports, photographic and artistic imagery, vociferous editorials, and political cartoons that condemned Captain Jack and the other Modocs. As the *Army and Navy Journal* described the national mood, "No event in connection with our Army since the Rebellion has created such excitement throughout the country as the news of the assassination."[68]

■ Shortly before the Modoc War became an international sensation, Mark Twain railed against the license given to the press. "I am putting all this odious state of things upon the newspaper, and I believe it belongs there," he told the Monday Evening Club of Hartford, Connecticut, on March 31, 1873. "That awful power, the public opinion of this nation, is formed and molded by a horde of ignorant self-complacent simpletons who have failed at ditching and shoemaking and fetched up journalism on their way to the poorhouse."[69] Twain was in a bad mood. But though his language was hyperbolic, he pointed to an essential truth about the relationship between the media and public opinion.

What had begun as a minor incident of frontier violence in an isolated and sparsely populated corner of the North American continent had become a national sensation as a modernizing media industry transformed this colonial conflict over land and resources into a spectacle of partisan bickering, political scandal, and feats of masculine adventurer journalism. Journalists sometimes reported the Modocs' point of view, but the media marketplace of remembering tended to marginalize Modoc motivations and obscure Indigenous perspectives as it transformed complicated and nuanced explanations into simpler arguments that established, sustained, and promoted American innocence. The attack on the peace commission and the deaths of Canby and Thomas propelled this coverage to new extremes.

Chapter Two

THE RED JUDAS

William Simpson, special artist for the *Illustrated London News* and famed veteran reporter of the Crimean War, the Franco-Prussian War, and the Paris Commune uprising, had a skilled hand at producing eyewitness accounts after the fact. Perhaps that is why he decided to interrupt his round-the-world trip to visit the Klamath Basin at the height of the Modoc War. Disembarking on March 21, 1873, from a Pacific Mail Steamship Company liner out of Tokyo, Simpson was in San Francisco, seeing the sights and visiting the nearby hot springs in Calistoga, when news arrived of General Edward R. S. Canby's death. "THE RED JUDAS: Based Treachery of the Modoc Indians. The Peace Commission Inveigled into a Death-Trap. General Canby Murdered," declared the *San Francisco Chronicle* in a full-page article. In the days and weeks following the April 11, 1873, attack on the peace commissioners, newspapers throughout the country and around the world picked up the story. The Republican-leaning *Yreka Journal* called it the "most dastardly assassination yet known in either ancient or modern history." The *Chicago Daily Tribune* condemned the "Indian Treachery" and added, "Christian Treatment of Untamable Savages Is a Sorry Delusion." *Harper's Weekly* described "the treacherous murder of General Canby and the Rev. Dr. Thomas" as "one of the most tragical events in the history of Indian wars." With newspaper publishers and editors throughout the country looking for material, Simpson boarded a train in San Francisco and headed north toward the remote battlegrounds of the Modoc War.[1]

During his eight-day visit to the region, Simpson produced several drawings. The most famous was "The Modocs—The Murder of General Canby" (figure 6). Simpson based his portrayal on information obtained,

Figure 6. "The Modocs—Murder of General Canby." Wood engraving based on a sketch by William Simpson. From Illustrated London News, *May 31, 1873; reprinted in* Harper's Weekly, *June 28, 1873.*

sometimes third- and fourthhand, from nearby ranchers and a few soldiers, none of whom were within a mile of the actual attack. His sketches were later made into a single twenty-two–by–sixteen-inch print that appeared in the *London Illustrated News* on May 31, 1873. Portraying Canby's death as a premeditated betrayal, Simpson's dramatic engraving reflected the national zeitgeist around the Modoc War in the spring of 1873. His composition evinced a sense of anticipated violence and brutal treachery and cast the conflict as a historic struggle between competing moralistic impulses. In the center stands Captain Jack, dressed in trousers, a long-sleeved shirt, boots, and a brimmed hat. He advances on General Canby, arm outstretched, a pistol leveled and aimed with calculated intensity. Opposite Jack, the general commands his attacker to stop, holding his right hand palm out. The two figures stand, eyes locked, frozen in a battle of wills. The background accentuates the image's metaphoric dualism. From the viewer's left, several armed Indian men rush toward their unsuspecting victims. On the right side, the peace tent where negotiations were to be conducted stands with its door open, evoking the possibility of a peaceful resolution, even at this final moment. This composition represents Jack and his people as guilty of a calculated and vicious crime while it portrays Canby and his men as innocent martyrs.

Although Simpson seems to have sympathized with the plight of the Indians—he later claimed that "the sense of justice in human nature must declare that these tribes have been cruelly wronged"—he nonetheless thought Jack's tactics were evidence of a moral failure. The Modocs, he believed, were virtuous warriors whose romantic feats were legendary. But their decision to attack the commissioners had tarnished their valor. "Had they not basely accomplished the deaths of General Canby and Dr. Thomas, few heroes could have been compared to them," Simpson subsequently wrote. "That crime put them beyond the pale of mercy, and extermination like vermin was decreed against them."[2] Simpson's engraving and commentary together constructed a narrative of innocence lost in which Indian violence was not irrational but tragic. In resisting a romantic death, the Modocs had made history but would be forever remembered as villainous criminals and brutal savages. Brimming with the racial and political tensions of the 1870s and tinged with Judeo-Christian as well as Shakespearean influences, Simpson's portrayal of the "Death of General Canby" is exceptional for its dramatic composition and narrative sophistication. And it soon became one of the most ubiquitous and influential images of the event.

In the weeks and months following the death of General Canby, the Gilded Age media transformed the conflict into an international sensation that focused on the victimhood of Americans and the savage criminality of Indigenous resistance. This coverage influenced the course of the war, contributed to the government's later legal justifications for trying the Modocs before a military tribunal, and mediated Americans' perceptions of these historical events as they unfolded. This chapter continues the story of how the media marketplace of remembering the Modoc War shaped historical memories and imprinted the conflict with narratives of American innocence, culminating in the trial and execution of Captain Jack and the other Modocs for "murder, in violation of the laws of war."[3]

■ General Canby's official state funeral occurred on April 18, 1873, in Portland. The day of remembrance began a few minutes before eleven o'clock in the morning with an intimate service for the family and a handful of close friends. Intended to shield the grieving widow from the impending media spectacle, the ceremony at the family's residence was as brief as possible. Following the service, Canby's body was marched through the city in a great funeral procession. At the head of the cortege was a hearse drawn by two black horses adorned with heavy black draping and spectacular plumage. On either side ranged the pallbearers; top-ranking officers in the Department of the Columbia represented the military, while Oregon Governor LaFayette Grover, district court judge Matthew Deady, Mayor Philip Wasserman, and other prominent politicians represented the civil authorities. The procession wound its way through the city's busy downtown area before stopping at Armory Hall, in what is today Portland's fashionable Pearl District, where the body, swathed in an American flag and wreathed with flowers, lay in state. "The solemn silence of death reigned," wrote one reporter, as an "immense concourse of people entered the building in single file to view the remains."[4]

For most Americans, the deaths of Canby and the Reverend Eleazer Thomas constituted a moment of deep betrayal and national trauma. To render the violence comprehensible, American newspaper reporters and commentators portrayed Modoc violence as deriving from a combination of the Indians' brutal and criminal character and the Klamath Basin's nefarious and demonic landscape. In the process, these journalists represented white soldiers, settlers, and religious officials as the innocent victims of Indian violence. "Go back to the Miltonian idea of the abyss to which the rebel angels were hurled," Samuel A. Clarke declared in the *New York Times*, "and I can describe it, perhaps, better than in any other way; for if the surface of the burning lake of hell had cooled, Satan and his legions would have such a region to inhabit as the Modoc lava beds."[5]

The burgeoning pictorial media marketplace of the 1870s transformed descriptions of the Lava Beds into phantasmal and demonic pictorial dreamscapes for eastern readers. Alongside news of Canby's death, *Frank Leslie's Illustrated Newspaper* ran an image of the Lava Beds shrouded in a dense fog punctuated by layers of jagged rocks. In the foreground, shirtless Indian warriors are preparing for an ambush atop towering colonnades, while a company of "union troops" advances (figure 7). Through the use of perspective, the illustrator emphasized the association of Indian violence with the landscape, suggesting that white vulnerability was a by-product of untamed western spaces and superior Indigenous knowledge of the terrain. Another engraving published in *Harper's Weekly* depicted a group of "Modocs in Their Stronghold" with long rifles perched on the rocks, ready to shoot. The Natives aim their primed weapons at an unseen target, yet in the background a lone soldier waves a white flag of truce, symbolizing the Americans' peaceful and innocent intentions. The composition of the scene evokes the moment of duplicity in which the Indians' betrayal is concealed

Figure 7. "Oregon—The Modoc War—Captain Jack and His Followers Checking the Advance of Union Troops in the Lava-Beds." Wood engraving. From Frank Leslie's Illustrated Newspaper, May 8, 1873.

by the rocks of the Lava Beds (figure 8). Although the arrival of photographers shifted the focus of printed imagery from representational landscapes to portraiture, by the war's end, journalists had used written and pictorial reporting to establish a relationship between U.S.-Indian violence and the physical landscape of the Klamath Basin.

Any earlier trace of public sympathy toward the Modocs vanished as newspapers across the political spectrum criticized President Ulysses S. Grant's administration and called for the resumption of war. "The policy of alternately coddling and killing the Indians has been tried long enough," declared the *Indianapolis Sentinel*. "There is nothing to be gained from preaching peace to the Indians in one section, and murdering them in another. The peace policy so called is fertile in war and massacre."[6] The *Daily Colorado Miner* also reproached the administration for its "experiments with the noble red man" and declared the paper's opposition to the peace policy: "Western experience, in this and adjoining Territories, is decidedly against General Grant and the preachers."[7] Perhaps most succinctly, the *New York Herald* suggested that the government return to the core principles behind its so-called Peace Policy: "Keep the peace or we shall kill you."[8]

News of Thomas's and Canby's deaths inflamed feelings throughout the country as American politicians and citizens vented their frustrations in the public sphere. The vast majority of newspapers relied on a racialized discourse of Indigenous savagery and criminality. In an open letter to President Grant, Minnesota's Republican governor, Horace Austin,

Figure 8. "The Modocs in Their Stronghold." Wood engraving.
From Harper's Weekly, *May 3, 1873.*

claimed that the "Modoc assassination" had residents of the Gopher State in an uproar. According to Austin, those familiar with the "Indian charac-ter from daily observation and sad experience" opposed the Peace Policy both in principle and in practice. "The Indians respect no policy that is not backed by power enough to enforce respect," he claimed, and there was no reason "the President should treat the Indians more leniently than he did the rebels." The governor looked forward to an "immediate" and "decisive" response from the Grant administration.[9]

While Minnesotans may have drawn inspiration from their use of a "discourse of savagery" during the Dakota War of 1862 to depict Indians as a threat to the nation requiring a severe response, Chicagoans bemoaned the president's "useless and vacillating Indian policy." The *Chicago Tribune* favored "the extermination of Capt. Jack's band of outlaws and the hanging of the murderers who attended the conference," while the *Inter Ocean* called for "the most summary measures." In contrast, the *Chicago Times* wanted to "lay the blame of the murders to the Indian policy" but did not advocate on behalf of extermination, while the *Chicago Journal* called for a combination of "the Quaker policy and Sheridan policy." A letter to the editor of the *New York Times* crystallized this approach. Laying the majority of blame for the Modoc War at the feet of "the vile class of border whites who have . . . 'inoculated' [the Indians] with all the vices of our civilization, and made them more depraved and vicious than they were by their own savage nature," the writer said, "Let Capt. Jack and his miserable crew be 'wiped out' for their recent atrocity, but let justice be meted out to these renegade and thoroughly brutal white men, who have preyed on the Indians so long; and let us not condemn the present Indian Policy."[10]

Even supporters of the administration's Indian policy had to walk a fine line between calls for justice and the excesses of vengeance. The *Boston Evening Transcript*, for example, believed that the Modocs must be punished but urged the nation to adopt "the calm judicial attitude which a civilized people should maintain" and to "not hastily abandon" the Peace Policy.[11] In an opinion piece that reached a much wider audience, *Harper's Weekly* adopted a similar view: "[The] fury of the savage blood has been illustrated [again] in the murder of the Peace Commissioners. . . . Their murderers should be punished as they deserve. But the innocent should not be confounded with the guilty. . . . Nor is it the custom of our people to encourage the cry of extermination. . . . Even against such treacherous murderers as the Modocs or their chiefs we are inclined to remember mercy, to spare the innocent, and not to impute the crimes of the few to the multitudes of their fellow-savages."[12] *Harper's*, like other pro–Peace Policy publications, thus called for a judicious application of violence.

A few commentators sought to explain the Modocs' actions by drawing on the Indigenous perspective portrayed earlier. The *San Francisco Chronicle*, picking up on Edward Fox's interview with Captain Jack and the other Modocs, suggested that their attack was in retaliation for the 1852 Ben Wright Massacre. Calling Wright's victims "Modoc Peace Commissioners," the *Chronicle* asked, "Are they avenging the murder of their ancestors?"[13]

William Simpson also believed the two events were connected and even suggested that Jack had used the same signal as Wright to commence the attack. "This is some of the history," Simpson wrote later, "which it is necessary to know in order to understand the late Modoc war."[14] Still others pointed to the long U.S. history of broken treaties with Indigenous nations. In a letter to the editor of the *New York Times*, "C.R." wrote, "The pen of the future historian of America . . . will calmly and truly tell the generation which succeeds us of the why and wherefore of this infamous deed. He will tell those living 200 years hence on the soil of America, that a so-called Christian people landed on this continent from Europe, and, coming into contact with its inhabitant . . . were treated by them with gentleness, if not affection . . . and he will tell them, to the shame and disgrace of the United States forever, that the Government has broken every treaty ever made with every Indian tribe."[15] These sentiments captured well the Indigenous perspective, which connected the Wright Massacre with the attack on the peace commissioners and the longer history of broken promises. But they were less of a defense than an explanation.

Indeed, any defense or explanation of the Modocs' actions was frustrated by the popular media's reliance on racialized discourses that viewed the conflict as the result of a lenient federal policy toward the nation's unruly minorities. *Frank Leslie's Illustrated Newspaper*, often careful to balance criticism of Indian "character" with calls for fair or humane treatment, responded to the public outcry with a political cartoon featuring President Grant asleep in bed. Captioned "The Head of the Nation's Nightmare: See What Dreams May Come from Too Free an Indulgence in the 'Pipe of Peace,'" the cartoon featured a smoldering calumet labeled "Modoc Massacre" beside the slumbering president. From the smoke, a bare-chested black man looms over Grant, and through the open window an Indian warrior menaces the nation's leader with rifle in hand (figure 9).

Juxtaposing the "Modoc Massacre" with the violent suppression and mass murder of more than one hundred freedmen in Colfax, Louisiana, on April 13, 1873, the cartoon rhetorically linked the Modoc War with an incident of racial violence that epitomized southern anxieties regarding Reconstruction.[16] Indeed, as literary critic Linda Frost suggests, reading the national coverage of local events through the prism of the era's many social upheavals sharpens our understanding of how Americans came to identify with the victims of frontier interethnic conflicts and of how these incidents were seen as attacks on the larger national community. Editorial cartoons such as "The Head of the Nation's Nightmare," then, transformed the Modoc War from a regional episode of frontier violence

Figure 9. "The Head of the Nation's Nightmare." Wood engraving. From Frank Leslie's Illustrated Newspaper, *May 3, 1873.*

THE HEAD OF THE NATION'S NIGHTMARE.
SEE WHAT DREAMS MAY COME FROM TOO FREE AN INDULGENCE IN THE "PIPE OF PEACE."

into an existential threat to the nation and in the process rendered white Americans the victims rather than the aggressors.[17]

If "The Head of the Nation's Nightmare" represented the Modoc War as a threat to the national community, it also evoked an evolving understanding of the reconstructed nation's future racial composition. By placing the Indian threat outside of the house and the former slave within, the image evoked the spatial division of Native and black bodies within Reconstruction-era America. Located outside of the house, the Modoc is depicted as an external threat to the nation, whereas the former black slave is a danger emanating from within the house of American society. This reading of the image is reinforced by historian Elliott West's observation that the federal project of Reconstruction had not been limited to the reintegration of the South back into the Union but also had to contend with the addition of many Western territories as a result of the war with Mexico.[18] Considered within the racially charged environment of this "Greater Reconstruction," the death of General Canby exposed tensions inherent in the federal government's approach to integrating American Indians into the nation's body politic. It also played into a general anxiety over the racial composition of the nation in the wake of Reconstruction-era reforms. Both of these were important aspects of the media marketplace of remembering the Modoc War.

While the press debated the future of the federal government's Indian policy, the army prepared to attack the Stronghold. On April 15, 1873, Colonel Alvan C. Gillem ordered a general assault on the Modoc position. In addition to the 675 soldiers and 4 batteries of artillery, 70 Warm Springs Indians had arrived the night before to assist in the fight against the Modocs. Earlier in the conflict, the federal government had enlisted dozens of Klamath Indians to serve as scouts. But rumors abounded that the Klamaths had aided the Modocs by supplying them with ammunition and by refusing to advance when ordered. "Our enlisted Klamath scouts have proved to be utter failures," Lieutenant Colonel Frank Wheaton, commanding officer of the District of the Lakes, had reported in a telegram to General Canby. "We want Warm Springs Indians. Donald McKay, my district guide, will take charge of them."[19] The grandson of John McLoughlin, chief factor of the Columbia Fur District for the Hudson's Bay Company and the son of Thomas McKay, a prominent fur trader, Donald had worked for the U.S. Army and Bureau of Indian Affairs for more than two decades. Throughout the 1860s, he and a company of Warm Springs Indian scouts under the command of his older half-brother, William McKay, had fought with General George R. Crook in his campaigns against the Northern Paiutes. By the spring of 1873, the War Department had authorized McKay to recruit and equip up to one hundred Warm Springs Indians to fight the Modocs. For two days after the death of Canby and Thomas, a combined force of U.S. Army soldiers and Warm Springs Indian scouts attempted to surround the Modoc position and cut off their access to water. According to the *Army and Navy Journal*, however, sometime after midnight on the morning of April 17, hours before the army's planned final assault, the Modocs abandoned the Stronghold, escaping under almost continuous fire from the artillery and mortars. The following morning, the soldiers advanced and captured a nearly emptied Stronghold; all that remained from the Modocs' hasty retreat were several articles of clothing, a few provisions, and a handful of elderly or wounded Natives. The army killed the wounded, burned the bodies, and turned the women over to the Warm Springs Indians.[20]

By capturing the Stronghold but allowing the majority of the Modocs to escape, the soldiers had failed in their primary mission. However, they soon suffered a far greater humiliation. On the morning of April 26, Captain Evan Thomas, with seventy-one soldiers and fourteen of McKay's Warm Springs Indian scouts, left to reconnoiter south of the Stronghold in an attempt to confirm the Modocs' location. Around noon, the group halted for food and rest at the base of Sand Butte in a flat grassy

*Figure 10. "Modocs Scalping and Torturing Prisoners." Wood engraving.
From* Harper's Weekly, *May 17, 1873.*

area surrounded on four sides by ridges. Caught unaware, Thomas and
his forces were attacked by more than twenty Modocs armed with rifles
and positioned atop the bluffs. Many of the troops fled in disorder, some
even mistakenly attacking the Warm Springs Indian Scouts who were
coming to their aid. Those who remained were pinned down for three-
quarters of an hour. In all, the army suffered thirty-six casualties, including Thomas and four other officers killed and one officer wounded.
And at the end of the fighting, Chĭkclĭkam-Lupalkuelátko, or Scarface

Figure 11. "The Two Vultures." Wood engraving. From Frank Leslie's Illustrated Newspaper, *May 17, 1873.*

THE TWO VULTURES.

"To the victor belong the spoils," *thinks the Modoc murderer who interrupts the feathered savage in his post-mortem repast.*

Charley, purportedly told the soldiers, "We've killed enough of you, now go home."[21]

News of the Modocs' escape from the Stronghold followed by the reconnaissance party's fiasco further inflamed public sentiment against the Modocs. The illustrated weeklies in particular used the battle as an opportunity to produce representations of the Modoc War that offered racialized images that evoked Indian savagery. *Harper's Weekly* published a full-page engraving of the "Modocs Scalping and Torturing Prisoners" (figure 10), while *Frank Leslie's Illustrated Newspaper* ran a political cartoon featuring a Modoc warrior scalping a soldier, with a bird of prey perched nearby (figure 11). The caption read, "'To the victor belong [*sic*] the spoils,' thinks the Modoc murderer who interrupts the feathered savage in his post-mortem repast." The juxtaposition of these "two vultures" would have been lost on few readers. But if these representations rendered the Modocs as bestial and savage, others transformed them into pests and vermin.

Extermination discourse, common before the attack on the peace commissioners, gained greater vehemence and rhetorical effect through the pictorial journalism of the 1870s. Despite initial calls for moderation, *Harper's Weekly* often portrayed the Modocs as bloodsucking insects.

Figure 12. "Uncle Sam Hunting for the Modoc Flea in His Lava Bed." Wood engraving. From Harper's Weekly, *May 10, 1873.*

Following the surrender of Captain Jack and the Modocs on June 1, the magazine ran a story that speculated on the prudence of extermination, placing the piece between an engraving featuring a swarm of mosquitoes "preparing and off for the summer campaign" and a picture of General William Tecumseh Sherman, President Grant, and an unidentified Quaker singing "Ten Little Indians."[22] If such intertextualism might seem innocuous, a month earlier, *Harper's Weekly* had printed a political cartoon, "Uncle Sam Hunting for the Modoc Flea in His Lava Bed" (figure 12), that depicted a Modoc as possessing the body of a flea. At this very moment, the U.S. Army was pursuing the Modocs and Sherman was declaring, "Now let extermination be the word. Let no Modoc live to boast that his ancestor had aught to do with the death of Gen. Canby." These images made explicit the connections among discourse, violence, and American innocence in the newspaper coverage of the Modoc War.[23]

While the popular press continued to promulgate extermination discourse and circulate racialized imagery to sell newspapers to an infatuated American audience, the Modoc War lurched toward its conclusion. Following the ambush of Captain Thomas, Colonel Jefferson C. Davis relieved Colonel Gillem of his duties and assumed command of operations in the area.[24] A veteran of the U.S.-Mexico and Civil Wars, Davis had considerable experience commanding volunteer forces and employed Donald McKay's Warm Springs Indian Scouts to greater effect. The result was that by early May, the Modocs had been forced into the more open southern and eastern corners of the Lava Beds. On May 10, the Modocs attacked a force of soldiers and scouts under the command of Captain Henry Hasbrouck in their camp on the shores of Sorass, or Dry, Lake. Caught by surprise, the soldiers panicked, but Hasbrouck rallied his troops. After the Warm Springs Indians led a surprise counterattack, the Modocs withdrew.[25]

Contemporary accounts are silent on what happened after the Battle of Dry Lake. But from subsequent accounts, it seems evident that the Modocs had suffered an irrecoverable blow to unity and morale. Based on the testimony of several Modoc women and children captured a few days later, the *Yreka Journal* reported that the Modocs had disagreed among themselves, resulting in "two thirds of the warriors decid[ing] there was no use in continuing the contest."[26] The cause of the disaffection, the *San Francisco Chronicle* asserted, was that Jack had "consulted a stolen chronometer" before the battle and after performing several rituals had declared that the Modoc warriors would "shed rifle-bullets as a duck does water and escape unharmed." When several warriors were killed and others wounded in the fight, "indignation then reigned supreme in Jack's household."[27]

The defeat exposed and deepened tensions among the Modocs. The loose confederation of autonomous villages—including the Lost River, Hot Creek, and Cottonwood bands—began to disintegrate. Indeed, as Steamboat Frank, a member of the Cottonwood band, later explained to reporters, the coalition broke down because Jack had formed an "aristocracy" within the tribe, favoring members of his village over others. "He had made the Cottonwood branch of the tribe bear the burden of the campaign. The Cottonwoods had to watch and fight at all times."[28] Others, however, claimed that Jack had lost his ability to lead. The ritual with the chronometer, which was supposed to confer invulnerability onto the warriors, had failed. Considering the fact that Jack had maintained his authority through prior successes in battle, it seems possible that some Modocs interpreted their defeat as evidence of Jack's declining power.[29] Regardless of the reason, the loose coalition that had lasted throughout the winter and spring of 1872–73 collapsed in the aftermath of the Battle of Dry Lake. As a result, seventy Hot Creek and Cottonwood Modocs, including many of those responsible for the Lost River settler's deaths, left Jack and headed west.[30]

Not long after this separation, the U.S. Army picked up the Hot Creek and Cottonwood Modocs' trail, and on May 22, the beleaguered band surrendered to Colonel Davis. But Davis and his men were intent on capturing Captain Jack. In exchange for sparing the lives of the defeated Modocs, he enlisted the aid of Hooker Jim, Bogus Charley, Shacknasty Jim, and Steamboat Frank to track down and capture the remaining Modocs.[31] On May 29, the army caught up with Jack and the others in the Langell Valley. For two more days, Jack evaded capture, but on June 1, in a canyon on Willow Creek, a tributary of the Lost River, Jack surrendered, reportedly saying that his "legs had given out."[32] Modoc descendants, however, later recalled that Jack's final words as a free man were, "I am ready to die."[33]

■ On July 5, 1873, Jack and five other Modoc defendants stood before a military commission to face charges of "murder, in violations of the laws of war."[34] Colonel Davis had been disinclined to give the Modocs a trial at all. When news of Jack's surrender reached him, the colonel ordered gallows built so he could summarily execute "eight or ten ringleaders." In a declaration of charges, Davis enumerated their crimes. "The history of your tribe is filled with murders of the white race," he declared. "For these crimes no adequate punishment has ever been visited upon the guilty. . . . Upon the contrary, the Government has tacitly overlooked them. A few years ago, regardless of these acts of treachery, it gave your tribe a reservation," he said. "You left the reservation; you spurned the kindness of the Government and even resisted the soldiers in the execution of their duty. . . . You decoyed the [Peace] Commission into your hands and murdered them. . . . These acts have placed you and your band outside the rules of civilized warfare. In other words you have made yourselves outlaws."[35] But the War Department ordered the executions postponed until the attorney general decided whether the Modocs were prisoners of war to be tried by military court or murderers and therefore under the jurisdiction of the civil authorities. Davis was irritated, but Sherman thought an attorney general's opinion might establish a precedent.[36] Davis ordered the gallows taken down—at least for a time.

Jack had temporarily avoided the gibbet; others were not so lucky. After Jack surrendered, Colonel Davis ordered all Modoc prisoners to be relocated from their various locations to the new military headquarters on the southeast side of Tule Lake. In accordance with this directive, on June 8, James Fairchild, John Fairchild's brother, left his ranch on Cottonwood Creek with seventeen Modoc men, women, and children. The Natives were put in a wagon drawn by four mules and without military escort. Around Lost River, Lieutenant Josephy H. Hyzer and a posse of Oregon Volunteers stopped Fairchild and questioned the rancher about his prisoners but allowed the party to continue unmolested. A few miles later, however, two gunmen intercepted the wagon train. When the firing stopped, four Modoc men (Little John, Tahee Jack, Pony, and Mooch) were dead and one Modoc woman (Little John's wife) was wounded. "It was a terrible scene; one I shall never forget," James Fairchild later remembered. "I shudder when I think what I saw and heard. The fearful voices of those women and children still ring in my ears."[37]

The Oregon Volunteers' use of vigilante justice played into a national debate about the fair treatment of Modoc prisoners. When news of the attack on the Modoc prisoners appeared in eastern newspapers, Benjamin Coates, a prominent member of the American Colonization Society, which had helped to establish the colony of Liberia to resettle free black Americans in West Africa, wrote to President Grant, urging the federal government to pursue the vigilantes who attacked and killed the Modoc prisoners with the "same effort" as they had pursued Captain Jack. "I do not ask . . . for the *'utter extermination'* of all the border ruffians of Oregon, and the women and children belonging to them. But I would suggest that the white murderers and the red murderers have meted out the *same punishment at the same time*."[38] A Philadelphia newspaper agreed. Echoing the rhetoric of Chief Justice Roger Taney, who had declared in his 1857 *Dred Scott* decision, which denied African Americans standing in federal court and rejected federal authority over slavery, that African Americans had "no rights which the white man was bound to respect," the editors wrote, "The theory which prevails in such a community is that an Indian has no rights which a white man is bound to respect." The Philadelphia editors thus used the specter of the injustice of *Dred Scott* to attack the government's approach to Indigenous issues. Since the victims fell under the protection of the federal government, the newspapermen insisted, the attack was equal to an attack on the government itself. "We earnestly hope that the authorities will take measures to secure the arrest of the perpetrators," they concluded, for "it is folly and madness to make war upon the Indians and to hold them to rigid accountability for their misconduct, and then to neglect to punish our own citizens for the same crimes."[39] Commissioner of Indian Affairs Edward Smith agreed with Coates and the humanitarian press: "Justice, Christianity, and the rights of man" demanded the punishment of these later offenders against law and life. But despite Smith's desire that the responsible whites be punished "at the same time, and in the same manner as the treacherous Modocs," no one was ever brought to justice for the assault on the Modoc prisoners.[40]

The government used the attack on the Modocs as an opportunity to rule out a civil trial for Jack and the other defendants, citing the impossibility of seating an impartial jury. The decision to try the Modocs in a military court, however, presented certain technical challenges. The key issue was whether the conflict could be called a war. In a lengthy brief, Major H. P. Curtis, the army judge advocate appointed to prosecute the prisoners, argued that the Modocs should be tried as war criminals. Drawing on language from Chief Justice John Marshall's landmark decision in *Cherokee Nation v. Georgia* (1831), Curtis offered a unique interpretation of the law. The Supreme Court had described the relationship between Indian tribes and the United States as resembling that of a "ward to its guardian," and as wards, the Indians were not foreign but "domestic dependent nations." Curtis agreed. But the use of violent resistance, he argued, created special circumstances. He claimed that because Indians were "domestic dependent nations" and were "in no sense citizens of the United States," they would "cease to be *dependent* nations, as soon as they resist the paramount authority of their guardian, the United States, and become so instant *independent* nations, at war with the United States ceasing to be so, only when again reduced to subjection by force of arms." Curtis argued that unlike in the case of Shay's Rebellion or the Whiskey Rebellion of the previous century, in which the combatants were judged by civil authority for treason, the unique status of the Modocs within the United States required that they be tried as enemy combatants of a foreign nation.[41]

Attorney general George H. Williams, a former U.S. senator and chief justice of the Oregon Supreme Court, wrote an attorney general's opinion regarding the Modoc Indian prisoners in which he concurred with Curtis's assessment. "It is difficult to define exactly the relations of the Indian tribes to the United States," Williams admitted. However, he concluded that they were equivalent to foreign nations for the purpose of waging war since they "have been recognized as independent communities for treaty-making purposes" and "frequently carry on organized and protracted wars" against the United States. Therefore, Williams concluded, "All the laws and customs of civilized warfare may not be applicable to an armed conflict with the Indian tribes upon our western frontier; but the circumstances attending the assassination of Canby and Thomas are such as to make their murder as much a violation of the laws of savage as of civilized warfare, and the Indians concerned in it fully understood the baseness and treachery of their act." Indeed, he continued, "According to the laws of war there is nothing more sacred than a flag of truce dispatched in good faith, and there can be no greater act of perfidy and treachery than the assassination of its bearers after they have been acknowledged and received by those to whom they are sent." The Modocs, then, were to be tried by a military commission for "offenses against the recognized laws of war," and if they should be found guilty, "they may be subjected to such punishment as those laws require or justify."[42]

The local media responded with approval. Reviling the Modoc prisoners and urging the military commission to set an example, William Irwin, a Democratic state senator and editor of the *Yreka Union*, declared, "No mawkish sentimentalism should be permitted to interfere with the course of justice in this matter. No desirable object could be accomplished by sparing the lives of these murderers and assassins." Irwin went so far as to recommend an appropriate mode of punishment. "It is said Indians dread death by hanging more than in any other form. This then is the mode of execution which should be adopted. . . . To strike a salutary terror among all other Indians who shall hear of it."[43] The *Yreka Journal*, a moderating voice in the community, nonetheless agreed: "Those whose hands are red with blood must pay the penalty of their crimes, and learn other tribes that treacherous murders . . . cannot pass unpunished."[44]

But not everyone agreed. The *New York Tribune*, for example, was more critical, denouncing the Modocs as "outlaws and marauders, no more entitled to belligerent rights than so many ruffians escaped from Sing Sing." But it claimed that to recognize the Modocs' sovereignty would be absurd since the United States had "never granted them the status of independence," and to suppose that they might declare war as "a foreign power" was just a politically expedient means to circumvent civil authority in these matters.[45]

For Indian rights advocates and East Coast humanitarians, the trial of Jack and the other Modocs by military commission was a cause célèbre that raised thorny questions about the nature of justice for Indigenous peoples in the post–Civil War era. In a public meeting at Cooper Union in New York City, a group of sympathizers including Indian rights advocates John Beeson and William Williams adopted a memorial to President Grant declaring the trial and the inevitable guilty verdict a "farce and a tragedy, the truthful history of which our posterity will blush to read."[46] On July 12, the Universal Peace Union, a transnational peace organization founded in 1866, added its voice when its representatives met with Grant and begged him to uphold the tenets of his own Indian policy: "However false, cruel or treacherous the Indians may have been . . . , we ask that they may not be brutally treated, and that your 'peace policy' be not departed from." Moreover, they insisted that the Modocs could not receive a fair trial because of the vengeful mind-set of the settlers in the region and expressed a desire for "executive clemency."[47]

But not all reformers agreed. The American Indian Aid Association interpreted the attorney general's opinion as freeing Indian tribes throughout the country from odious state laws and called on "the friends of justice and humanity to see to it that this decision does for the red men substantially what President Lincoln's emancipation proclamation did for the black men."[48] For the association, federal jurisdictional supremacy over Indigenous relations was preferable to state jurisdiction since the federal government was believed to be less hostile and more likely to strictly interpret treaties, providing Indians with at least a chance at equal justice. Within this view, the case of the Modocs paradoxically represented the possibility of preserving the bright promise of inclusion that Reconstruction had briefly offered. But they did not know that the military commission had found Jack and the other Modocs guilty of all charges several days earlier.

■ The trial of Captain Jack, Schonchin John, Black Jim, Boston Charley, Barncho, and Slolux was a farce. It was held in the adjutant's office at Fort Klamath during the first week of July 1873. The defendants sat on a bench along one side of the room with their legs shackled, while uniformed soldiers stood guard armed with rifles and bayonets. Major Curtis served as judge advocate and represented the U.S. government in the trial. The Modocs were denied the benefit of counsel and so had to trust the military commission to protect their interests. Elijah Steele had asked E. J. Lewis, an attorney from Calusa, California, to defend the Modocs, and he had agreed. But the military commission proceeded without delay, and Lewis arrived at Fort Klamath on the last day of the trial, too late to be of any material assistance.[49] Compounding the lack of counsel, the commission included several biased officers. Of the six members of the commission, four had served under General Canby, and three had seen combat against the Modocs. They were therefore passing judgment on defendants they had fought and who were charged with murdering their commanding officer.[50]

The commission also failed to follow its own rules and procedures, further undermining the legitimacy of the proceedings. Since some of the defendants spoke little English, Frank and Toby Riddle were employed as translators. As officers of the court, the interpreters should have been impartial third parties. Yet both Riddles testified on behalf of the government.[51] Furthermore, at least one observer believed that the Riddles had compromised the proceedings. In a letter to the secretary of the interior, H. Wallace Atwell, a reporter covering the trial for the *Sacramento Record*, stated, "We know that the general belief is, the interpreter employed is unworthy of evidence. We know he is illiterate; can neither read or write; cannot translate the idioms of our tongue; cannot even understand good English." Moreover, he accused Frank Riddle of "shield[ing]" his wife's relatives "in his interpreting at the expense of others."[52] These objections notwithstanding, the trial proceeded with alacrity.

The prosecution began its case on July 5 and presented the testimony of eleven witnesses over four days. The testimony offered by Frank Riddle, L. S. Dyer, Alfred Meacham, assistant surgeon Henry McEldery, and H. R. Anderson, Canby's assistant adjutant general, focused on establishing the presence of the defendants at the incident and determining who fired at whom and whether the wounds Canby and Thomas received were fatal. The prosecution also offered the testimony of several Modocs, including Toby Riddle, Shacknasty Jim, Steamboat Frank, Bogus Charley, Hooker Jim, and William (or Whim), whose statements were dedicated to establishing premeditation on the part of the defendants, who had agreed to bring weapons to the meeting.[53] The Modoc defendants never cross-examined any of the witnesses.

While the lack of counsel prevented the Modocs from receiving anything like a fair trial, they nonetheless seized the opportunity once again to explain the conflict from their perspective. On July 8, the defense began its case, calling just three witnesses and then concluding with an address to the commission, delivered by Jack. Their first witness was Scarface Charley, who said almost nothing about the attack on the commissioners and instead dedicated his testimony to detailing the several occasions in which the Klamath Indians, under Link River Jack and Allen David, had encouraged the Modocs to fight by supplying ammunition and promising not to shoot at them. Another Modoc, Dave, reiterated in his testimony that "Allen David had told him to tell the Modocs to fight and not to give up to the soldiers—not to make peace." And he testified that Allen David had said, "The Klamaths are your friends and have given you ammunition, and will give it [to] you whenever you want it." The defendants' final witness, another Modoc, One-Eyed Mose, repeated these essential points and further indicted Allen David and the other Klamaths.[54]

Why were the Modoc defendants so emphatic about establishing a conspiracy between themselves and their Klamath allies? At the time, observers scorned Jack for what they believed was an attempt to shift blame. The *New York Times* called these accusations "a tissue of lies," while the

Boston Globe and others reproached Jack for being "anxious to shoulder the responsibility of the deed upon [others]."[55] Historians have also accused Jack of hoping to displace blame. Keith Murray, the most prominent twentieth-century historian of the Modoc War, described Jack's defense as "a cry of distress, rage, and frustration" and compared it to "a child about to be punished for misdeeds."[56] But the fact remains that there may have been some truth to Jack's accusations that the Klamaths had conspired with the Modocs. It is likely the Klamaths did indeed supply ammunition and weapons and that Jack felt disinclined to bear all the blame for what had happened. The Modocs' defense, however, might also have been an attempt to explain the Indigenous political landscape of the Klamath Basin and the network of obligations that compelled Jack to participate in the attack on the commissioners. In Klamath and Modoc society, a headman never acted of his own free will but was always bound to enforce the wishes of the community, whether or not he supported them. A powerful leader might influence the community to act as he desired, but as he declined in power, he often found himself carrying out the wishes of others—a point Jack tried to make clear in his closing statement.

Showing his usual savvy, Jack began his final statement with an appeal to the court's conscience by reminding it and the spectators who had gathered to hear his defense of his unfamiliarity with the etiquette of the proceedings. "I hardly know how to talk here. I don't know how white people talk in such a place as this; but I will do the best I can." In substance, however, Jack's speech suggested a considerable level of understanding, for he offered as a defense the entire history of U.S.-Indian relations in the Klamath Basin. He began by explaining how he and his people had lived in peace with the settlers and had even emulated their behavior. "I considered myself as a white man; I didn't want to have an Indian heart any longer," he observed. He insisted that the commission members did not understand how he had maintained peace in the region and he blamed Major Jackson for precipitating violence by coming to his village in the morning and shooting his men and women. Jack reiterated that he had not intended to fight after the Battle of Lost River but that the other Modocs got scared when they heard how the settlers intended to lynch them. In particular, Jack blamed Hooker Jim, who Jack said was the leader of those who killed the Lost River settlers. "None of my people had killed any of the whites," he said, "and I had never told Hooker Jim and his party to murder any settlers." Then, in an outburst of anger, he yelled at Hooker Jim, "What did you kill those people for? I never wanted you to kill my friends. You have done it on your own responsibility."[57]

Finally, Jack explained that he had been the primary advocate for peace among the Modocs but that duplicity on the part of the commissioners had undermined his authority and influence. He had wanted to meet with the commissioners back in March, but "an old Indian man," an Indian woman, and a settler, Nate Beswick, had told them that the commissioners were going to "burn me, and I was afraid to come."[58] Jack concluded his closing remarks by explaining,

> Your chief makes his men mind him and listen to him, and they do listen to what he tells them, and they believe him; but my people won't. My men would not listen to me. They wanted to fight. I told them not to fight. I wanted to talk and make peace and live right; but my men would not listen to me. . . . By my being the chief of the Modoc tribe, I think that the white people all think that I raised the fight and kept it going. I have told my people that I thought the white people would think that about me . . . but they would not listen to me. I told them that they run around and committed these murders against my will. . . . I thought that it would all be laid on to me, and I wondered to myself if there could be any other man that it could be laid upon.[59]

Despite Jack's attempt to explain the complex Indigenous political landscape of the Klamath Basin, the system of chiefly obligations that compelled him to participate in the attack, and the inexplicable arrival of Major Jackson at the villages on the Lost River, the military commission determined that the testimony introduced by the defense "was wholly irrelevant."[60] After adjourning briefly to deliberate, the commission found Captain Jack, Schonchin John, Black Jim, Boston Charley, Barncho, and Sloluck guilty of all charges and sentenced them "to be hanged by the neck until . . . dead."[61]

A guilty verdict and the sentence of death elicited expected responses along familiar battle lines. The local press approved of the trial's outcome but cried foul after learning that the Modocs indicted for murdering the Lost River settlers had been pardoned.[62] East Coast humanitarians and those sympathetic to the Modocs, in contrast, advocated clemency for Jack and the other condemned men. Throughout July and August, President Grant and secretary of the interior Columbus Delano were inundated with requests for executive clemency. The American Indian Aid Association decried the "ridiculous farce of administering justice by erecting the gallows" even before the trial began and rejected "the fallacy of assuming that the extinction of the Indian race is owing to manifest destiny."[63] Elisha Steele, John Fairchild, H. Wallace Atwell, and Sheriff William Morgan of Siskiyou

County signed a petition asking for executive clemency until a "full and fair investigation of the causes of the war" might be conducted.[64] These petitions, however, were to no avail.

The only successful petition came from Major Curtis, the judge advocate who prosecuted the Modoc defendants. "I would like to have said a word in favor of lenity towards Barncho and Slocuk," he wrote in a private letter to an officer in the judge advocate general's office in Washington, D.C. "The others were all involved deeply in the plot to murder, consulted about it with each other, and acted as ringleaders, I have no doubt." But Barncho and Slolux he regarded "as common soldiers" and he believed it "an unnecessary outlay of national venge[a]nce to put [them] to death."[65] On September 10, Grant modified the sentence by commuting Barncho and Slolux's punishment to life imprisonment on Alcatraz Island.[66]

As the weather cooled, Fort Klamath prepared for the execution. Throughout September, the Modoc prisoners were kept under guard in a stockade erected for the purpose. Relatives or friends from the Klamath Reservation, often in groups as large as fifty, visited the prisoners with some regularity. Toward the end of September, Hiram Fields, the post carpenter, erected the gallows anew.[67]

The day before the execution, newspapers ran headlines featuring the Modocs' last words. Published in excerpts in newspapers across the country, which probably sold hundreds of thousands of copies, many featured versions of these men's final speeches along with detailed accounts of their execution. "I am not a bad man, but have a good heart and was always friendly to the whites," Jack told reporters. "I tried to keep peace and opposed the murder of the Peace Commissioners." He again reminded his audience of his long political alliance with the United States and expressed his desire to discuss his punishment with the president. "The Great Chief is a long way off. There have been representations made to him, and if he would come and talk face to face, he would let [me] live." But Jack was told that the president's people were "numbered by millions" and that he would not come to meet with the Modoc chief. Seeing that his death could not be averted, Jack despaired. "It is terrible to think that I have to die. When I look at my heart I would like to live till I died a natural death."[68]

Many papers published speeches from each of the condemned men. Slolux was defiant: "I was arrested, ironed, and chained under misrepresentations. My child died yesterday and I am here in the guardhouse and unable to be with the mourners. Show me a man that will say that I was present at the time of the massacre." He demanded to know who had testified that he had attacked the commissioners: "Perhaps it was Riddle's wife.

I am innocent. I took no part in the murder of the Peace Commissioners, and I am here on the representation of Tobey." Barncho, too, declared his innocence and denied that he had played any part in the attack: "I was not there till the killing was done, but was some distance away with the other Indians." For his part, Boston Charley corroborated Jack's claims to innocence: "I killed General Canby, assisted by Steamboat Frank and Bogus Charley. . . . Captain Jack has implicated others, but I see it would be too late. I know that our chief men, Captain Jack and Schonchin, were not at the bottom of that affair; that they did not take as prominent parts as some of the younger men. I am young; know but little, and cannot say much. I only know what I see with my eyes." Like Slolux, Boston Charley concluded his statement with an accusation aimed at Toby Riddle: "Toby, Riddle's wife, understood that there was a plot on hand to kill the Commissioners. Toby said: 'To kill the four.' Bogus said to her: 'Go with me to General Canby's tent.' That was the evening before the massacre. I am telling what I know to be true—nothing more. I am done."[69]

In many accounts of the Modocs' last words, Schonchin John gave the final speech of the morning. He spoke with resignation, like a leader betrayed by his followers: "I have always tried to be a good man, and have always given my young men good advice, and was always ready to shake hands with white men when they came into my country; but here I am in irons and condemned to die." He believed that he was innocent and ought not to be executed but took solace in knowing he might again see his father: "I have always thought that I would like to see him in the Spirit Land. If I die now, perhaps I will see him with the Great Spirit." Above all, Schonchin regretted that the president had "formed the opinion that I was a wild savage Indian" and "did not know that I used my influence to prevent the young men from doing such great wrongs." He said, "War is a terrible thing, and we see the effects of it here to-day when we look at these chains." But "the Great Chief is a long way off; if I could see him face to face he might listen to me; but it is just the same as if I was at the bottom of a long hill and he on the top and I cannot see him. He has made his decision so let me die. I have talked much to-day, and you think I believe that by talking, I can escape the penalty, but I think no such thing. There is no way of crossing the line the Great Chief has drawn. When I saw the young men taking the lead I did not think I was a great criminal, and I do not talk to save myself, but that you may know my heart. I am not afraid to die."[70]

■ Gauging readers' reactions to the Gilded Age newspaper industry's coverage of the Modoc War is fraught with difficulties. But the memoir of

James Williams, a fugitive slave who escaped from a Maryland plantation and traveled to California in 1851 in search of gold, provides a glimpse into one man's evolving perspective on the Modoc War. His memoir was published in several editions throughout the 1870s with additional material and commentary added in each printing. At first, Williams expressed outrage at the news of Canby's death. The Modocs had "slaughtered our soldiers too shamefully to record," he wrote in a summer 1873 edition. They had "sent three of our best men, Gen. Canby, Dr. Thomas, and Colonel Wright to the grave . . . and the idea of letting the best men be killed! It is a disgrace, according to my belief, to the American Government."[71]

Reflecting on the popular press's ability to cultivate racial enmity to the point of violence, however, Williams observed after the execution, "I believe that they were trying to deal with Captain Jack like they deal with the freedmen down South, but Jack didn't see the point. . . . They were playing on Captain Jack, but he would not stand it, and you hung him." To a man who had escaped slavery and read with horror accounts of lynchings in newspapers, the popular press's accounts of the Modoc War struck a familiar chord. He drew powerful connections among the public persecutions of former slaves, the preferential treatment given to white Americans, and the negative treatment of American Indians by the military and the media. Williams believed that "it was wrong to hang [Jack], because there was no law established by Congress to hang him." Comparing Jack to the former president of the Confederacy, Jefferson Davis, Williams asked, "What do you think of him? He was the cause of thousands of lives being lost, and widows distressed to-day in our land; cause of our President of the United States being assassinated. Was there no law to hang Jeff Davis, according to Congress? I say there was. Then why didn't you do it? If he had been a poor Indian, we would. Remember, my reader, God created the Indian, the same as any American."[72]

For Williams and many other readers, historical understandings of the Modoc War were negotiated within the marketplace of the Gilded Age popular press. Williams's initial outrage reflected the national mood, but his subsequent disavowal of the execution, while shared by many, was a minority opinion. Between November 1872 and October 1873, journalists and editors transformed a minor incident of frontier violence into a national sensation. Their tendency to dwell on the Modocs' supposedly savage and duplicitous nature—especially after the death of General Canby—and their penchant for representing Indian violence as illegal, immoral, and directed toward the nation as a whole revealed something fundamental about the American experience of the Modoc War. Despite the romantic and sentimental humanitarianism of abolition-inspired liberalism, most mid-nineteenth-century Americans preferred to view the military conquest of Indigenous peoples as a necessary, justified, and inevitable response to the victimization of white settlers.

Far from presenting a unbiased version of events, the Gilded Age press imposed cultural concepts of progress and modernity onto racialized representations of the Modocs and in the process turned actual American Indians into ideological, symbolical, and disposable caricatures.[73] Indeed, on the day Captain Jack and the others were executed at Fort Klamath, the *Daily Alta California* declared—incorrectly—that "The Modoc have already filled their space in the world, nine[ty] days have passed since their capture and the public evidently care very little about them now."[74] Having performed their part in the romance of Manifest Destiny by assuming a brief and eventful role on the national stage, the Modocs were now free to vanish and make way for white prosperity.

Beyond promulgating the inevitability or justified nature of U.S.-Indian violence, the newspaper coverage of the Modoc War highlights the often-overlooked connection between the imaginings of journalists and the physical violence of colonialism in the history of the United States. As was the case when the *San Francisco Chronicle* described Jack as a "Red Judas" or when *Harper's Weekly* depicted the Modocs as fleas to be exterminated, the reproduction and dissemination of racialized representations of the Modocs created hierarchical relationships that influenced the course of the conflict. These representations, moreover, transformed a complex colonial conflict into a story of personal betrayal and moral failure and contributed to notions of American innocence and the spectacle of violence and retribution. But even as reporters and editors mediated Americans' perceptions of the Modoc War and imprinted the conflict with narratives of white victimhood and Indigenous criminality, they were laying the foundations for future historical interpretations.

Coda

AMERICAN INNOCENCE
IN MY INBOX

When I began researching this project, I set up a Google Alerts for the term "Modoc War." Each time the Google search engine identified a new web page, news article, blog post, or discussion thread with the term "Modoc War," I received an email notification. My inbox soon filled with a steady trickle of innocuous blog posts or antiquarian references to military history forums or California tourism articles. Or at least they seemed innocuous enough to me at first. But in the spring and summer of 2008, I noticed something unusual amid the background noise. The term "Modoc War" had appeared somewhere in a post discussing the use of so-called enhanced interrogation techniques on suspected al-Qaida operatives or designated enemy combatants in the U.S. Global War on Terror. What was this all about? Why had the Modoc War come up in a discussion of twenty-first-century terrorism? Was there an actual connection here, or was this just some random happenstance of the Internet? I was surprised by what I found.

Shortly after the attacks of September 11, 2001, the George W. Bush administration began constructing its legal response to the perceived terrorist threat. This response consisted of a series of legal opinions from the Department of Justice, many of them written by John C. Yoo, a University of California law professor who was then serving as a deputy assistant attorney general. The memorandums provided legal arguments to support the administration's claim that detainees from the war in Afghanistan did not enjoy the protections of either the U.S. Constitution or the Geneva Convention and that the War Crimes Act of 1996 also did not apply.

Despite considerable disagreement from Secretary of State Colin Powell and others, the administration went ahead, and by December 2002, the Defense Department had drafted detailed policies for interrogation techniques. Then, in early March 2003, Yoo authored one of his most sweeping legal briefs in what came to be known as the infamous Torture Memos.[1] In it, he set out not only a legal justification but also a historical connection between unlawful combatants in the current conflict and Indigenous peoples in the nineteenth century.

Reading the eighty-one-page memorandum after it became available to the public in April 2008, I was surprised to discover that Yoo relied on U.S. attorney general George H. Williams's 1873 opinion regarding the Modoc Indian prisoners for this justification. The opinion had provided the legal justification for trying the Modocs for murder by a military tribunal, using a legal interpretation of U.S.-Indian violence that sustained claims to American innocence. "It cannot be pretended that a United States soldier is guilty of murder if he kills a public enemy in battle," Williams wrote, "which would be the case if the municipal law was in force and applicable to an act committed under such circumstances."[2] The Modocs, he argued, could be legally killed by the U.S. military as long as they were first declared criminals; the U.S. Army, in other words, could kill Indians who were deemed murderers without themselves becoming murderers. Indeed, this is the "transit of empire" Chickasaw scholar Jodi A. Byrd describes wherein "all who can be made Indian . . . can be killed without being murdered, yet they are held to the standards of U.S. law that make it a crime . . . to kill any American soldier." And in the transit of empire, American innocence is maintained.[3]

One hundred thirty years later, Yoo resurrected this legal theory to support his expansive articulation of executive power and to maintain American innocence in the Global War on Terror. "The strictures that bind the Executive in its role as a magistrate enforcing the civil laws have no place in constraining the President in waging war," Yoo argued.[4] Enhanced interrogation techniques, including waterboarding, could be used on so-called unlawful enemy combatants because federal criminal laws prohibiting assault and battery simply do not apply to such criminals. Embedded in the logic of this justification was an exceptional circumstance that transformed Indigenous peoples into the first enemy combatants. "All the laws and customs of civilized warfare may not be applicable to an armed conflict with Indian tribes upon our western frontier," Williams conceded in 1873, "but the circumstances attending the assassination of Canby and Thomas are such as to make their murder as much a violation of the laws of savage as of civilized warfare, and the Indians concerned in it fully understood the baseness and treachery of their act."[5] Yoo concurred. The enemy combatant is a criminal because the Modocs were criminals; the Global War on Terror is justified because the Modoc War was justified.[6]

Legal theories matter. Even those theories that were born in a nineteenth-century military tribunal to legitimize the murder of Indigenous criminals can rise again to assert American innocence. Yoo's reliance on Williams's opinion and its legalistic explanation for the judicious use of state violence reveals the interconnectivity between the marketplace of remembering nineteenth-century U.S.-Indian violence and the perpetuation of claims to American innocence today. Indeed, the opinion itself was at least partly the product of the Gilded Age newspaper industry's penchant for partisan sensationalism and racialized representations of Native peoples to advance arguments for Indigenous criminality and white victimhood on the frontier. Amid a national outcry for vengeance, Williams constructed a legal opinion to justify the ends. But in doing so, he created a means to an end for others.

Are we to be surprised, then, that American innocence permeates our historical memories of the Modoc War and other incidents of nineteenth-century U.S.-Indian violence? Journalists in the Gilded Age proclaimed the Modocs to be criminals and American settlers and soldiers to be victims. The courts confirmed it. And ever since, Americans have claimed to be innocent in their wars of empire. In the nineteenth century, Williams's opinion transformed citizens of a domestic dependent nation into criminals from a hostile foreign nation to execute them. In the twenty-first century, Yoo and the Bush administration performed the same alchemy to detain and interrogate. Much separates the Modoc War from the Global War on Terror, but perhaps not as much as we once thought or hoped.

Part Two

Performing

Chapter Three

POCAHONTAS OF THE
LAVA BEDS

Seventeen years after the execution of Captain Jack and the other Modocs, the U.S. Congress passed a bill granting Winema, a Modoc woman, a pension of twenty-five dollars per month for "prov[ing] herself to be the friend of the white man at the risk of her own life." In particular, Congress believed she deserved a pension for her service as interpreter during the Modoc War and for saving the life of peace commissioner Alfred Meacham. Representative Binger Hermann of Oregon, the bill's author, cited Winema's bravery in warning the commissioners of her people's "intended treachery" and for "running from one [attacker] to the other, turn[ing] the[ir] pistols" as she frantically fought to save Meacham from her "murderous" relatives.[1] Hermann viewed Winema as a Pocahontas-like figure who intervened to save Meacham's life. Others portrayed her as an Indigenous Florence Nightingale. According to one account, she "heard [Meacham's] groans, went to him, tore strips from her dress to stanch the blood from his wounds, dragged him to a cave near by, and then fed and nursed him until he could escape." The precise details of how she saved Meacham notwithstanding, all accounts agreed that once her fellow Modocs discovered Winema's treachery, they banished the brave woman and forced her into the degrading position of cleaning houses and even begging to survive. Fortunately for Winema, her supporters discovered her miserable condition and appealed to Congress for her relief.[2]

Through the text of the bill and other accounts from the 1890s, Winema emerges as an Indian princess. Positioned as she was between the innocence of Manifest Destiny and the savagery of Indigenous resistance,

81

Winema proved her devotion to civilization by rescuing a white man from the dangers of male Indian violence. This interpretation of Winema's life was not confined to the halls of Congress or to the columns of reform-minded newspapers. In 1926, John B. Horner, a prominent Oregon historian, wrote that Winema was a "Modoc Princess [and] Heroine of Early Oregon Days [whose] courage and valor ... entitles her to rank along with Pocahontas and Sacajawea in American history." Half a century later, Dee Brown made a similar argument in *Bury My Heart at Wounded Knee*, casting Winema as a cultural go-between in his tragic narrative of the Modoc War.[3]

Behind these erstwhile attempts to give the story of Winema a celebratory meaning, however, lies an opportunity to explore the distorting effects of the marketplace on subsequent histories of the Modoc War. For far from being a "negotiator of change," Winema was in reality the stage name of Toby Riddle, the Modoc translator who between 1874 and 1876 toured the United States as part of the Alfred B. Meacham Lecture Company and became the subject of numerous dime novels and Wild West shows. Indeed, by adopting the persona of a latter-day Pocahontas, Riddle embraced gendered representations of Indigenous women as rescuers of white men to create a space for herself within the postbellum traveling Indian show industry. Considered within this context, the bill introduced on her behalf was not simply a posthumous act of nostalgia or an isolated case of mythmaking. Rather, it was the direct result of a highly gendered and sexualized marketplace dominated by representations of Indian women as rescuers of white men, in turn shaping historical memories of nineteenth-century U.S.-Indian violence.

Gendered discourses of civilization and savagery have long defined Indianness in American history. And many scholars have commented on the metaphoric power of the Pocahontas story to reduce the identities of all Indian women to their sexualized relationship to men.[4] But while critiques of the Pocahontas narrative have exposed how Americans have used images of Indian women rescuing white men to construct the nation's racial and imperial identity, the significance of these literary devices to the lived reality of Native women who presented *themselves* as Pocahontas figures is less well understood. Indeed, these representations require a closer examination precisely because scholars have tended to overlook their contribution to the economic lives of those who performed these acts of remembering. If constructions of Indianness influenced political debates, reflected broad cultural expectations, and contributed to settler-descendant identity formation and understandings of the nation-state,

they also created opportunities for those who sought to utilize those constructions to further political, economic, and social agendas. Establishing
this connection and tracing its contours and origins is a central objective
of this chapter.

To that end, my aim here is to consider the forgotten career of Toby
Riddle and in the process explore how one woman used existing narratives
of violence and gendered tropes of civilization and savagery to become
a national celebrity, earn a federal pension, and emerge as a local legend. But the story of Winema does not end with her public career. Rather,
her mythic self remains a popular icon throughout the Klamath Basin
and beyond. Indeed, the cultural landscape of southern Oregon and the
historiography of the region are the result of both Indigenous men and
women participating, out of necessity, in the mystification and romantici-
zation of their past and of later scholars glorifying and reproducing these
narratives. Within this tradition, the fetishization of Winema's decision
to abandon her people to save a white man reveals Americans' desire to
portray the conquest of Indigenous peoples as a tragic clash of cultures
and therefore ultimately innocent. This chapter, then, considers the life
of Toby Riddle/Winema to explore how she transformed the Modoc War
into a cross-cultural romance in the context of the traveling Indian shows
of the 1870s and 1880s. The story begins on a dusty stage three hundred
miles south of the Lava Beds, on the evening before Jack and the others
were hanged.

■ On October 2, 1873, Alfred Meacham took the stage at Mercantile Library Hall in San Francisco and changed the way Americans remember
the Modoc War. Speaking in a strained voice and appearing with his head
still bandaged from his near scalping, Meacham recounted for the audience the history of the Modoc War. The conflict, he argued, had resulted
from the government's failure to fulfill its obligations and to maintain
good faith with its Native wards. He blamed the government for its re-
luctance to prosecute settlers for their crimes and for its overreliance on
corruptible agents rather than religious philanthropic organizations. But
Meacham's version of events blended the political with the sensational.
He ended his lecture with the tragic meeting of the peace commissioners
with the Modocs and described in harrowing detail how they had drawn
their concealed weapons and fired on the commissioners. He painted a
dramatic picture of Edward Canby's and Eleazer Thomas's deaths. And he
concluded the emotional final scene with his own timely rescue by "Toby
Riddle, womanlike . . . who failing in all else, clapped her hands and cried

out 'Soldiers!,'" thereby saving him from almost certain death. Following the lecture, many in the audience bought tickets to his next performance and lingered around the speaker's podium, wishing they could see the Indian woman who had saved this gaunt and pale man.[5]

Unbeknownst to Toby Riddle, her career as Winema—the heroic savior of white men—had begun. But Meacham's lecture contradicted earlier versions of the event. According to court transcripts of the trial of Captain Jack and the other Modocs, Toby Riddle stated that during the attack, she had been knocked to the ground, where she remained until the soldiers arrived. Meacham concurred when he testified that Riddle had thrown herself on the ground when the fighting began and that his attackers had knocked him unconscious. But he added that he regained consciousness only after "hearing the voice of Colonel Miller. . . . That is the first sound I remember."[6] There is no doubt that Toby Riddle had warned the commissioners of the Modocs' plan to attack. She may have even prevented one of the Modocs from scalping Meacham. But contemporaneous sources from the spring of 1873 emphasize the chaos of the day and omit the soon-to-be famous rescue narrative of later retellings. On the stage at Mercantile Library Hall in San Francisco, however, Meacham took advantage of his audience's dramatic expectations.

Meacham was not alone in lecturing on the Modoc War. Many people hoped to capitalize on the conflict's sensationalism and notoriety. Even before the conflict ended, *Captain Jack of the Modocs*, a play by John F. Poole, opened at Wood's Theater in Manhattan. The following spring, the Bowery Theatre debuted *White Hair; or, The Last of the Modocs*. And by November, Wood's Theater followed Poole's drama with one starring Oliver Doud Byron, *Donald McKay, the Hero of the Modoc War.*[7] Not content to have his fame claimed by another, the real Donald McKay, together with his brother, William, organized a traveling Indian show of his own. Bringing together a troupe of twelve former Warm Springs Indian scouts as well as mountaineer and fur trader Joe Meek, the McKay brothers intended their show to include both a historical lecture—based on Frances Fuller Victor's book *All Over Oregon and Washington* (1872)—and rousing demonstrations of Indian skills.[8] The troupe gave its first performance in early March 1874 in Portland, where audiences flocked to see "The Modoc Slayers."[9] Having perfected the show in Portland, the McKays hired Samuel Parrish, Malheur Reservation's well-liked agent, as manager, and the troupe began performing in eastern cities in the spring of 1874. Essential to the success of any tour was a well-organized schedule with sufficient advertising and suitable arrangements made in advance. Unfortunately for the McKays and the other Warm Springs Indians, Parrish was not up to the task, and they were soon deep in debt. In June 1875, Donald McKay was arrested and placed in a Boston poorhouse.[10]

William and Donald McKay's 1874 failure may well have been attributable to managerial incompetence. But the 1870s were a period of great opportunity for western-themed melodramas. Their popularity resulted in no small part from the employment of Indigenous actors, who came to represent living and breathing trophies of western progress. In 1872, William Frederick Cody, better known as Buffalo Bill, began his career by performing before a backdrop of Indian actors. Indeed, the 1870s represented a renaissance for Indigenous actors as a new generation of eastern urbanites came of age in the United States when the appearance of Natives had become a novelty. In the context of this explosion of interest, Meacham and the McKays sought to perform the history of the Modoc War.[11]

As the McKay troupe traveled around the United States, thrilling audiences and falling deeper into debt, Meacham began establishing the groundwork for his own traveling Indian show. Following his inaugural lecture at Mercantile Library Hall, Meacham delivered two additional performances in San Francisco to judge the financial profitability of his lectures. Well aware of the need for his performances to have a more authentic Indian flare, Meacham wrote to Oliver Applegate on the Klamath Reservation asking him to supply a series of "Indian phrases" that Meacham might use "cleverly" in his lectures. Throughout the winter and into the summer of 1873–74, Meacham worked on a book-length account of the Modoc War while recuperating at his father's farm near Iowa City.[12]

Titled *Wigwam and Warpath; or, The Royal Chief in Chains* (1874), it was written in defense of the humanitarian reform movement and its commitment to righteous administration of Indian affairs. The book presented the Modoc War as the shameful result of the U.S. refusal to recognize the individual rights of American Indians. "Read the history written by our own race, and you will blush," Meacham wrote, to find "the record of battle-grounds where the red man has resisted the encroachments of a civilization that refused him recognition on equal terms before the law." American history was littered with the "graves of innocent victims of both races," he insisted; "you will find scarce ten miles square that does not offer testimony to the fact that it has been one continuous war of races, until the aborigines have been exterminated at the sacrifice of an equal number of the aggressive race."[13] Infused with passionate paternalism and committed to notions of liberal individualism, *Wigwam and Warpath* sought to strike a balance, castigating the government's Indian policy without condoning the Modocs' attack on the peace commission.

After completing his book, Meacham began turning it into a series of lectures. In May 1874, at the invitation of famed abolitionist Wendell Phillips, Meacham traveled to Boston and delivered a lecture, "The Tragedy of the Lava Beds," at the Park Street Church to a group interested in Indian policy. The event was a tremendous success, convincing Meacham that he should organize his own lecture company.[14] "I have an enterprise that I think has money in it," he wrote to Applegate in the fall of 1874, "and in order to carry out my designs I must find some reliable man acquainted with Indian life." Meacham's plan was to bring together some former members of Jack's band of Modoc Indians, a few Klamath Indians, and a few others. But above all, he wanted to recruit Toby Riddle and asked Applegate to help arrange it.[15]

While Applegate coordinated recruitment in the Klamath Basin, Meacham traveled to Indian Territory. Arriving in November at the Quapaw Reservation, where some of the Modocs had been relocated, he had little difficulty convincing several to join his troupe. The horrid conditions and lack of economic opportunity on the Quapaw Reservation added to their willingness. Incidences of illness were high among the new arrivals, especially children. Of the 153 prisoners who arrived by cattle car in the winter of 1873, one-third died of illness in the first six years. Further exacerbating matters, the Quapaw Reservation was infested with nepotism, corruption, and fraud. Eleven of the twelve employees working at the agency were relatives of Hiram Jones, the Indian agent, or Enoch Hoag, the head of the Central Indian Superintendency in Lawrence, Kansas.[16] Jones had also embezzled agency funds, purchasing rancid meat and otherwise swindling the Modocs out of their meager rations. And to make matters worse, he restricted their access to trade with local merchants, refusing to allow them to do business with any merchants from the surrounding white community of Seneca, Missouri, thereby providing a monopoly for Superintendent Hoag's first cousin, T. E. Newlin, who operated the reservation store.[17] Faced with such conditions, the opportunity to make money by participating in public performances such as Meacham's doubtless seemed appealing.

Despite the prospect of financial gain, government administrators disapproved of Meacham's plan to employ Modoc actors. Secretary of the Interior Columbus Delano suspected that Meacham might abandon the Indians if his public exhibitions proved unprofitable. In an attempt to limit Modoc involvement, the government required Meacham to provide for the actors' well-being and transportation and insisted that he guarantee that his traveling show would cost the government nothing. In the end, three Modoc Indians were allowed to participate in Meacham's exhibitions: Steamboat Frank, the former headman of the Oklahoma Modocs; Scarface Charley; and Shacknasty Jim.[18] All arrangements having been made, Meacham traveled back to Sacramento for his troupe's debut.

If the Oklahoma Modocs saw Meacham's lecture tour as an economic opportunity, those who remained on the Klamath Reservation viewed it as a political opportunity when Meacham's representative, Oliver Applegate, asked them to join. The Klamath Tribes had been having problems with their annuities for more than a decade, and a promised mill had only materialized after years of delay. In selecting participants for Meacham's traveling Indian show, the Klamath headmen wanted someone who could speak directly to the president about conditions on their reservation and advocate for the fulfillment of specific annuities. Their choice was David Hill, a man of considerable influence on the reservation who spoke English fluently and could represent all the chiefs when he arrived in Washington, D.C.[19]

The specific issues they wished Hill to bring to the president were expressed in a letter dictated by the principal chiefs in 1875. Henry Blow, for example, wanted Hill to ask Grant to provide funds for the position of chief, as the original treaty stipulated. "I understand that no provision has ever been made for pay of Head Chief on this Agency," he wrote, but previous headmen had been promised pay. "I want you and Oliver & Meacham to talk to the Hias Tyee [president] about this. . . . I want Dave Hill & Tecumseh to know what the Tyee says about this."[20] Blow was concerned about the matter since giving gifts, feeding constituencies during meetings, and providing for the needy were among the headmen's duties, and he wanted Grant to understand. "We have cut our hair . . . and try to be like white men. I live up to the treaty and am all right. . . . I help Mr. [agent Leroy S.] Dyar and we are both big men. I know about Gen. Grant and I want him to know that I help him in keeping my people straight. I want him to know what I say today. I have not sent him any talk for a long time."[21]

The Klamaths would enter the marketplace of remembering the Modoc War on their own terms. In addition to bringing treaty issues before the president, Hill was also charged with carrying several personal requests for the tribe. One headman calling himself Captain wanted Hill to ask President Grant for a wagon: "I want a wagon. I want you to tell this to the Tyee at Washington. . . . Allen David, Blow La-Lakes, Chiloquin & Jack have wagons and other things. Now I am chief I also want them. I have become like the Boston man [Americans] and I want these things." Henry Blow wanted Hill to request a "mowing machine so that we can cut more hay for our cattle." Allen David, the principal headman of the reservation, wanted Hill to tell Grant about the new mill they had built and ask the president what he thought of it and how they might improve on it. He also wanted Hill to inform Grant that "bad men are trying to get our lands and are lying to the President." He advised Hill as their representative to "tell the whole truth to him and . . . not chaco tenas tumtum [become discouraged] at whatever he might say or do. Don't be afraid of him, but tell him all about these things."[22] The Klamath headmen viewed Hill and Tecumseh's involvement in Meacham's traveling Indian show as tantamount to a delegation sent to address their specific concerns to Grant. They were to ask the president to fulfill treaty obligations and other needs as part of a long-term relationship between the Klamaths and the U.S. government.

With Hill and Tecumseh signed on, Applegate visited Frank and Toby Riddle at their home in Yreka. It is not known what Applegate promised them, but the Riddles soon joined Meacham's troupe. They may have seen the tour as an opportunity to educate their nine-year-old son, Jeff, in the wider world. We might well imagine the Riddles receiving the invitation with excitement and only a tinge of anxiety. Perhaps like many Indigenous actors who joined traveling Indian shows, Toby Riddle sought money and adventure. It is possible she wanted to see her husband's hometown in Kentucky. Or maybe, like the Oglala medicine man Black Elk, Ogliasa, and many of the Lakota who joined Buffalo Bill's Wild West show, she agreed to go because she enjoyed traveling and wanted to see more of the country.[23] Regardless of the reason, shortly after New Year's 1875, Frank, Toby, and Jeff Riddle boarded a train bound for Sacramento, the first of many trains they would ride in the months and years to come.

■ On March 29, 1875, the "San Francisco Minstrels" took the stage of the Robinson Hall in New York City. For two months, they had traveled across the country, lecturing on the shortcomings of federal Indian policy while acting out the romantic and stirring scenes of the Modoc War. Every evening and twice on Wednesday and Saturday afternoons, Oliver Applegate; Frank, Toby, and Jeff Riddle; David Hill; Tecumseh; Scarface Charley, Steamboat Frank, and Shacknasty Jim; and a Rogue River Indian, George Harney, and his wife, Maggie, appeared on stage in a kind of tableau vivant as Meacham delivered his set lectures. Meacham had tried to convince Natchez Overton, brother of the soon-to-be famous Paiute activist

Figure 13. "Alfred B. Meacham Lecture Company," 1875. Left to right: *Shacknasty Jim, Steamboat Frank, Frank Riddle, Jeff Riddle, Toby Riddle, and Scarface Charley. Courtesy of Klamath County Museum, Klamath Falls, Ore.*

and educator Sarah Winnemucca, to join the group. Overton would have been a popular addition to the tour. But he was more interested in continuing the struggle for his Paiute people and declined, traveling instead to Reno to lobby senators and others for food to feed his people.[24]

Even without Overton, the Meacham Lecture Company appealed to a wide audience. Descriptions of its performances are scarce, but extant accounts suggest the troupe members sought to balance eastern audiences' desire for authentic, stereotypical Indians with Meacham's reformist and humanitarian agenda. A studio photograph taken in Boston captures this tension (figure 13). Appearing in fringed shirts and feathered headdresses, the Modoc actors regaled their audiences with hokum performances and feats of skill. Shacknasty Jim in particular soon became famous for his archery skills. During one performance, according to a witness, Jim asked Applegate to stand at the front of the stage and hold a six-inch-wide pine board over his head while Jim and the other Modocs stood arrayed throughout the auditorium. The audience watched with amazement as the archers planted their arrows with great precision. And they received a standing ovation when Jim, spinning around like a top, loosed an arrow and planted it in the center of the target.[25] These performances, together with the performers' stylized dress, excited the crowds.

But Meacham sought to edify as well as entertain. As an active reformer and future founding editor of a humanitarian journal, *Council Fire*, he was keen to present Indigenous peoples in a positive light. To accomplish this goal, the troupe emphasized the role Toby Riddle had played in the war and sensationalized her relationship to Meacham and American civilization in general. Dressed in a high-necked and uncorseted tea gown, Riddle served as the interpreter on stage, translating the Modocs' speeches into English for the audience while David Hill attested to their eagerness to embrace American culture (figure 14). At the end of each performance, according to the *Sacramento Record*, "Mr. Meacham paid a glowing tribute to the devotion, truth, and sagacity of Toby Riddle, and declared her a heroine of the highest order."[26] The Meacham Lecture Company's performances blended the humanitarian lecture style of the antebellum abolitionists with the more rowdy novelties of the traveling medicine or vaudeville shows.

The commercial lyceums of the 1870s operated on razor-thin margins and required considerable business acumen and organizational talent. To aid in the daunting task of organizing a national tour, Meacham hired James Redpath's Boston-based Lyceum Bureau to manage his troupe's accommodations. Redpath was well suited to the task. In addition to having organized tours for Mark Twain and the American debut of Gilbert and Sullivan, he was also adept at drawing large crowds for shows of the exotic and the foreign. In 1875 alone, Redpath organized a debate in St. Louis between two Confucian and Zoroastrian philosophers; in New York, he secured an appearance for illusionist Harry Kellar before a substantial audience; and he even managed to arrange for the Ottoman consul general to appear on stage in full native dress and demonstrate some Muslim worship practices. Yet Redpath was also a passionate reformer who believed that by presenting their story on the national stage, Indian actors would prove to the American people that they deserved peace.[27]

Passion and talent, however, did not insure success. Unforeseen obstacles soon exposed divisions within the group. In February, Meacham and his group arrived in Washington, D.C., and traveled to the White House and Capitol Hill to meet President Grant and speak with Edward P. Smith, commissioner of Indian affairs. But the experience disappointed David Hill. When the delegation met the president, Hill was surprised by

Figure 14. "Winema and Her Son Jeff," 1876. Courtesy of Klamath County Museum, Klamath Falls, Ore.

the lack of grandeur surrounding the "Hias Tyee" of the United States. As Hill later recounted, the president "looked just like any other man. I was not afraid of him." But when he spoke to Grant, delivering the Klamaths' wishes and concerns, Hill was disheartened by the president's lack of interest. "I intended to tell him what my people wanted, but his ear was to [*sic*] small, he could not hear me. I brought all the things in my heart away." The delegation's visit with Smith likewise ended in disappointment. "He had large ears," Hill recalled, "he seemed to listen to what I had to tell him, but I looked him in the eye. He did not put the things I told him in his heart. My heart got sick, because I had came a long way with Colonel Meacham to see these men, but they would not take the words I gave them."[28]

With his political mission a failure, Hill decided he no longer wanted to conform his performance to the demands of the marketplace. He abandoned Meacham and the rest of the troupe without telling anyone and returned home to the Klamath Reservation. Using money he had saved to buy a train ticket, he departed New York in late April and got as far as Chicago before he ran out of money. As he walked west, Hill found occasional work making hay for white farmers in western Illinois and Iowa, saving money and traveling by rail whenever possible. In Fremont, Nebraska, he discovered that a local conductor allowed local Indians to ride free of charge as long as they rode on the platforms and tops of the boxcars. "So I painted myself a little, and . . . taking my place on the top of a car, I found it went well . . . being first a Sioux, then a Shoshone, then a Piute, and finally a California Digger." Traveling so disguised, he returned to the Klamath Reservation in early August.[29]

Hill's departure caused considerable concern among the rest of the performers. Meacham contacted the New York police and hired a private detective to investigate Hill's absence. Meacham publicized the disappearance, sought assistance from local charities, and even enlisted the services of a spiritualist to conduct a séance, all to no avail. By happenstance or by design, an enterprising group of imposters contacted Meacham several weeks after Hill had left, claiming to have him held captive. At first, the purported kidnappers demanded one thousand dollars for his safe return. However, once it became evident that Meacham would not part with such funds without proof, the gang withdrew its demands and was never heard from again.[30] When news reached Meacham and company that Hill had returned to the Klamath Reservation, Meacham called the entire affair a "cock and bull" fabrication.[31]

To make matters worse, Hill's sudden departure and the considerable expense it caused were not the troupe's only misfortune. Through the generous support of several prominent humanitarians, Redpath and his associates had managed to raise a considerable sum—as much as thirty thousand dollars—to support and promote Meacham's Lecture Company. In early May, however, the Boston bank in which Redpath had deposited the funds failed.[32] Bankrupt, Meacham had no choice other than to send Applegate and all the Modocs home in June 1875. Only Toby, Frank, and Jeff Riddle remained of the original company.[33]

The financial failure took its toll on Meacham and affected Toby Riddle particularly hard. Of all the members of the troupe, she had been least influenced by the uncertain circumstances they encountered. Traveling with her family, she had greater emotional support. Moreover, she had enjoyed traveling by train, marveling at the beauty of the great American prairies.[34] For his part, her son, Jeff, found the fantastical and macabre attractions of the eastern cities unforgettable. Indeed, as he later recalled, while walking along Pennsylvania Avenue during their visit to Washington, D.C., Jeff saw a large crowd gathered outside a tent, in which it was said a great Indian chief was on display. Paying the entrance fee, Jeff later recalled, "I expected to see a living Indian [and] looked for such. To my dismay I saw Captain Jacks head in a large jar pickled. I knew the instant it was Jacks head . . . the sight of the chiefs head in a big glass jar struck me with such force so far from home I have never forgotten it and [never] will as long as I live."[35]

But with the departure of the others, Toby Riddle turned morose. In September, her homesickness took root. In a letter to Applegate, already back at the Klamath Reservation, Frank Riddle disclosed that "Toby wants to here [sic] from her people very bad" and wished for news of life back home.[36] As the troupe's debts mounted, she fell into a deeper depression. In December, Frank became terribly ill. His son wrote, "I think my Father cannot live much longer in the great City of New York."[37] By June 1876, Toby's mental state had worsened. In a heartbreaking letter to a friend back in Oregon, Frank poured out his despair: "I don't know what to do with [Toby], she has them fits every day or too [sic] now. I have to watch her to keep her from killing her self she thinks she will never get home. . . . I think if we don't get away from here soon, Meacham and her both will go crazy." He concluded his letter with an appeal for help. "I want you to see the Indians as quick as you can and let me no [sic] what you and them can do."[38]

In the midst of this financial and personal crisis, Meacham and Riddle collaborated to create the Winema-as-Pocahontas narrative. In debt and desperate to send Toby Riddle home before she committed suicide, the troupe published and began selling a novel that would change her life. Written by Meacham, *Wi-Ne-Ma (The Woman-Chief) and Her People* (1876) was intended to raise funds to support the troupe's performance (figure 15). Priced at one dollar per copy, *Wi-Ne-Ma* valorized Toby Riddle by casting her as a mythical chieftainness. Excising all evidence of her previous identity as Toby Riddle, Meacham wrote, "Of the several characters developed by [the Modoc War], none stands out with more claim to an honorable place in history than Wi-ne-ma, (the woman-chief) who is the subject of this sketch."[39] During the lecture tour, Toby Riddle had played the role of Meacham's savior, but she had never claimed to be a Modoc chieftainness. Nonetheless, *Wi-Ne-Ma* claimed for Riddle a central role in almost every aspect of the war. From the very beginning of the conflict, according to the novel, she rode around on horseback, carried messages, negotiated peace agreements, and commanded Modoc troops (31–37, 51–69).

Beyond exaggerating her role in the Modoc War, the novel also chronicled in minute detail Winema's growing fascination with white society and

Figure 15. Title page of Alfred B. Meacham, Wi-ne-ma (The Woman-Chief)
and Her People *(Hartford, Conn.: American, 1876).*

her commitment to assimilation. According to the novel, Winema learns
to speak English after nursing a sick white man she finds in the woods.
While attending to the man—the first of many she will save—she hears of
all the cities Americans have built and the wonders of industrialization.
"Her heart . . . fired by her first lessons in the white man's history," she
dedicates her life to learning all she can about the "higher life of the white
man" (22). Ultimately, her desire to embrace white society draws her to
Frank Riddle, her future real-life husband, who enchants her with "stories
of civilized life" (27). After they are married, Winema rejects Indigenous
dress and learns to cook European foods and keep a European-style house,
attaining "the distinguished title of 'a first-rate housekeeper'" (27).

The novel portrays Winema as a model for civilizing Indigenous
peoples through acculturation. The evident superiority of white society draws Winema to reject the savage ways of her people, and once
introduced to white society, she never falters in assimilating herself
and others. Indeed, according to the novel, she became "a teacher and
missionary to her own race," speaking with them for hours about the
"wonderful things she had seen among the white people" (37). The com-
pleteness with which she embraced white society is further suggested by

her distinct lineage. "Her mother is said to have belonged to a family of Indians remarkable for one peculiarity, that of having very fine brown or red hair" (20). In addition to supplying Toby Riddle with a new stage name, the book also gave her the basis for claiming a deep and profound admiration for American society and even hinted at the civilizing benefits of racial mixing.

The complexity of Winema's romantic relationships and the centrality of her union with a white man are further revealed in the character of Uleta, her "savage" lover. Early in the novel, Winema tries to inspire Uleta to embrace white society, but he is "so thoroughly Indian" that her tales do not interest him (23). Her first civilizing project revealed as a failure, Winema rejects her Indian lover and turns her attention toward finding a partner among the whites. Consumed by madness, Uleta plots to kill Frank Riddle during the tribe's annual bear hunt. But Winema intercedes, adding yet another saved white man to her list of accomplishments. His love rejected and his revenge thwarted, Uleta throws himself from his canoe and drowns (24–30).

Within the context of the novel, not only does Winema choose to marry a white man but she also assumes the role of a protector of Indigenous women's virtue. Locating Toby Riddle within another historical event, the novel portrays her as an agent of colonialism when it asserts that she supported the Oregon superintendency's 1870 declaration that all enslaved Indigenous people must be freed and that Indian women could live with white men only if they were legally married. According to the novel, Winema embraced the project and crusaded to have Indigenous women and settler men married. Indeed, her involvement in this project is used to explain her friendship with Alfred Meacham. Winema's sexual relationships and her commitment to interracial marriages, then, presage her eventual choice to betray her people and save Meacham's life.

Winema's romantic relationships are critical to presenting her as a Pocahontas-like character. But her role as a rescuer of white men and as a peacemaker is central to the novel's portrayal of the Modoc War. It tells of her efforts to secure peace between Euro-Americans and the Modocs as well as between the warring Indigenous nations, saving the lives of many. And in one particularly dramatic scene, she negotiates a cease-fire between the Modocs and the U.S. Army and further delays bloodshed by physically placing herself between General Canby and Captain Jack when negotiations falter. As Meacham declares in the novel, "I have not the slightest doubt that but for her presence our party would have been attacked and slain" (45).

Despite her role as peacemaker, Winema cannot delay the inevitable violence and the novel, like the traveling show, features her rescue of Meacham. In the dramatic scene, Schonchin John discharges his pistol at Meacham's head. "Before the next shot, Wi-ne-ma was between [Schonchin] and his victim, grasping his arms and pleading for" Meacham's life. The beleaguered commissioner is afforded time to retreat "while my heroic defender struggled to save me." But the attacker pursues, and Winema is described as "running from one [attacker] to the other . . . turn[ing] aside the pistols" until Meacham loses consciousness (60–61). Believing him dead, she persuades the Modocs not to scalp the commissioner by shouting that the soldiers are coming, and they are content only to strip the body, leaving her to grieve. By portraying Winema's rescue of Meacham as the climactic event at the center of the Modoc War, the novel transforms an otherwise complex moment in U.S.-Indian relations to a recognizable demonstration of Indian savagery redeemed through the loyalty of an Indigenous woman to white civilization.

Was there any factual basis for the fantastical version of her exploits portrayed in the novel? Although it seems evident that some of the details contained are factual and may have been provided by Toby Riddle herself, the vast majority of the text is the product of Meacham's imagination. Far more important, the novel provided a figurative paper trail for the Winema-as-Pocahontas narrative. Indeed, this version of Meacham's rescue is almost identical to the one presented in subsequent pension bills and in fact serves as the source for all accounts of Winema's rescue of Meacham.[40] Although the illiterate Riddle may not have collaborated in the writing of the novel, she nonetheless embraced its romanticized presentation of her life. But her options were limited. Indeed, the literary devices that Meacham could use to tell the story of Riddle/Winema were shaped by the accepted roles of Indian women in nineteenth-century popular culture. The ways these stereotypes came to shape and influence Riddle's career as Winema reveal the centrality of American innocence to her public persona.

■ In the winter of 1875, Toby Riddle agreed to meet with Edwin F. Bacon, a phrenologist from Oneonta, New York. Having heard of the heroine of the Modoc War, Bacon traveled to New York City to examine the head of a Pocahontas. When Riddle met with Bacon, she conversed amiably with him while the phrenologist felt the bumps and depressions of her skull that would reveal her personality and character. He was interested in her faculties for conscientiousness as well as approbation and anything that distinguished her as different from other Indigenous people. "She has more Combativeness than Destructiveness while her people generally have more Destructiveness than Combativeness," he observed regarding the relative size of the various regions of her skull. "She has large Consciousness, and loves justice as well as honor," he reported. Not surprisingly, Bacon found that her faculties corresponded exactly to his expectations of what a Pocahontas-like heroine would possess. "She has very strong social feelings. She is true to her friends, and would be a devoted lover. She is fond of home, friends, and society. . . . She has more open bravery, but not so much severity or cruelty, or artfulness, as most people of her race."[41] Like all Modoc children, Riddle's mother had altered the child's skull by rubbing her soft forehead. But as far as Bacon was concerned, Toby Riddle's cranium proved she had the compassion, bravery, and devotion necessary to be the Pocahontas of the Lava Beds.

The conclusions of Bacon's examination reveal the degree to which Riddle's self-representation had to conform to cultural expectations for a Pocahontas-like person. The character of Winema that emerges from Meacham's novel was the product of a century of popular literary and dramatic representations. To make her role legible, Toby Riddle's stage persona had to conform to the literary conventions of the day. As an Indigenous woman, long-established plot devices of the genre circumscribed her rescue of a white man.[42] Historical precedents structured the story of Winema.

Throughout the nineteenth century, Pocahontas-like figures populated the American literary and theatrical canon. Catharine Maria Sedgwick's Magawisca, in *Hope Leslie* (1827), was the strong-willed, outspoken, caring, and loyal daughter of chief Mononotto and a childhood friend of the book's protagonists, Hope Leslie and Everell Fletcher. Magawisca's role as a latter-day Pocahontas is revealed when Mononotto, in revenge for the death of Samoset, decides to kill the young Everell. At first, Magawisca tries to reason with Mononotto, but her pleas are ignored until the chief is about to behead Everell with an axe. "Magawisca, springing from the precipitous sides of the rock, screamed—'Forbear!' and interposed her arm. It was too late. The blow was leveled—force and direction given—the stroke aimed at Everell's neck, severed his defender's arm, and left him unharmed. The lopped quivering member dropped over the precipice."[43] Magawisca's selfless actions are motivated by her love for Everell and symbolize her rejection of her father and his violence. Her intercession allows Everell to claim the tempering experience of Indigenous violence yet live to see another day.

Magawisca represents one variant on the Pocahontas story, but adaptations of the narrative were quite common throughout the antebellum period and beyond. These works often borrowed elements of Pocahontas's life—her rescue of John Smith, for example—but discarded others. And the genre included such characters as James Kirke Paulding's Aonetti, or Deer Eyes, in *Koningsmarke* (1823); William A. Caruther's Wyanokee in *The Cavaliers of Virginia* (1834); Anne L. Snelling's Onona in *Kabaosa; or, The Warriors of the West* (1841); Ann Sophia Stephen's *Malaeska* (1860); and John Neal's Lily-Pad in *Little Moccasin* (1866). By recasting the life of Pocahontas in the form of other Indigenous women, nineteenth-century authors could preserve aspects of the story that presented these relationships as ones in which Indian women rescued and redeemed white men while avoiding or at least revealing the tragic consequences of miscegenation.[44]

If romance authors portrayed Indian women as rescuers of white men, Indigenous men were often represented as tragic heroes, valiant leaders of anticolonial wars of resistance who were destined to die violent deaths as iconic martyrs. Indeed, a veritable craze for Indian tragedies sprung up during the antebellum period: James Wallis Eastburn and Robert Charles Sands's *Yamoyden* (1820); John Augustus Stone's *Metamora* (1829); Joseph Doddridge's *Logan* (1868); Lydia Maria Child's *Hobomok* (1824); John Richardson's *Tecumseh* (1828). In the process, these authors and playwrights transformed previously fearsome and dreaded Indian adversaries into doomed but noble foes ready to deliver eloquent speeches before exiting stage right.[45] By viewing all Native men as chiefs and all Indian women as Pocahontases, American audiences projected their own values and desires on Indigenous bodies as part of a process of translating the conquest of North America's Indigenous peoples into a tragic love story.

This process of literary translation is evident in Meacham's traveling Indian show in lectures such as "The Tragedy of the Lava Beds" and "The Royal Chief in Chains." But far more Americans experienced the transformation of the Modoc War into a tragic romance through the publication of dime novels. Captain Seth Hardinge's *Modoc Jack; or, The Lion of the Lava Beds*, published in the first week of October 1873, presented the Modoc War as the ultimate consequence of Jack's tragic desire for revenge.[46] Although Hardinge's novel is largely a compilation of published newspaper accounts, including a verbatim account of the hanging of Jack published days earlier in the *San Francisco Chronicle*, it nonetheless dwelled on Jack's adolescent motivations. Drawing on themes popular in other dime novels, Hardinge opens with the capture of Bright Feather, Jack's fictionalized father, by whites, an event that elicits a moving vow from the young Jack that he will avenge his father's betrayal: "The time will come when the Son of Bright Feather will avenge his father's wrong, when he will drink the blood of the palefaces as the hunted deer laps the water of Nondagura." Plotting his vengeance, Jack indentures himself to an English family in Santa Barbara, California, returning to his tribe only after enacting his vengeance on his employers, whom he blames for the death of his mother and father. Returning to his tribe, Jack becomes embroiled in the Modoc War. Yet despite his thirst for vengeance, Jack is portrayed as a character consumed by his tragic flaws. The novel ends with a hasty account of Jack's capture, his trial, and his sentencing before lingering on the Modocs' heroic speeches from the scaffold.[47]

Hardinge's Jack fits at times awkwardly within nineteenth-century imaginings of the tragic chief; other dime novels more successfully translated Modoc women into Pocahontas-like characters. In *The Squaw Spy; or, The Rangers of the Lava-Beds* (1873), T. C. Harbaugh, writing as Captain Charles Howard, tells the story of Artena—a fictional version of Artena Choakus, the Modoc translator who aided Edward Fox on his trip into Jack's cave and received considerable mention in the national popular press. She assumes the role of Pocahontas by helping the fictional Kit South rescue his daughter, Teresa. By placing Artena at the center of the Modoc War, Howard's novel suggests that Americans were eager to find a Pocahontas-like character in the story of the Modoc War. Moreover, the book's various set pieces presaged many of the stories and episodes that Toby Riddle would adopt for her stage persona.[48]

While dime novels like Hardinge's and Howard's cast the Modoc War in popular literary categories, two works by Joaquin Miller, the Poet of the Sierra, were far more instrumental to Toby Riddle's career: *Life amongst the Modocs* (1873) and *The Tale of the Tall Alcalde* (1871). The first, published in the summer of 1873, as news of the Modoc War continued to titillate readers, was titled to capitalize on the almost instantaneous popularity of anything connected to the Modocs. Blending biography with fiction, *Life amongst the Modocs* anticipated the arguments of Helen Hunt Jackson a full decade before she wrote her influential indictment of American Indian policy, *A Century of Dishonor* (1881), or her popular romance, *Ramona* (1884). "This narrative is not particularly of myself, but of a race of people that has lived centuries of history and never yet had a historian; that has suffered nearly four hundred years of wrong, and never yet had an advocate," Miller wrote. "When I die I shall take this book in my hand, and hold it up in the Day of Judgment, as a sworn indictment against the rulers of my country for the destruction of these people." But

Miller often reproduced humanitarian-inspired colonial discourse of Indigenous extinction even as he positioned himself as the self-appointed official historian of the Modocs. "I shall endeavour to make a sketch of my life with the Indians . . . true in every particular," for they were "a race of prophets . . . moving noiselessly from the face of the earth."[49]

Miller presented his book as connected with the political moment surrounding the Modoc War. "As I write these opening lines here to-day in the Old World, a war of extermination is declared against the Modoc Indians in the New." While he acknowledged the crimes for which the Modocs had been condemned, he nonetheless intended his account to provide a measure of understanding. "Peace commissioners have been killed by the Modocs, and the civilized world condemns them. I am not prepared to defend their conduct . . . but I could, by a ten-line paragraph, throw a bombshell into the camp of the civilized world at this moment, and change the whole drift of public opinion. But it would be too late to be of any particular use to this one doomed tribe."[50] In later editions of his book, Miller claimed that he had written it because "a war of extermination, it seemed to me, was being waged against my best friends, and it was imperative that I should strike hard and at once."[51]

Life amongst the Modocs begins when the fourteen-year-old Joaquin Miller runs away from home to find adventure among the Indigenous communities around Mount Shasta. His sojourn into the idyllic world of the Modocs is shattered when the young Miller discovers the savagery of white civilization while viewing a painting in a saloon. "An Indian scalp or two hung from a corner of this painting. The long matted hair hung streaming down over the ears of the bear and his red open mouth. A few sheaves of arrows in quivers were hung against the wall, with here and there a tomahawk, a scalping knife, boomerang and war-club." Confronted with the ambiguity of the boundary between civilization and savagery, Miller is awakened to the injustice of U.S.-Indian violence: "For every white man that falls the ghost of a hundred Indians follow . . . killed in cold blood by the settlers, and the affair is never heard of outside the country where it occurs."[52]

If Miller's realization about the truth of U.S.-Indian relations is at the center of the book, his evolving relationship with the beautiful Paquita is its emotional core. Described as "tall and lithe, and graceful as a mountain lily swayed by the breath of morning," Paquita is revealed to be an industrious and intelligent woman who is respected by her people even though she cannot embrace their ways.[53] Miller marries Paquita, and they live an ideal romance until Miller is wounded in battle and he is forced to turn to a life of thieving and raiding. The book's climax involves Miller's arrest and imprisonment in Shasta City for stealing a horse. Languishing in prison and besieged by charlatan lawyers, Miller despairs until Paquita arrives and sets him free. But as they flee across the Sacramento River on horseback, the lovers are ambushed by pursuing soldiers, and in the ensuing battle, Paquita is wounded in the act of saving Miller's life. The scene ends with Paquita dying in her lover's arms.

Though a far more complex work than the hackneyed dime novels of Hardinge and Howard, Miller's novel nonetheless portrays the Modoc War within the same intellectual framing. Indigenous men are tragic heroes whose eloquent deaths are all the more mournful for their inevitability; Indigenous women exist to save settler men. Thus, even before Toby Riddle joined Meacham's traveling Indian show, both dime novels and international bestsellers such as *Life amongst the Modocs* had set the groundwork for her rendition of the Modoc War. But while all these novels helped Riddle craft her persona, another poem, also by Joaquin Miller, was the source for her stage name.

Published in the spring of 1871, Joaquin Miller's *The Tale of the Tall Acalde*, part of his anthology, *Song of the Sierra*, was written in the florid prose for which Miller became famous. The poem tells a "tale of lovers who are star-crossed by the cross-cultural."[54] And it is a biographical rehearsal of his relationship with Paquita, though in this version, his lover and rescuer is named Winnema. As in *Life amongst the Modocs*, Miller becomes imprisoned and in need of a savior. Unlike the story of Paquita, however, to rescue Miller, Winnema must sacrifice her body to the jailer's sexual advances: "And all his face was as a fire as he said, 'Yield to my desire.'"[55] When Winnema comes to rescue Miller, she is desolate. "Still sadder—so that face appears, seen through the tears and blood of years—than Pocahontas bathed in tears."[56] Having freed Miller from his captivity and nursed him back to health, Winnema assumes her place by his side as they ride away. But Winnema's betrayal of her people and her tainted sexual purity haunts her, and although they escape their pursuers, she cannot return Miller's love. "O touch me not, no more, no more, 'tis past, and my sweet dream is o'er."[57] The poem ends with Winnema's sacrificial self-murder: "Oh the peril and the pain I have endured! The dark stain that I did take on my fair soul, all, all to save you, make you free, are more than mortal can endure: but fire makes the foulest pure."[58] Plunging a dagger into her breast, she dies so that Miller, rescued from danger, might not be burdened with her impure body.

The poem, with its motif of an Indian princess laying down her life for her white lover, echoes the prominence of the Indigenous woman as rescuer that would so dominate Toby Riddle's future career. Winnema, then, emerges from Miller's poem as an archetype for the Pocahontas-like character, sacrificing herself to rescue white men before dying to avoid burdening the white man with her past transgressions. Indeed, as Miller observed in a commentary on the poem in the *New York Tribune*, "The Indian girl is permitted to perish because it is in the order of things. She represents a race that is passing away. It would have been contrary to the order of things to have allowed her to escape. There is not one Indian in all my songs that survives, not one Indian woman that does not die a violent death, because that is as it is. I have done my work advisedly, such as it is, and if I have created a sympathy for the Indian girl that compels an outcry, it is surely more perfect than I had thought."[59] Although Toby Riddle would have disagreed with Miller's insistence on her inevitable self-murder, she nonetheless shared his desire to produce sympathy in the hearts of American audiences.

The decision to present Toby Riddle as a latter-day Pocahontas was influenced by nineteenth-century representations of Indigenous women as the rescuers of white men. But did Riddle's choice of Winema as a sobriquet hold any deeper meaning? Is it possible that Toby Riddle might have seen a similarity between her circumstances and those of Miller's Winnema? It is likely that Meacham read novels and poetry to the Riddles in the evenings during their traveling show, and we know he tutored young Jeff. Did she hear the story of Winnema and see her present circumstances in it? She was homesick and stranded, after all, thousands of miles from her people. We know she was suicidal, and she probably felt "sadder than Pocahontas bathed in tears" while in New York. Did Toby Riddle choose the name "Winema" because she felt a dark stain on her soul, so far from her people? Overcome by despair at the prospect that she might never return home, did she long for the release of a dagger or the purifying flames of a traditionally built pyre? Or did Meacham simply think the name might sell a few more tickets and so choose it from among the spectrum of options?

We do not know. I like to think she had some part in choosing the name. It seems unlikely that Meacham would have chosen the name for commercial reasons since Miller's poetry was not particularly popular in the United States; it was valued much more in Europe, where the poet lived at the time and where his writings were published. But whether or not Riddle initially chose the name, she unquestionably adopted the persona of Winema following the publication of Meacham's novel. In the context of nearly a century of literary representations, her choice to borrow a name from Miller's poem and her decision to mystify her past to create a new present becomes both logical and necessary. To render her fictional self legible to late-nineteenth-century traveling Indian show audiences, Riddle knew it was best to accept Meacham's rendering of her as the Pocahontas of the Lava Beds. Unlike the Winnema of Miller's poem, however, Toby Riddle did not die but lived for a very long time, playing out her theatrical persona.

▪ In the summer of 1903, Julia Frather left her house in Klamath Falls and traveled the forty or so miles to the Klamath Reservation, where she camped along the banks of the Wood River and observed the Indians' Fourth of July celebrations. Staking her tent in the midst of the Indian campground, Frather was glad to see that almost the entire tribe had gathered in the meadow, for she sought one individual in particular. Among more than a thousand people who were singing, dancing, gambling, and plying their wares to tourists such as her, Frather was overcome by the sense of abundance. As she walked among the tents, she noted that although some contained only the barest of necessities, others were well provisioned with tables and tablecloths, glass and decorated china, healthy amounts of fresh white bread and green vegetables, and succulent jellies. It is perhaps for this reason that when she finally located the person she was looking for in a well-stocked tent, Frather was indignant at the high price she demanded for a photograph. "Wi-ne-ma . . . was obstinate and proved mercenary," she later wrote. For more than half an hour, they haggled until they reached a deal and Riddle agreed to have her photograph taken. At that moment, the affluence Frather had seen in the tents like Riddle's perhaps became a little less mysterious.[60]

In the years after her time in Meacham's traveling Indian show, Toby Riddle continued to capitalize on her popularity in the American imagination. In addition to bartering with tourists who wished to take her picture, her house on the Sprague River in Yainax was a popular destination for anthropologists and others interested in gathering accounts of the Modoc War. In 1888, Riddle asked Representative Binger Hermann to introduce a bill in Congress that would award her a pension for her service in the Modoc War. In 1895, the popularity and sympathy generated by the Winema story led Jane Stanford, the widow of railroad tycoon Leland Stanford, to build Toby Riddle a new house and pledge to provide for her needs for the rest of her life.[61] And by the turn of the century, the name "Winema" had become so popular among Oklahoma Indians that she seems to have been the source for Alice Callahan's title character, "Wynema."[62] Even as her story grew in popularity, Toby Riddle continued to use the name "Winema" and everything it stood for to earn a living.

Callahan, however, was not alone in adopting the name and fame surrounding Winema for her own stories. Following the failure of their first traveling Indian show, William McKay (of Daring Donald McKay fame) returned home to Oregon while Donald, after a brief period of imprisonment for debt, traveled to Europe with his future business partner, Colonel Thomas Augustus Edward, performing before the queen of England and other monarchs.[63] In 1876, McKay and Edward returned from Europe and participated in the national centennial celebrations in Philadelphia. For the next couple of years, Donald McKay traveled and participated in various Indian shows, including "Texas Jack" Omohundro and the Kickapoo Indian Medicine Company in Boston.[64] Around 1880, Donald joined the Oregon Indian Medicine Company, which sold a cure-all tonic, Ka-ton-ka, in bottles shaped to look like Daring Donald McKay and his daughter, Minnie McKay. However, when Minnie died from a respiratory illness in 1884, the Oregon Indian Medicine Company had to find a replacement. They recruited a young Warm Springs Indian woman who assumed the stage name "Wi-ne-mah, or, Bird of the Mountain" and replaced Minnie as the face behind the product. According to the company's pamphlet, Wi-ne-mah was "a beautiful little Indian maiden . . . mild and gentle unless aroused to anger." While traveling as part of the company, Wi-ne-mah was in charge of making the "Great Indian Medicine, KA-TON-KA," for which she received many presents out of gratitude from whites.[65] The image of Winema continued on long after her personal career had ended.

Throughout her life, Riddle's identity and reputation were mystified as the story of Winema became appropriated by others and used for a variety of reasons. Around the turn of the century, settler descendants in the Klamath Basin began using the name "Winema" to mark various cultural and technological achievements. Mont Hutchinson, for example, named his hotel the Wi-Ne-Ma in her honor, for which Toby Riddle gave his son a horse. In 1905, Totten and Hansbury ran a contest to name their new luxury steamboat, nicknamed the "Grand Lady" or the "Queen of the Lake." The winner was Mrs. F. W. Jennings, who had proposed that the largest steamboat ever to sail in the Klamath Basin should be named the *Winema*.[66] Such adulations came to dominate Riddle's public persona, rendering her into a latter-day Pocahontas. Indeed, when she died on February 18, 1920, the local newspaper wrote that Winema, supposedly the Modoc word for "descendent of a long line of Modoc chieftains," was "loyal to the whites" despite her kinship with Captain Jack and the "Modoc rebellion." Within a decade, many things besides the steamboat would be named "Winema." Even after death, Toby Riddle's stage persona lived on as the mythic "good Indian" of California's last Indian war.[67]

Coda

A DRIVE THROUGH SETTLER
COLONIAL HISTORY

In the summer of 2008, while driving south along scenic Highway 97 between Bend, Oregon, and Klamath Falls, I was confronted with the continuing importance of Winema's story in the Klamath Basin. A few miles north of the struggling town of Chemult, a brown-and-yellow sign announced that I had entered the more than one-million-acre Winema National Forest, established in 1961. More than 50 percent of the Winema comprises former reservation land declared surplus following the termination of the Klamath Tribes in 1954 and incorporated into the Department of Agriculture to stabilize lumber prices by preventing the introduction of the whole Klamath Reservation into the market at one time. Continuing south, I next passed the Chief Schonchin Cemetery, near the former reservation town of Beatty, where a Daughters of the American Revolution monument stands: "In memory of Winema, Modoc Heroine" for her "Courageous and Loyal Service" in the Modoc War.[1] From Beatty, I drove into Klamath Falls, where I found an enormous mural dedicated to Winema on the side of the Winema Inn, next to the Winema Dance Hall. A few blocks from downtown, I bought batteries at the Winema Electronics Store. Through conversations with locals, I soon discovered that several schools in southern Oregon have been named after Winema, and there are numerous Winema Ways and Drives in cities throughout the state. Today there remains a Winema Lodge near Tule Lake, a theater in Scotia, California, and even a Christian summer camp in northwestern Oregon. And after half an hour of Internet searching, I learned that her name has even been used on a sleeping bag for women manufactured by

Sierra Design and that when Oregon State University developed a species of red potato specifically for the Klamath Basin, they designated it the "Winema."[2]

At the time, I had just begun to question the standard narrative of Winema. And as I tallied up the places and things named in her honor, I began to ask myself, "Why does she continue to occupy such a prominent place in the Klamath Basin's collective memory? What can this memorial tradition tell us about the meaning of the Modoc War in American life today? Who was the real Winema?" Everywhere I looked, I found traces of her presence on the southern Oregon landscape. So I set myself the task of reading everything I could about her life. Rummaging through scrapbooks and subject files in the Klamath County Museum and the Shaw Historical Library at the Oregon Institute of Technology, I learned that her legacy ran deep in local lore. Pawing over volumes of amateur, antiquarian, and academic histories of the conflict, I learned that for more than a century, virtually every historian of the Modoc War had found Winema to be an irresistible subject. But they all told the same story.

Historians of the region have reproduced fanciful narratives of Toby Riddle's life that adopt the story of Winema whole cloth. They have ignored the backstory of how Riddle, Meacham, and others actively mystified their own history to create narratives of the Modoc War that conformed to the representational dynamics of the late-nineteenth-century marketplace for traveling Indian shows. Why? Why have historians not told the story of her career as Winema the stage character? Why has the Winema-as-Pocahontas narrative persisted while the conditions that produced it remain always on the edges of the story? I left the basin that summer with few answers.

But the following summer, I returned. I had spent the previous year learning more about the history of Indians such as Toby Riddle and David Hill and the rest. And I became convinced that one reason their story had not been part of most histories of the Modoc War stemmed from our general lack of understanding of the experiences of Indigenous performers in these traveling shows. Indeed, scholars have largely ignored their experiences because these traveling Indian shows reinforced persistent stereotypes. Focusing on these performances as sites for producing racism and victimhood, historians have ignored how they also functioned as sites of economic production. By 1890, a show Indian could expect to earn between twenty-five and ninety dollars a month, salaries that far exceeded those available to Indians on reservations and that equaled those of the best paid of Bureau of Indian Affairs employees.[3] Did Toby Riddle see her performance, her fictional narrative of her life, in these economic terms? Was it part of her strategy for surviving and thriving in the face of American settler colonialism?[4]

I asked these questions of Christine Allen, Toby Riddle's great-granddaughter, and Debra Herrera, her great-great-granddaughter. Allen is a slight, soft-spoken woman, thoughtful and quick-witted. Herrera is the family's genealogist and a regular museum consultant on Modoc history and culture. And when I spoke with them in the summer of 2010, both women emphasized how after the war, Toby Riddle returned home to the Klamath Basin to live a quiet life. But her fame persisted. "She was a person that a lot of people said used to have dreams, visions, of what was going to happen," Allen told me. She also struggled, they said, to shake her reputation as a cultural go-between. "Some of her own family members really didn't care for her because they looked at her as a traitor because she worked for the government in going against Captain Jack," Herrera confided. "But then you have others like my mom and I and several of our closer family members that believe she did a great thing." According to Herrera and Allen, Riddle really had no choice. "She was married to a white man and she's Modoc and they have a son. So she had to be on both sides. She had to do what she had to do."[5]

"She had to do what she had to do." That, in a nutshell, is the story of Winema. But the story of how Toby Riddle became Winema in the popular imagination offers us more than a tale of individual contingency in the face of adversity. Indeed, it offers us an opportunity to think about the relationship between historical knowledge production and American colonialism. For what concerned me as I delved deeper into her story and legacy was how popular culture, professional historians, and even her descendants in the Klamath Basin have perpetuated the Winema narrative and in the process fetishized her story, participating in what Maureen Konkle and Vine Deloria Jr. term "the intellectually satisfying" act of portraying Indigenous people as "torn between two cultures."[6] Rather than exploring the economic and political motivations that contributed to the production of the Winema narrative, historians and others had reproduced it and thereby produced the expected image of the Modoc War as a clash of cultures wherein only one woman stood between these two tragically different people.

In writing about the intersection of mythology and Indigenous peoples, historians have focused on how settler societies create and then revel in their construction of the Indigenous. But as Philip Deloria has suggested, we should not be surprised to find Indigenous peoples capitalizing on dominant conceptions of Indianness.[7] Riddle and other Indigenous women presented themselves as Pocahontas-like figures because that was how society expected them to appear in the public sphere. In omitting the active role played by women such as Toby Riddle in the making of historical narratives, historians have overlooked the importance of the marketplace in the production of historical memories of U.S.-Indian violence and of the stories that continue to sustain American settler colonialism.

This tendency to write about U.S.-Indian violence within the paradigm of American innocence and to present conflicts such as the Modoc War as an inevitable clash of two cultures is particularly concerning in light of the inexorable interconnectivity of colonialism and the politics of making history.[8] The reason the Winema narrative continues to hold such currency is precisely because it embodies Americans' desire to view the conquest and colonization of the West as an unavoidable cultural conflict. If only the other Indigenous peoples or the settler descendants had been more like Winema, the story goes, this tragedy could have been avoided. This narrative, of course, comes out of a particular historical moment, one in which its proponents would have been considered progressive for their views. But despite its multicultural political correctness, the culture-clash narrative perpetuates the belief that colonization was inevitable and cloaks nineteenth-century U.S.-Indian violence in a veneer of American innocence. After all, "she had to do what she had to do."

By the time I had thoroughly investigated the life and legacy of Toby Riddle, I had become more convinced than ever that histories of nineteenth-century U.S.-Indian violence should connect the present with the past to expose the role of professional history and historical memory in the colonization of western Indigenous spaces. When I set out to meticulously reconstruct the story of the making of the Winema narrative, I did so hoping to undo her fetishization by the marketplace. I wanted to place the story of Winema at the center of my narrative of the Modoc War. But I wanted to avoid the tendency to portray the war as a culture conflict. Historians had silenced the political and economic nature of colonial violence in the American West and twice-silenced the political and economic nature of *remembering* that violence. And I did not want to repeat that mistake.

The story of Winema contains layers. It is a story of a woman trying to make do in the face of American settler colonialism. It is a story of compassion. It is a story of loss. But above all, it is a story that reaffirms American innocence. And its persistence *in professional historiography* and the popular culture of the Modoc War is one example of our inability to think of settler colonialism outside the culture-conflict paradigm. The story of Winema is a myth. But it is a myth many Americans have accepted because they want to believe that version of events. By using the mythical name "Winema" instead of Toby Riddle, Americans can have their "history" without the messy details. They can celebrate an Indigenous woman who saved a white man and thereby preserved the fundamental innocence of American history. That is the legacy of Winema. And it is today written onto the very landscape of the Klamath Basin.

Part Three

Commemorating

Chapter Four

THE ANGELS OF PEACE AND
PROGRESS

On the Fourth of July 1893, more than twenty-five hundred people gathered around the barracks and buildings of the recently decommissioned Fort Klamath to mark the twentieth anniversary of the Modoc War and to rewrite history. For almost a week, nearly the entire population of the Klamath Basin participated in a variety of activities. Exhibition baseball games pitted local teams against one another, while ethnic and civic organizations sponsored picnics, outdoor dances, footraces, and demonstrations of horsemanship. German, Irish, Italian, Russian, and other recent settlers strolled through the fort grounds, visiting the graves and the guardhouse. Hundreds of Klamath Basin Indians also participated in these midsummer revelries. They entered their children in "best baby" contests and participated in displays of patriotism. But the culmination of this leisurely summer celebration and civic exposition was the elaborate reenactment of the region's most notorious Indian war before the largest crowd ever to gather at Fort Klamath.[1]

The performance began at around nine o'clock in the morning, when Captain John Siemens strolled across the promenade to a small group of pines, where he sat, reading a newspaper, beneath an American flag. His examination of the day's news was interrupted when Gus Melhase, on cue, burst from the tree line without hat or coat. "They have murdered our families and burned our dwellings," he cried. "They are now in that belt of timber." With the alarm sounded, the reenactors fell into a ragtag line, firing stray volleys at unseen enemies. But the attack from the woods was a ruse, and the attacker's main force of more than one hundred mounted actors, led by a white-plumed chief, flanked the small force and descended from the opposite side. The *Klamath Falls Express* described the dramatic scene in vivid detail: the Indigenous actors ("paint-bedaubed savages, uttering their fearful war-whoops") encircled the beleaguered settler actors ("Uncle Sam's defenders") as they prepared to make their final stand. Suddenly, the white-plumed chief, who had remained apart from the assault, sprang forward and raised his hand in peace. "The whites are victorious!," he declared before lifting his headpiece to reveal "the features of Captain Ivan D. Applegate, the pioneer defender of western homes, the noted scout of three Indian wars, the honored and respected citizen of Klamath county." A cheer broke forth from the crowd as the mock battle ended.[2]

Sitting in a circle on the parade grounds, the reenactment concluded with the actors—both Indigenous and settler-descendant—smoking a ceremonial peace pipe while a dozen Native women returned the horses, guns, and swords the troopers had lost during the performance. The participants then "drew up the written compact of friendship which has existed between the whites and the Klamaths since the latter first met their pale-faced brethren." They ended the event by singing the national anthem. "Powder and bullets have given way to education," the *San Francisco Examiner* proclaimed. "Probably it will be impossible to ever have in the Klamath country another spectacle similar to the one just concluded. The civilizing influences of churches and schools have extinguished the war spirit in even the older Indians."[3]

The first reenactment of the Modoc War performed in the Klamath Basin marked a pivotal moment in the region's collective memory of U.S.-Indian violence. Bathed in patriotism and nostalgia, the performance recast the Modoc War as the originative moment of cooperation between the area's Indigenous and settler communities. Indeed, by surrendering at the moment of their victory and declaring the Americans triumphant, the performance signified the voluntary participation of Indians in the conquest of the Klamath Basin. The Native women's symbolic act of re-arming the soldiers, coupled with the acknowledgment of their collective contractual agreement, confirmed the legality of Euro-Americans' ownership of the region. The effusion of patriotism and the inducements of educational and civic institutions, moreover, encoded the event with a narrative of progress that affirmed the inevitable ebbing of the region's Indigenous peoples before the onslaught of civilization. In other words, within the framework of American innocence and the performative text of the reenactment, the Modoc War marked a rupture in the region's history, signifying the beginning of the Klamath Basin's transformation from savagery to civilization, its incorporation into the nation-state, and its embrace of modernity.

But this performance marked a pivotal moment in the region's collective memory of U.S.-Indian violence in more material ways, too. Throughout the 1870s and 1880s, small-scale agriculture and ranching dominated the Klamath Basin's meager economy. Isolated from national markets as a consequence of the lack of railroads and other infrastructure, settler-promoters nonetheless presented the region as a settled frontier to attract Euro-American migrants. In this vision of the Klamath Basin as a closing but not yet closed frontier that was committed to a shared agrarian future, they sought to improve the Klamath Basin's frontier mien by marginalizing or forgetting the Modoc War as an aberration on the path from wilderness to civilization.

Indeed, the 1890s heralded a new era in how both Indians and settler-descendant communities remembered the Modoc War. Congress's 1887 passage of the General Allotment Act (the Dawes Act) empowered the U.S. government to distribute reservation lands to individual tribal members. The stated goals of this abridgement of Indigenous sovereignty were to eliminate tribal governments and to have individual Native landowners embrace American citizenship. But allotment had unintended consequences, too. It coincided with a national timber boom and the concurrent near exhaustion of the Great Lakes forests, leading American businesses to clamor for access to the vast timber stands located on many western Indian reservations. This was especially true in the Klamath Basin, where almost 1.5 million acres of ponderosa pine lay within the Klamath Indian Reservation. As midwestern railroad tycoons and timber capitalists raced to open the Klamath Basin and its vast stands of prime timber, Euro-American migrants and some Klamath Basin Indians began embracing narratives asserting the Modoc War as the harbinger of prosperity and peace in the region.

The reconciliatory narrative of the Fourth of July 1893 reenactment arose out of this anticipation of profound transformations in the region's economy. But it was not to last. The expansion of lumber production in a region dominated by an agricultural economy altered the dynamics of interethnic relations. Almost overnight, with allotment coming soon, the vast forests of the Klamath Reservation were transformed from being of little market value to some of the most desirable land in the country. The unrealized promises of economic prosperity that accompanied calls for allotment, moreover, bred first resentment and then open hostility among many Klamath Basin Indians toward the federal government and Euro-American settlers in the area. In this environment, the promises espoused by turn-of-the-century reformers proved illusionary, and Klamath Basin Indians found their sovereignty threatened. By the second decade of the twentieth century, many Klamath Basin Indians had rejected the narrative embedded in the 1893 reenactment; in the process, they articulated their own versions of the past, drawing direct connections between the Modoc War and their present circumstances. This story, then, is about how capitalism and settler colonialism shaped retellings of the Modoc War to reaffirm American innocence in the Klamath Basin at the turn of the twentieth century.

■ Throughout the 1880s, Klamath Basin promoters sought to entice new migrants by constructing historical narratives of the region that located Indian violence in the distant past. Indeed, the post–Civil War years were a period of considerable promotional effort throughout the American West, as developers distributed pamphlets, brochures, newspaper articles, novels, maps, editorials, cartoons, and personal letters to tens of thousands of readers across the country and around the world. These texts shared certain characteristics: exuberance regarding the various opportunities afforded by settlement; a desire to assuage fears and to banish any of the notions of hardship or danger so often associated with "frontier living"; a commitment to presenting the region as a bastion of cultural and social institutions; and above all, a confidence in the area's historical trajectory from wilderness to postfrontier civilization. In short, boosters presented their western places as landscapes of opportunity in which the frontier was closing but not yet fully closed.[4]

Oregon promoters in general were adept at presenting their state as a "closing frontier." Dubbed "America's Sunset Land" by the Oregon State Board of Immigration, they claimed it was "the last among the states to be touched by those physical achievements, which have made man so irresistible and invincible in his wresting and heroisms with the rugged and defiant in nature."[5] Robert E. Strahorn, an ardent and prolific Northwest promoter and railroad speculator, praised Oregon as America's final frontier: "Where this region meets the sea ends the American 'course of empire.' Here, if not before, must our wondering capital and industry forever make its stand."[6] Lest the state's frontier demeanor deter perspective settlers, boosters in Portland and beyond were keen to emphasize cultural and civic attainments. As the Southern Pacific Company advertised, "Western Oregon does not suggest pioneer conditions" but rather possesses the "conveniences and privileges of far older States with the opportunities of a new one—that is to say, pioneer advantages without pioneer privations."[7]

Less precocious than their brethren on the Columbia River, southern Oregon promoters nonetheless embraced the practice of boostering with verve. Emphasizing the region's suitability for agriculture and ranching, the Klamath County Board of Immigration touted it as ideally suited for the production of cereals and grasses, fruits (especially cranberries), potatoes, and livestock. The Klamath Basin was not without its obstacles; owing to its altitude—four thousand feet above sea level on average— farmers were periodically troubled by midsummer frosts. But, as the Board of Immigration observed, "It is the history of all new countries in the temperate zone . . . that they are subject to summer frosts during their infancy." With the "progress of settlement and cultivation," however, these "occasional disadvantages" would be "greatly modified, if they do not wholly disappear."[8] Rain and sunshine, in other words, had historically followed the plow and would do so again.

But promises of productive land, culture, and benign climate were often not enough, since the Klamath Basin had become notorious for its U.S.-Indian violence. To combat these perceptions, promoters often turned to historians to convince others—and themselves—that such incidents were a thing of the past. Harry Wells's *History of Siskiyou County* (1881), for example, presented the region as a postfrontier whose lands—through natural and evitable historical processes—had come into the possession of American settlers as if a "magic wand" had "waved over the mountain tops, and a new race came to supplant the old." Couching the supposed extermination of Klamath Basin Indians within the racialized extinction discourse of the era, Wells claimed that they had "melted away before the advance of the Caucasian race like snow before the warm rays of the sun."[9] But Wells's vision of a postfrontier Klamath Basin extended beyond the vanishing Indian trope. When discussing Siskiyou County's Indian wars, he categorized Indian violence as savage, illegal, provocative, technologically inferior, and the remnant of an ancient way of life while categorizing settler violence as civilized, legal, retributive, technologically superior, and the precursor of industrialized modernity.[10] These binaries, moreover, carried over to Wells's rendering of the Klamath Basin's landscape, which he depicted in nearly one hundred engravings as a neatly ordered, modern agricultural space dominated and owned by Anglo-American families. These idyllic scenes of yeoman urbanity consolidated U.S. territorial claims while revealing American anxieties and insecurities regarding a still-wild landscape.

Despite the unrestrained optimism of promoters, outsiders' perceptions of the region changed little throughout much of the nineteenth century. The Modoc War had transformed Linkville from a hamlet with forty inhabitants to a bustling village of three hundred. But by the late 1870s, its promising growth had slowed to a trickle, with potential settlers often hearing disparaging descriptions of the town before confirming their suspicions on arrival. A group of settlers from Mono County, California, passing through in 1884 considered whether "they dared entrust their lives and property to this den of cut-throats." Herman Werner, a cavalry officer stationed at Fort Klamath, found the area less the home of thieves than a region scared by its recent, violent past. During an 1881 reconnaissance of the area, Werner noted the presence of burnt-out cabins throughout the Lost River Valley and local settlers' penchant for regaling travelers with tales of Modoc atrocities. The Reverend R. W. Hill, who visited the region a year later, confirmed rumors that Linkville possessed all the "disagreeable features of a frontier town" with "nothing to entice one to linger long, save the lakes, and the cold fog." In other words, the Klamath Basin was "decidedly a frontier region, as not only the country but the people indicated."[11]

Beyond the Klamath Basin, the word "Modoc" had become a vandals' moniker associated with civil disobedience or general thuggery. In Mississippi, a group of Confederate veterans opposed to federal Reconstruction assumed the alias "the Modoc" as they terrorized and tortured freedmen who dared to exercise their political rights. According to one account, the hooligans pinned a black man to the ground by driving pegs through his wrists and ankles, cut out his tongue, and shot him in the stomach before leaving him to die. In another instance, they broke into the home of a woman holding a vigil for her murdered husband and brother-in-law and taunted the mourning family. In Indiana, a secret society known as the Modocs gained notoriety when it declared war on the Burnville Turnpike Company, dismantling and stealing property to prevent the construction of a toll road through the area. And in San Francisco, a nativist gang calling themselves the Modocs terrorized Chinese residents while using nicknames such as "Captain Jack," "Schonchin," and "Bogus Charley." They attacked Chinese laundrymen, breaking the windows of their establishments before fleeing to a lumberyard dubbed the Lava Beds by local residents.[12] With such associations circulating, it is no wonder that the Modoc War remained a persistent reminder of the Klamath Basin's recent history of U.S.-Indian violence.

While promoters sought to downplay that history, disputes over land and resources throughout the 1880s exacerbated interethnic relations and gave rise to fears and rumors of a second Modoc War. The roots of the scandal stemmed from an 1864 congressional land grant to the Oregon Central Military Wagon Road Company to finance the construction of a public road through the area. The land grant predated the establishment of the Klamath Reservation's boundaries by a few months, but the bill had not designated the road's precise route. Three years later, after the reservation boundaries had been established, the wagon road company made public its plans to include a southern detour that ran "diagonally through the whole length of the Klamath Reservation, a distance of sixty miles or more, traversing the very best portions," as agent Leroy S. Dyar fumed to his superiors. It had been designed to capture "more than one-half of all the land upon the reserve suitable for cultivation or for winter grazing."[13] Despite opposition from Indian affairs, Oregon governor George L. Wood certified the 420-mile long road completed on January 12, 1870, and authorized the company to claim 806,400 acres of land, approximately 111,385 of which lay within the boundaries of the Klamath Reservation. Subsequent investigations, however, determined that much of the road was never built or was just a rudimentary trail through the sagebrush. But by then, the company had transferred its assets to a holding company, the California and Oregon Land Company.[14]

Many observers thought that the Military Road's land grant constituted a direct violation of the Treaty of 1864. But with the Modoc War just concluded, Dyar wanted to avoid any further violence. "It is my honest conviction that, if a public announcement were made to-day . . . we would stand upon the verge of a war by the side of which the late difficulty with the renegade band of Modocs would be dwarfed to insignificance," he told the commissioner of Indian affairs in October 1873. Rumors of the land grant, however, soon began circulating as petitions flooded the governor's office. Despite several attempts by the California and Oregon Land Company to assert its claims, the legal status of the land grant remained uncertain throughout the nineteenth century in the absence of any definitive action.[15]

Klamath Basin Indians faced other threats to their land base as well. Beginning in 1877, Euro-American cattlemen began running livestock on lands to the north of Klamath Marsh and within the Sycan Valley, lands that the Klamaths believed were theirs. When they complained about the ranchers, Dyar assured them that "the white people were only stopping for awhile, and they would soon go away."[16] When John R. Roork replaced Dyar later that year, the new agent began investigating the matter and soon concluded that the initial 1871 survey (known as the Mercer Survey) had excluded perhaps as much as a half million acres from the reservation as stipulated by the treaty.[17] Yet despite the fact that everyone—including George Mercer, the original surveyor—believed that the established boundaries were inaccurate, the secretary of the interior disregarded the Klamath Basin Indians' rights and previous land claims, declining to act because, he insisted, the department lacked the resources to finance a new survey. "Besides," he told the commissioner of Indian affairs, "settlers have located upon the desirable portions of the disputed territory, and their claims have been recognized by the General Land Office."[18]

For a decade, the boundary issue remained unresolved, compounding already difficult conditions and spreading discord across the reservation. Visiting the Klamath Basin in May 1885, Jeremiah Curtin, an employee of the Bureau of Ethnology, found the Klamaths outraged and unwilling to cooperate with any government employees. They had become distrustful of anyone sent by the federal government and charged him twice the rate approved by the bureau for working on his vocabulary. "I had considerable difficulty in getting Indians to give me words and assist me in learning their language," he later recalled. Although many factors contributed to an overall sense of discontent on the Klamath Reservation, the vexing matter of the boundary was paramount for many. Indeed, as one observer noted, "To the Indians . . . their deprivation, without consent or compensation . . . presents itself as an ever-present outrage of the most inexcusable and flagrant character, and naturally creates bitter feelings among them."[19]

Two separate and at first seemingly unrelated events in the summer of 1886 forced the government to act. On May 1, President Grover Cleveland declared Fort Klamath "no longer needed for military purposes" and ordered the garrison closed. This was a significant blow to the region's economy since soldiers at the outpost bought beef, hay, wool, flour, lumber, and manufactured products from both Indians and Euro-American settlers. But the loss of an important commercial center would have gone unnoticed by the Office of Indian Affairs except that two months later, a group of ranchers fenced off a large tract of land owned by the Klamaths in the Sycan Valley, reigniting concerns about the reservation's eastern boundary. In response, agent Joseph Emery ordered the cattlemen off the reservation and employed several Klamaths to help round up the wayward stock. During or shortly after the roundup, a German settler, Fritz Munz, shot and killed one of the Indians. And although the sheriff arrested Munz for murder, he jumped bail and disappeared.[20]

Settlers responded to news of the garrison's imminent closure and the Klamath man's murder by raising the specter of a second Modoc War.

On September 28, 1886, they convened a public assembly in Linkville to discuss the events. Firing off petitions, letters, and telegrams to western congressmen, the assembly struck a melodramatic tone. Jonathan Baxter Harrison, an observer for the Indian Rights Association and a special correspondent for the *Boston Herald*, noted that the settlers "talk[ed] without end about the horrors of savage warfare, the midnight attack on the lonely cabin, the scalping-knife, the red flames curling through the crackling roof, and all the rest of it."[21] No one claimed that the Klamaths and Modocs had actually done anything, and many even admitted that the settlers were guilty of many transgressions. Nevertheless, they demanded that Fort Klamath remain open. The Klamath Reservation, they reminded their elected officials, had "always required the presence of a strong military force." In addition, they insisted, "the inadequacy of the military force" had caused the Modoc War. They even suggested that the fort was necessary "to protect the Indians from trespass and injury by whites" as much as to protect Euro-American settlers—all to no avail. On August 9, 1889, the U.S. Army abandoned the post, designating a small detachment to oversee the transfer of the former garrison to civilian authority within the year.[22]

On the Klamath Reservation, the specter of a second Modoc War impressed on the administration the need to resolve the boundary issues. On October 15, 1886, in response to the Linkville resolutions, the secretary of the interior at last approved funds for a new survey and, at the request of the commanding officer of Fort Klamath, ordered that the true boundary be ascertained "by mutual concord." In the ensuing investigation, Emery found that few Euro-American settlers recalled anything from the actual negotiations and the Klamaths' opposition surprised them. "I do not remember that the Indians ever expressed to me or in my presence any dissatisfaction with the boundary line as located by George Mercer," Oliver Applegate testified, echoing the sentiments of many. But if the settlers feigned ignorance, Mosenkosket and other Klamath Basin Indians were resolute in what the agreement had been. "Mr. [J. W. P] Huntington [superintendent of Indian affairs for Oregon in 1864] told the Indians that all of Sycan Valley . . . and all of Sprague River Valley would be in the reservation, and that Indians could go there and gather roots without a pass." Faced with what Emery described as "contradictory and unsatisfactory" oral evidence, he recommended that the northern and southern boundaries be expanded by only two and three miles, respectively, while confirming Mercer's description of the eastern boundaries. The commissioner of Indian affairs agreed, concluding that maintaining the inaccurate boundary would be "the easiest way out of the difficulty."[23]

The incomplete and unsatisfactory resolution of the Military Road's land grant and the reservation boundary issues revealed the tensions simmering in the Klamath Basin in the decades following the Modoc War. Indeed, throughout the 1870s and 1880s, Klamath Basin Indians found their ownership of the land threatened by Euro-American settlers who saw little reason to honor the Natives' legal rights. Quality lands for farming and raising livestock were, after all, the keys to wealth in the regional economy. Faced with such material realities, both Indigenous and Euro-American settlers returned again and again to retellings of the Modoc War, undermining efforts to imagine the Klamath Basin as a postfrontier. As the nineteenth century gave way to the twentieth, however, the federal policy of allotment dovetailed with developments in the national timber industry to remake the Klamath Basin's economy and, in turn, its history.

■ A 1909 Klamath Development Company promotional pamphlet captures the multiple economic and political forces then transforming the Klamath Basin. Published in cooperation with the Southern Pacific Railroad, *Klamath Falls, Oregon: The Distributing Point for a Vast Timber, Live Stock, and Agricultural Empire* featured a centerfold map of the region with railroads connecting major towns to markets across the country and around the world and declared that "endless trains and cars laden with merchandise" would fuel the region's growth (figure 16). Federal irrigation canals and reclamation projects were likewise transforming the region into a landscape of progress and modernity. But the vast and productive forests of the Klamath Basin were the keys to its economic future. "In these forests are twenty billion feet of timber," one caption proclaimed. "Cutting at the rate of one-half million feet per day. It would take approximately two hundred years to exhaust the supply of standing timber." Perhaps most insidious, the map announced in bold print where precisely that timber would come from: "Klamath Indian Reservation 1500000 acres soon to be opened."[24] The Klamath Basin's future economic prosperity, then, would depend on the exploitation of Indigenous lands and resources.

This vision of the region's future little resembled the economy of a generation earlier. Isolated from major markets and situated at an average elevation above four thousand feet in the moderate rain shadow east of the southern Cascades, the Klamath Basin had for most of the nineteenth century featured an economy dominated by Euro-American sheepherders, livestock growers, and small-scale agriculturalists. In the 1880s, a handful of farmers tried hardier crops such as rye and alfalfa for local

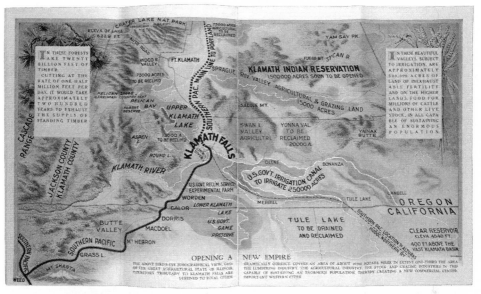

Figure 16. "Opening a New Empire." From Klamath Development Company,
Klamath Falls, Oregon: The Distributing Point for a Vast Timber, Live Stock,
and Agricultural Empire *(San Francisco: Sunset, 1909). Courtesy of Yale*
Collection of Western Americana, Beinecke Rare Book and Manuscript
Library, Yale University, New Haven, Conn.

consumption, but the region's sole exports remained livestock and a modest amount of wool. Economic conditions on the Klamath Indian Reservation were little different. Successive years of drought and damaging
midsummer frosts had convinced even the most obstinate Office of Indian
Affairs bureaucrats that agriculture was impractical on a reservation better suited for livestock. By 1883, Indigenous ranchers were raising beef to
fulfill regular contracts with the agency as well as nearby Fort Klamath.[25]

Throughout the nineteenth century, the region's modest lumber industry was limited to local consumption. In 1870, the Klamath Indians
completed the area's first commercial mill and commenced a brisk and
lucrative trade with Fort Klamath and surrounding communities. But
government regulations and prohibitions against commercial cutting
forced the practice underground. By 1896, a considerable black market
had emerged, with demand for reservation timber estimated at 250,000
board feet per year. Beyond the reservation, a handful of settlers ran commercial mills as well. Throughout the 1870s, Daniel Gordon operated
two small mills near Bonanza and the present-day town of Keno. In 1877,
William Moore established a mill near downtown Linkville. Yet despite

these modest operations, the Klamath Basin's lumber industry remained small.[26]

A series of events altered the Klamath Basin's economy toward the end of the nineteenth century. In early December 1889, snow began falling in the Klamath Basin, and by February, some areas reported more than twenty feet of accumulation. The unusual winter wreaked havoc across the Pacific Northwest, destroying railroad and telegraph lines, burying houses, collapsing barns, and devastating livestock. In the Klamath Basin, the cattle industry was crippled for more than a decade, with at least one operation losing more than 90 percent of its herd. If the hard winter was not enough, fires destroyed the town of Linkville in the fall of 1889 and again in summer of 1892, damaging the region's fledgling commercial district.[27]

The destructions of the region's cattle industry and its major business center were severe blows that forced settlers in the area to reconsider their economic future. As the town rebuilt, some residents felt they should re-place the diminutive name "Linkville" with the more development-oriented appellation "Klamath City." The new name, it was argued, would stow ideas of smallness and evince a notion of growth and opportunity. But Isa Les-kard, an engineer who had come to the area to help rebuild, suggested a slight alteration. The name "Klamath Falls," he argued, "advertises the fact that there are falls here, thus giving the town an advantage. . . . There is a great deal in the name of a town situated by a heavy cataract," Leskard explained. For its supporters, the new name signaled a new future: the seat of Klamath County would be no longer a mere "ville" but would become the wellspring and anchor of an ambitious industrial region. On February 6, 1893, the town of Linkville ceased to exist and the city of Klamath Falls was born.[28]

To realize their aspirations, Klamath Basin promoters had to attract considerable outside investment to expand the railroads to transport their timber. In the summer of 1892, Oliver Applegate traveled to Minneapolis to attend the Republican National Convention and to meet with Freder-ick Weyerhaeuser, a German immigrant whose vast syndicate of lumber interests controlled production on the Mississippi and Minnesota Rivers. Applegate's timing could not have been better. With newspaper reports and industry experts predicting an imminent decline in the timber supply coming out of the Great Lakes region, the 1890s were a period of transi-tion as midwestern lumber capitalists and railroad tycoons scoured the country for cheap and accessible forests to exploit. Many looked to the vast stands of southern yellow pine around Nashville, Chattanooga, and

St. Louis, but others, including Weyerhaeuser, believed that the Pacific Northwest held greater promise. A few years after meeting with Applegate, Weyerhaeuser began buying timber rights in the Klamath Basin, and by 1908 he controlled 158,000 acres of forestlands.[29]

Railroad interests were pursuing projects in the region as well. On December 17, 1887, the Southern Pacific Railroad completed a line connecting Portland to Redding, California, with a Golden Spike ceremony in Ashland. Over the next several years, the lumber towns of Klamathon, Thrall, and Ager sprang up in the southwestern corner of the Klamath Basin, near the Southern Pacific line. In 1899, a syndicate of local investors formed the Oregon Midland Railroad—later renamed the Klamath Lake Railroad (KLRR)—with the intention of constructing a line connecting Klamath Falls to the Southern Pacific. But after four years, the KLRR had laid just twenty-five miles of track and was still less than halfway to its goal. In 1906, while the KLRR languished, E. H. Harriman, the president of the Union Pacific and Southern Pacific Railroads as well as half a dozen other interests, secretly began building a railroad that would connect Klamath Falls to the Southern Pacific via Weed, California. Operating as the California Northeastern Railway, the group purchased the Weed Lumber Company and its twenty-two miles of track between Weed and Grass Lake in 1905 before building the remaining sixty-four miles of track. On May 20, 1909, the Southern Pacific's first train steamed into Klamath Falls, heralding a period of almost twenty years of unprecedented growth.[30]

As timber capitalists and railroad interests raced to connect the Klamath Basin with outside markets, federal agents on the Klamath Reservation proceeded with their plans for allotment. Sometimes mistakenly described by its proponents as an Indian counterpart to the Homestead Act, the General Allotment Act of 1887 and its subsequent amendments were supposed to promulgate equality by dissolving allegedly abusive tribal governments and investing American Indians with the freedom of individual property rights. Under the provisions of the original act, each individual was to receive between 40 and 160 acres, depending on age and marital status, to be held in trust by the U.S. government for twenty-five years, after which a legal ownership of the land (patent-in-fee simple) and U.S. citizenship would be conferred on those who renounced their tribal citizenship and adopted "the habits of civilized life." Transforming tribal citizens into liberal economic and political individuals, allotment was supposed to accelerate their assimilation into American society as equals. Instead, however, allotment led to devastating land loss and sowed the seeds of inequality for generations to come.[31]

Tribes such as the Cherokees, Choctaws, Creeks, Osage, and others at first objected vehemently to the idea of allotment. But many residents of the Klamath Reservation embraced the policy as a means of securing greater autonomy. Pressured by the encroachment of Euro-American ranchers on the tribal land base, the majority of Klamath Basin Indians had come by the mid-1880s to believe that private landownership might prove to be a preferable alternative. Indeed, in 1885, several tribal members, on the advice of their attorney, renounced their tribal citizenship to claim tracts of land under the Homestead Act near Tule Lake. Others embraced landownership because they saw the potential to earn money if leasing was allowed. But not everyone agreed. Tribal members without business connections beyond the reservation opposed allotment, pointing out that leftover reservation lands would be declared surplus, inviting more encroachment and thereby undoing the protections proponents sought. Despite some misgivings, many Klamath Basin Indians supported allotment, with more than 800 of the 933 eligible individuals enrolling for allotments in the first year.[32]

Once begun, however, the process of allotting the Klamath Reservation faced numerous setbacks stemming from disagreements over the still-unresolved Military Road's land grant. In 1888, David Hill, Jesse Kirk, Henry Jackson, and Dan Schonchin wrote to the commissioner of Indian affairs, requesting funds to support a tribal delegation to Washington, D.C., to discuss the Allotment Act and to resolve any outstanding claims on reservation lands.[33] They were denied funding. But the following year, the federal government filed a forfeiture suit against the California and Oregon Land Company, claiming that their grant lands were invalid because the Oregon Central Military Road and two other roads had never been completed. The Supreme Court, however, confirmed the holding company's land grant in March 1893 because it had been a purchaser "in good faith." The court reasoned that since the California and Oregon Land Company had purchased the land grant from the Oregon Central Military Road Company without knowledge of the fraud, the land company could not be penalized after the fact.[34]

Having lost its suit to regain the land grant in full, the federal government, in its capacity as guardian of the Klamath Basin Indians' trust status, next attempted to void the company's land claim within the reservation. On June 30, 1900, Judge Charles B. Bellinger, a federal district court judge in Portland and a veteran of the Modoc War, ruled against the California and Oregon Land Company, stating that although the treaty was not ratified and proclaimed until 1870, the fact that Congress had appropriated funds in fulfillment of the treaty in 1867, 1868, and 1869 suggested the treaty was in effect prior to the issuing of the land grant. Justice Oliver Wendell Holmes Jr. and the U.S. Supreme Court, however, reversed the lower court ruling in 1904, declaring that although the Klamaths' claims had merit, they should have been included in the general forfeiture suit. Failure to do so tied the court's hands, Holmes insisted, and precluded any other legal recourse. Vacillating legal opinions, however, had not forestalled the process of assigning individual allotments, and by 1897, more than three-quarters of Klamath Basin Indians had claimed their allotments.[35]

The Supreme Court's decision threw into doubt the allotments that had been granted almost a decade earlier. But it provided the California and Oregon Land Company (now controlled by the Booth-Kelly Lumber Company) the opportunity to trade its odd-numbered alternate sections of agricultural land for a consolidated, continuous tract of timberland. When the Central Military Road was originally designed, it had avoided the region's vast timber stands because the developers had considered them of little value. The transformation in the region's economy, however, had altered that calculation. To resolve the situation, Congress authorized a trade wherein the Klamath Tribes would receive $108,750 and retain their allotments—approximately 110,000 acres—in exchange for 87,000 acres of some of the finest ponderosa pine in the world. The Klamath Tribes rejected the offer, viewing it as a scandalous undervaluing of their resources. But the death of the most vocal opposition leader, Jesse Kirk, left the movement disorganized. And in the winter of 1906–7, the tribe reluctantly accepted the deal.[36]

The agreement was an exceedingly bad one for the Klamath Tribes. In arriving at the deal, the secretary of the interior had valued the timberland at $1.25 per acre. One contemporary observer believed the government had undervalued the land by as much as two or three million dollars, an opinion confirmed a decade later when the Long Bell Lumber Company purchased the tract of land for $3,700,000. Although the Klamath Tribes received $5,313,347.32 in additional compensation from the Indian Court of Claims in 1938—the market value of the timber plus interest—the affair had soured their experience with allotment and sowed the seeds of resentment and anger between Klamath Basin Indians and Euro-American business interests.[37]

Federal policy influenced development in the Klamath Basin in other ways, too. On June 17, 1902, President Theodore Roosevelt signed the Newlands Reclamation Act, which authorized the Department of the Interior to fund large-scale federal irrigation projects with the proceeds from government land sales. In the Klamath Basin, a land of abundant water but little rainfall, the Newlands Act contributed to significant alterations in the landscape. Several irrigation projects had previously been undertaken. In 1878, a group of citizens formed the Linkville Water Ditch Company to provide water to town lots. Four years later, Dan and Clint Van Brimmer undertook a far more ambitious project when they cut a small channel from White Lake to irrigate 4,000 acres in the Lost River Valley. The Reclamation Service expanded these private interests by connecting existing canals to irrigate around 210,000 acres and by draining several sections of swamp and marshland as well as almost all of Lower Klamath and Tule Lakes. "Battle Ground to Be Garden," the *San Francisco Call* declared when news of the Klamath Project (figure 17) was announced; "Scene of Modoc Outbreak in the North to Be Made a Rich Region by Irrigation." In 1917, the Reclamation Service began accepting applications from Euro-American settlers who wanted to homestead on reclaimed land, a practice that would continue until 1949.[38]

The Klamath Basin's abundant water provided local entrepreneurs, especially Euro-Americans, with the opportunity to pursue less capital-intensive means of developing the region's transportation system. For agricultural products and dried goods, pack trains and horse- or mule-drawn freight teams—many of them owned by Indigenous entrepreneurs—would suffice. But as local demand for timber, rock, and sand increased, more efficient means of transportation were necessary to bring these goods to market. The first steamboat in the Klamath Basin was the *Mary Moody*. Built around 1872 and named after the owner's Indian wife, this small boat hauled black-market lumber from the Klamath Indian Reservation as well as trade goods and occasionally military supplies to Linkville.[39] For the next two decades, several other small vessels plied the lakes and rivers of the Klamath Basin, with at least three boats making regular trips to destinations across Upper Klamath Lake.

These modest vessels facilitated development by moving goods throughout the Klamath Basin. But the golden age of steamboat transportation in the area was the 1900s. In 1901, the double-decker *Alma* was brought into service to carry barge loads of lumber and wool from Pelican Bay to Klamath Falls, returning with logging equipment, sawmill machinery, and supplies. The *Tule*, *Ewauna*, and *Jessie* joined the *Alma* two years later. And by 1909, approximately fifteen commercial vessels of various sizes— all of them owned by Euro-American settlers—were in service throughout the Klamath Basin, sustaining a network of transportation and trade that fueled uneven growth in the region.[40]

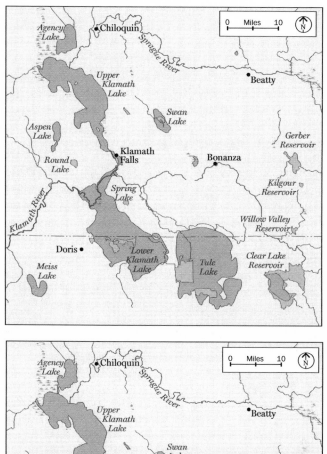

Figure 17. The Klamath Basin Project, 1904–1970. The top map is of the Klamath Basin in approximately 1904; the bottom map shows the basin as it appeared once the project was completed in 1970.

With improved transportation networks, attractive reclaimed land for Euro-American settlements, and a diversifying economy, the Klamath Basin experienced unprecedented growth in the first quarter of the twentieth century. Klamath Falls underwent its first great construction boom. In 1905 alone, developers started ninety new buildings at an estimated cost of $250,000. Three years later, the California Fruit Canners established the first box factory in Klamath Falls, introducing a lucrative new industry that would employ hundreds of Euro-American and perhaps some Indigenous residents. Indeed, benefiting from southern California's expanding fruit industry, the Ewauna Box Company, which began operation in 1912, was the second-largest box factory in the United States by the end of the decade.[41]

Beyond Klamath Falls, the turn of the twentieth century saw the establishment of several new predominantly Euro-American communities. In 1903, the town of Merrill was incorporated; within a few years, it had become the agricultural business center of the southern basin.[42] In 1909, a group of Czech migrants from Omaha, Nebraska, and members of the Bohemian Colonization Club founded the Colony of Malin along the northern shore of Tule Lake. Settling on land owned by J. Frank Adams and his associates, residents of the colony prospered as new migrants settled on reclaimed land.[43] Not all towns were successful. Established in 1905 near the California border, White Lake City boasted two hundred residents within a few years, but it soon failed. In 1910, the *Klamath Republican* referred to it as the "Lemon City," and by 1919, the town site had been deserted.[44]

The allotment of the Klamath Reservation, the advent of the railroads, and the maturation of the region's manufacturing, timber, and irrigated agriculture industries brought dramatic change. Indeed, for almost four decades, the population of the Klamath Basin doubled every ten years, rising from 2,444 in 1890 to 32,407 by 1930.[45] But the transformation of the Klamath Basin's economy from one dominated by small-scale agriculture and ranching to one focused on timber production was anything but smooth. The influx of new migrants and the formation of new communities left the newcomers grasping for a shared identity and history. Moreover, the encroachment on Indigenous sovereignty as a result of allotment and the unsatisfactory resolution of the Military Road's land grant further strained relations. In the face of such uncertainty and change, both Klamath Basin Indians and Euro-American settlers remembered the Modoc War in an effort to articulate their place in the rapidly modernizing Klamath Basin.

■ Long a symbol of the region's frontier character, the Modoc War around the turn of the century came to symbolize the genesis of the modern

Klamath Basin. Several factors contributed to this reinterpretation: railroad and steamboat technology provided Euro-Americans with an opportunity to proclaim their inclusion in the modern economy; new migrants and new communities looked to the region's past to construct collective identities; and the newfound importance of timber, the vast majority of which remained on the Klamath Reservation, led Euro-American promoters of the Klamath Basin to emphasize the civilized and benign nature of the region's Indigenous population. This neat story of modern transportation development and abundant resource exploitation gave rise to an appropriation of Indigenous land, resources, and above all, history that celebrated the romance of the Modoc War.

The spirit of technological and economic progress that infused the Klamath Basin around 1900 manifested itself in historical narratives of the Modoc War, many of which drew a direct connection between the conflict and the community's aspirations to modernity. The 1895 souvenir edition of the *Klamath Falls Express* blended boosterism with historical revisionism when it touted the region's many advantages to prospective migrants. The Klamath Basin was ideal for growing alfalfa or raising cattle; its towns were thriving centers of business; and the numerous lakes, rivers, and springs provided ample opportunities for irrigation, transportation, and leisure. The present lack of a railroad and want of capital to finance investments hindered development, but in the natural course of civilization, these privations would no doubt give rise to innovation, prosperity, and industry for all.[46]

Central to this Euro-American vision of the Klamath Basin was a replacement narrative of historical progress in which the violence of the Modoc War gave birth to the modern Klamath Basin. The "short, terrible, dramatic" history of the Modoc War "abounded in thrilling incidents and startling adventures," the *Express* acknowledged. "But the times are changed. The angel of peace has spread her bright wings over our fair land. We trust we shall hear no more the call to arms or the dreadful war-cry, but as an enterprising, grateful and appreciative people, surrounded by plenty, enjoy the blessings of an all-wise giver, as we unite to develop the great resources of our own Klamath land."[47] For Euro-American boosters of the Klamath Basin eager to portray the region as a land of opportunity, the Modoc War proved a convenient marker of the region's progression toward modernity.

While the promotional campaigns of the 1870s and 1880s sought to marginalize Klamath Basin Indians as savage relics of the past, the booster literature of the turn of the twentieth century depicted the continuing presence of Indigenous peoples as a source of opportunity rather than malice. A promotional pamphlet from 1900 described the Klamath Basin as an area "rich in historical associations" but passed over the "stubbornly contested" Modoc War in a single sentence. Rather, the panegyrist was more interested in advertising the recent allotment of the Klamath Reservation, the residue of which, "some million and a quarter acres[,] will probably be opened for settlement this fall or next spring." Indeed, the writer assured prospective migrants that Klamath Basin Indians had "been at peace with the nation" since the Modoc War and that they now "conducted their affairs in a business-like and profitable manner, thus illustrating the advantages of industrial, business, and social education as a civilizer of a wild or barbarous people."[48]

Historical memories of the Modoc War and the continuing presence of Klamath Basin Indians often became symbolically entangled with the physical technologies of their new economy. Steamboats, for example, served as potent symbols of the region's transition from a frontier characterized by U.S.-Indian violence to a modern, industrialized society. Graced with names like the *Modoc, Klamath, Captain Jack, General Canby*, and the *Winema*, steamboats allowed Euro-American settlers to appropriate historical memories of the Modoc War and recast them as icons of progress and modernity. This figurative transcription is rendered visible in a postcard-sized photograph of the *Winema* that juxtaposed the massive steamer with an elderly Indigenous couple's fishing boat (figure 18). With the caption "The Old Way and the New," the image captured visually the Klamath Basin's turn-of-the-century zeitgeist: as the "old" gives way to the "new," so, too, must Euro-American progress and mobility supplant the region's Indigenous, primitive, and violent past. The historical renarration implicit in this double appropriation of Klamath Basin Indian identity, in other words, excluded Indigenous peoples from the region's story of social-technological advancement while declaring that transformation complete.

No one appropriated Indigenous history and embraced the romantic glorification of the Modoc War more than William Drannan. The son of French emigrants who settled in Tennessee, Drannan's early life is the subject of considerable controversy, and little is known for certain. It is believed that Drannan made his way west as a young man, trapping in New Mexico and Montana or farming and ranching along the Sacramento River before moving to the Klamath Basin around 1870. Settling in the Lost River Valley, he served as a civilian contractor during the Modoc War, delivering supplies to the army in the field. After the war, Drannan may have remained in the Klamath Basin or moved to Santa Rosa,

Figure 18. "The Old and the New Way," ca. 1906. Maud Baldwin Photograph Collection. Courtesy of Klamath County Museum, Klamath Falls, Ore.

California, in 1878. Whatever the case, by 1887 he had again relocated to Seattle, Washington Territory, where he was the part owner of the River Side Restaurant. Drannan's career as a restaurateur, however, was short-lived. On June 6, 1889, the Great Seattle Fire destroyed the entire business district, including his establishment. Little is known of the next nine years of Drannan's life, but in 1899, he showed up in Chicago, this time as "William Drannan, Chief of Scouts": he claimed that he was the adopted son of famous scout Kit Carson and that he had captured Captain Jack in the Modoc War. The following year, he published *Thirty-One Years on the Plains and in the Mountains.*[49]

The reinvented William Drannan of *Thirty-One Years on the Plains* was equal parts Horatio Alger and Buffalo Bill. Calculated to capitalize on themes of uplift and individual success, the book tells the story of Drannan's alleged adoption by Carson. The fictional memoir recounted Drannan's travels with Carson on his various escapades and Drannan's education in the ways of the frontier. Central to Drannan's story is his alleged role in the Modoc War. Having learned all he could from Carson, Drannan heads out on his own, settling in the Klamath Basin, where he becomes friends with Captain Jack. Drannan's depiction of the Modocs is racist if sympathetic. Indigenous men are referred to as "young bucks" who are "as a general rule treacherous and barbarous." Jack is described as "a very intelligent Indian," but his speeches are rendered in a kind of pidgin English: "My people heap hungry and Applegate no give us anything to eat, no let us leave reservation to hunt."[50]

Throughout his account, Drannan borrows from published histories of the Modoc War, substituting himself into all the lead roles. When the Modoc War begins, Lieutenant Colonel Frank Wheaton recruits Drannan to serve as the government's principal scout, in which capacity he supposedly captured all the Modoc "ringleaders." Indeed, although his language is vague at times, Drannan claims to have captured at least thirty-one Modocs, including seventeen warriors, at a rate of "one or two Modoc everyday" for a period. Elsewhere, Drannan replaces Frank and Toby Riddle with "George Meeks and his squaw" as the army's interpreters. Later, he claims credit for having warned the peace commissioners of the Modocs' plans. And in a particularly poignant example of appropriating Indigenous history, he steals a moment from Meacham's Lecture Company's performance, casting himself in the role of the young Jeff Riddle, who, with "his father's revolver and field-glass," climbed a bluff and witnessed the death of General Canby.[51]

Sold by newsboys on trains and by Drannan himself on street corners and at public readings and performances, the book was successful and may have been published in more than one hundred editions. Its success resulted in part from its subject matter—Kit Carson was a perennial favorite. But it may also have resulted from the popularity of the emerging genre of the pioneer reminiscence. Modestly published and voraciously consumed by both American lay readers and by members of the historical societies proliferating across the United States, these texts became a veritable cottage industry after 1900. In the specific case of the Klamath Basin, these works almost without exception located the Modoc War at the center of the region's early history. Popular titles such as Cyrus Townsend Brady's *Northwestern Fights and Fighters* (1907) and William Thompson's *Reminiscences of a Pioneer* (1912) combined a simplistic and popular style with a powerful western mythology stretching back to Francis Parkman and borrowing from Frederick Jackson Turner and Theodore Roosevelt, who represented the pioneer as a citizen-soldier bridging the chasm between civilization and savagery. As a perfect example of the pioneer reminiscence cum frontier adventure fantasy, Drannan's *Thirty-One Years on the Plains* may have been the decade's most widely read and popular version of the Modoc War, but its popularity provoked a forceful response from members of the Klamath Basin's Indigenous community.

Despite visions of a modern Klamath Basin freed from the legacy of the Modoc War, persistent and intractable disputes over the reservation's boundaries and other scandals dampened enthusiasm among many Klamath Basin Indians. Indeed, according to anthropologist Theodore Stern, who worked with Klamath Tribes for more than forty years and trained generations of graduate students specializing in Oregon Indigenous cultures, their anger and frustration found expression in an interpretation of history that placed the blame for their current disempowerment squarely on the shoulders of the federal government and local Euro-American settlers. Around the turn of the century, many Klamath Basin Indians began insisting that before the Modoc War, they had lived in a "golden age," unfettered by outside forces. "The Klamaths were a great nation," declared former headman Chiloquin in a representative formulation of this halcyon past; "[We] never lost prisoners and [we] were always able to avenge all wrongs committed against [us] by other tribes, and they were all afraid of us." This image of an unworried past constituted Klamath Basin Indians' articulation of their own version of history that differed from that presented by Euro-American settlers.[52]

Opposition to dominant representations of the Modoc War assumed many forms. School-aged children on the Klamath Reservation subjected to the boarding school experience began resisting the historical explanations offered by their teachers. "We studied in history at school about the Indians and about how they warred. I didn't know what to think about it. I felt that it was not all true," a Klamath Basin Indian identified as T.L. told anthropologist Hiroto Zakoji many years later. "Sometimes they used to say, 'Now you have to go by way of books and teaching,'" but T.L. responded that the "white man was at fault. He drove the Indians from his home into the hills." Another informant recalled being told that the Klamaths and Modocs were "guilty" of the violence that led to the Modoc War. Through discussions with Klamath Basin Indians who were children around the turn of the twentieth century, Zakoji concluded that in opposing these historical narratives of the Modoc War, Indigenous students emphasized their Indianness in the face of a white majority.[53]

Indigenous resistance to the appropriation of land, resources, and history by settler descendants extended beyond the classroom. At some point between 1898 and 1905, superintendent Oliver Applegate came up with the idea of celebrating the first "battle" between Klamath Basin Indians and Euro-Americans, which occurred when John C. Frémont attacked and destroyed the Klamath village of Dokdokwas in the early morning hours of May 10, 1846. Informed of the superintendent's plan,

Leon Lelu, who had been a young boy at the time of the attack, publicly denounced the commemoration. "There was no Fremont Battle," he declared. "I watched it and saw the Fremont men shoot the Indians. I just saw the people killed and my mother killed. I won't go to celebrate the Fremont battle."[54] Resentment continued to simmer among many Klamath Basin Indians. On the Fourth of July 1916, Sheldon Kirk summarized their feelings. Looking back over the history of his tribe and its relations with recent American settlers, he concluded his public remarks by declaring, "I stand before you an aborigine of this country, a ward of a nation, but not a free man."[55] In various ways, then, Klamath Basin Indians began deconstructing and challenging settler colonial representations of the region's past.

Resentment of the government's heavy-handedness and the belief that Euro-American settlers had abused and distorted Klamath Basin Indian history found expression in Jeff Riddle's *The Indian History of the Modoc War*. Written between 1908 and 1911 and published in 1914 by David L. Moses, Riddle's history of the Modoc War offered a complex and subtle rebuttal to more than three decades of settler colonial histories of U.S.-Indian violence in the Klamath Basin, though it began with a not-so-subtle proclamation: "To the Public: In writing this little book I want to say, I did what I thought was my duty. I have read so many different works on or about the Modoc war of 1872 and '73. The books I read were so disgusting, I must say that the authors of some of the books . . . must have dreamt of the Modoc war." He took umbrage at one work in particular. "I have read Capt. William T. Drannan's book, 'Thirty Years on the Plains,' where he wrote about the Modoc warriors. According to what he says, he captured and killed more Modoc warriors than Capt. Jack really had when he commenced fighting." And it is writers like Drannan "who mislead the public in regards to Indian wars," Riddle explained. "Mr. Drannan certainly was not anywhere near the lava Beds at the time of the Modoc war of 1872 and '73 as I do not remember meeting him at that time." Riddle concludes his preface with a declaration: "In my work, I aim to give both sides of the troubles of the Modoc Indians and whites. The Indian side has never been given to the public yet."[56]

Representing his historical narrative of the Modoc War as an unbiased and unembellished account, Riddle intended to present an allegory for the usurpation of Modoc sovereignty that revealed the injustice and cruelty inherent in American settler colonialism. To accomplish this interpretative reframing, Riddle adopted a personal approach that employed the historical literary conventions of the day without reproducing its racist or romantic trappings. This approach allowed Riddle to confound neatly delineated categories of civilization and savagery and obliquely reject romantic representations of Klamath Basin Indians as timeless, irrational, nature-bound children of the forest while still appealing to and persuading a non-Indigenous audience. Riddle argued that U.S.-Indian violence in the Klamath Basin started when Jim Crosby, a quasi-official vigilante from Yreka, attacked and killed several Modoc women and children. "They came along and killed my people for nothing," Captain Jack's father explains during a council following the massacre. "Not only my men, but they kill our wives and children. I did not give the white men any cause to commit these murders." Later, Riddle again portrays non-Indigenous violence as illegitimate and savage when directed toward women. After describing the Battle of Lost River, Riddle intones bitterly, "Mind, kind reader, these men that shot the squaws and children were white men, government soldiers, supposed to be civilized. Jack, a born savage, would not allow his men to do such a coward's work, as he called it." Elsewhere, he described the soldiers as debating the best way to cook and eat "Modoc sirloin." Inverting the classic accusation of cannibalism so often leveled at Indigenous peoples, Riddle's descriptions of the white soldiers' behavior are contrasted with those of the Modocs, confounding expected categories of civilization and savagery.[57]

While Riddle's history inverted simple binaries and romantic tropes, it also challenged the preclusion of Klamath Basin Indians from modernity by representing his people as existing in the present and in possession of a future. His history is rooted in the experiences of his own family. The book includes photographs of his grown children as well as a frontispiece depicting Riddle and his wife, Amanda, well if simply dressed in a modest photo studio (figure 19). Perhaps most important, Riddle's history suggested that the continuing suffering of Klamath Basin Indians was a result of the Modoc War. In a particularly revealing juxtaposition, Riddle discusses the Klamath Basin Indians' opposition to H.R. 16743, a 1909 bill that would allow those Modoc Indians exiled to Oklahoma following the Modoc War, to return to Oregon and receive their allotments from the Klamath tribal land base, with an image of "One-Eyed Dixie. Present Day." The placement of this image of a human face ravaged by war beside his explanation of contemporary political struggles over allotment and the imposition of Washington policies reinforced the relationship between the violence of the past and the Klamath Indians' present-day political battles. As Riddle concludes his book, "Quite a number of Klamath Indians are protesting against this move the government did for the Modoc, but of

Figure 19. "The Author and Wife, Jeff C. Riddle & Manda." From Jeff C. Riddle, The Indian History of the Modoc War and the Causes That Led to It *(San Francisco: Marnell, 1914).*

course they are powerless to do or undo what Uncle Sam has already did, so this closes the chapters of the struggles of the Modoc Indians."[58]

Riddle's *The Indian History of the Modoc War* received favorable reviews in the *Oregonian, San Francisco Chronicle, Los Angeles Times, Boston Transcript, Nation,* and *Indian's Friend.* "Klamath county's latest claim to literary fame is through an Indian, Jeff Riddle," proclaimed the *Minneapolis Morning Tribune.* "It will be the only Indian history ever written giving the Indian side of the struggle and its real cause."[59] Popularity among the reading public at large was important, but Riddle's history also garnered a level of acceptance among the wider historical profession. In the *Mississippi Valley Historical Review,* the predecessor to the *Journal of American History,* historian O. G. Libby declared, "The Indian story of Captain Jack and the Modoc war is a singularly convincing piece of testimony."[60] By addressing a Euro-American audience while claiming to tell the "Indian side" of the story, Riddle presented a critical view while carving out a place for his own history in the marketplace of remembering the Modoc War.

But understanding Riddle's book requires viewing it within the longer history of American Indians' intellectual engagement with American settler colonialism. As Robert Warrior, Maureen Konkle, and others have observed, works of nonfiction—including histories, memorials, autobiographical writings, and critical essays—have been the primary form used by Indigenous authors in both developing their own literary cultures and communicating with the colonial state.[61] Including Jeff Riddle alongside Charles Eastman, Ella Deloria, Zitkala-Sa, and Arthur Parker opens a space for exploring how Klamath Basin Indians remained engaged and involved as historical memories of the Modoc War were transformed by the region's changing economy.

■ The Modoc War had put the Klamath Basin on the map and made it a household name. But throughout the nineteenth century, it remained on the margins of American settler colonialism. Euro-American settlers in a region dominated by small-scale agriculture and ranching sought to forget the Modoc War, preferring to view the conflict as a small bump on the road to civilization and modernity. The turn of the twentieth century, however, brought about a radical transformation of the Klamath Basin with the arrival of industrialized timber production and railroad construction, changes that led many area residents to embrace the rhetoric of modernization. With new expectations for the future came new and competing understandings of the region's history.

Narratives of the past often depended on the teller's present perspective and expectations of future prosperity. For the Euro-American land promoters and boosters who were benefiting from the region's industrial transformation, the Modoc War represented a rupture in the progressive history, a turning point in the Klamath Basin's inevitable ascent to modernity. They looked to the collective history of U.S.-Indian violence and saw a story of civilization persevering over Indian savagery. They inscribed the conquest and colonization of the Klamath Basin with a narrative of inevitability and innocence. And they insisted that Manifest Destiny was benign, benevolent, and beneficial. But for Klamath Basin Indians who saw their tribal sovereignty circumscribed and their economic livelihood threatened by corrupt land dealings, the Modoc War came to represent the end of a halcyon era of Indigenous autonomy and the beginning of their present-day exploitation.

The marketplace of land development and promotion, then, shaped and influenced historical retellings of the Modoc War. But while many Klamath Basin Indians and especially tribal historians rejected these self-serving narratives, not all did. Indeed, for Klamath Basin Indians seeking veterans' benefits for their service in the Modoc War as scouts for the U.S. Army, locating their service within a benign narrative of Manifest Destiny and the Modoc War could prove beneficial in navigating the racialized bureaucratic requirements of the veterans' benefits system.

Chapter Five

FAITHFUL AMERICANS

On the morning of April 3, 1914, a Paiute Indian calling himself Louie walked into the Burns, Oregon, office of attorney A. W. McGowan. He appeared before McGowan as a man broken by hard service. His shoulders were narrow, sapped of their strength by a bullet lodged in his back. He walked with an uneasy gait, the consequence of a wounded leg. And a deep scar ran the full length of his neck, starting just below his left ear and ending somewhere beneath his collar. These wounds told of Louie's intimate familiarity with the cost of war. Practicing law on the border of the former Malheur River Indian Reservation in east-central Oregon, McGowan had represented several Natives and pursued their issues as an elected representative. But Louie's request left McGowan uncertain. The Paiute wanted help securing a federal pension for his service as a scout for the U.S. Army in the Modoc War.[1]

Louie's first attempt to receive a pension came later that year. But it was rejected automatically, since no legislation extended veterans' benefits to individuals who served in an Indian war after 1860.[2] Three years later, new legislation, the Keating Measure, named for Representative Edward Keating of Colorado, provided Louie a second chance. He obtained letters of support and affidavits attesting to his identity and his record of service under the command of Donald McKay. But he was again denied a pension, this time because although the new legislation covered the Modoc War, no derivation of Louie's name appeared on any of the official muster rolls. "Apparently, his name never was put on the roll by McKay," special examiner C. M. Lane reported years later. "I examined this list today very carefully and do not find Louie, Louis, Quama, Wama, Sap po or Pa to si or any name having any similarity with the names just written thereon."[3]

Undeterred, Louie continued to battle Washington bureaucracy, with little success. In 1928, the Bureau of Pensions opened a special investigation to explore Louie's claim. After two days of lengthy depositions, in which Louie recounted his experiences during the war and the many wounds he received as well as attested to his loyalty and desire for citizenship, the claim was rejected.[4] On two subsequent occasions, Louie petitioned his congressmen to introduce special bills on his behalf. But in both cases, the measures failed in committee. Despite the sworn testimony of numerous officers to Louie's "forceful and loyal" character, he died in 1935 without receiving a dime in veterans' benefits.[5]

The story of Louie's efforts to receive benefits for his service provides a glimpse into the byzantine corner of the Bureau of Pensions reserved for Indigenous veterans of the Indian wars. An arbitrary and at times capricious system, it emerged over the course of the nineteenth century from a patchwork of legislation designed to reimburse states and Euro-American settler citizens for damages resulting from U.S.-Indian violence. The formation of several fraternal veterans' associations in the early twentieth century brought Indian war veterans together and created for the first time a united voice in Washington for their issues. Bolstered by their lobbying efforts and their newfound identity, these veterans and widows of the Indian wars soon became a powerful national political force.

Perhaps unexpectedly, the system these lobbyists created also provided hundreds of Indigenous veterans the opportunity to apply for and receive benefits. In the case of the Modoc War, at least fifty Indians applied, and thirty-six eventually received benefits. And these were not inconsiderable. An Indigenous veteran whose claim had been approved on September 4, 1922, for example, was entitled to a lump sum of $1,380 retroactive to the passage of the Keating Measure on March 4, 1917, plus $240 a year, increasing to $600 in 1927. A widow under similar circumstances would receive retroactively $792, with an annual pension thereafter of $144, increasing to $360 later.[6] These payments represented a significant source of income. In 1928, 96.4 percent of American Indians nationwide had an annual earned income of less than $200, and the pensions these Indigenous veterans and widows received would have ranked them among the wealthiest 2–3 percent of American Indians.[7]

But the benefits system did not willingly admit Indigenous veterans. Like Louie, they confronted a set of profound challenges and contradictions. A claim to veterans' benefits began with a simple application, listing the claimant's name, date of birth, date of service, regiment, rank, commanding officer, and physical condition. Department officials processed the application and assigned it a number before calling for additional evidence. The claimant then provided certified evidence, including affidavits; birth, marriage, and death certificates; discharge papers, and anything else he or she thought would support the claim. When evidence was lacking or documentation could not be obtained from the War Department or Office of Indian Affairs, the bureau rejected the claim. For complicated cases, a special examiner interviewed claimants and gathered additional material from local sources. The Bureau of Pensions offered no exceptions for exigent circumstances.

While the system dictated the forms in which these memories were transmitted, it also structured the narratives that were deployed. It transformed poignant memories of service into boxes to be checked, and the government's stringent and racialist requirements forced applicants into recounting narratives of their service that reduced complex historical moments to tidy chronological accounts of durations of service, positions held, and dates of discharge.

Here I explore the larger social, cultural, and material context within which veterans produced these particular narratives as they sought to monetize their experiences within a system dedicated to American innocence. Like their settler-descendant counterparts, these Indigenous veterans and widows relied on specialists, networks of cooperation, and communally developed evidence. But the legalistic requirements of the Bureau of Pensions often compelled veterans of the Modoc War to reimagine the meaning of their service as part of a strategy for negotiating the system, revealing the interconnectivity between historical memories of U.S.-Indian violence and the material reality of American settler colonialism. This chapter, then, considers the Indian War veterans' pension system to understand how Indigenous veterans and widows who served with the U.S. Army against their brethren helped reproduce notions of American innocence as they remembered their service in the Modoc War, a story that begins with the emergence of a social welfare system that forever changed the lives of those Americans who called themselves the "winners of the west."

■ Writing from his desk in Klamath Falls, Oliver Applegate was on the front line of the veterans' benefits movement. As an active member of the Indian War Veterans of the North Pacific Coast and the Oregon state commander of the National Indian War Veterans, Applegate was a prodigious letter writer who pestered every Republican congressman in the Pacific Northwest to support pension legislation. "Risking their lives and enduring untold hardships, in the interest of American civilization and settlement," he wrote to Oregon senator Charles L. McNary, Indian war veterans "believe that they should, in equity, share in such measures of relief as may be accorded the Civil War Veterans." Deploying the language of hardship, patriotism, and service, Applegate and hundreds of other veterans of the Indian wars lobbied for pensions in recognition of their service.[8]

In many ways, Applegate relied on methods perfected first by an earlier generation. Indeed, Civil War veterans have dominated the story of veterans' benefits and social welfare policy in the Gilded Age and Progressive Era to the virtual exclusion of other interest groups, and for good reasons. The Grand Army of the Republic (GAR), a fraternal organization turned Washington lobbying group of Union veterans of the Civil War, far outnumbered any other veteran cohort at the time, peaking at four hundred thousand members in 1890. The GAR's lobbying efforts influenced national politics and helped to transform veterans' benefits into a viable alternative to a national system of public old-age and disability services. But the key to the group's success was a compelling narrative. They were not looking for handouts. Rather, they cast social welfare as a contractual obligation between the nation-state and its male, native-born, and predominantly white veterans. Portraying pensions as an honorable benefit system, veterans and politicians recast social welfare, and as a result, more than one out of every four dollars spent by the federal government between 1880 and 1910 went to veterans.[9]

Civil War veterans, however, were not the only ones to organize or to make claims on the state. Veterans of the Indian wars also formed numerous associations. But unlike the GAR, these early organizations were not designed for lobbying as much as for fostering fraternal connections among an elite class of American soldier-pioneers. The Society of Veterans of Indian Wars of the United States, which later became the Order of Indian Wars of the United States, for example, was an elite organization that sought to define and valorize the legitimate veterans of the Indian wars. The Society of Veterans of Indian Wars required substantial membership dues and limited its membership to commissioned officers who served during an Indian war, their lineal male descendants, and Medal of Honor or Certificate of Merit recipients.[10]

These organizations not only provided social distinction but also served a commemorative function. Publishing accounts of their "heroic service and personal devotion" and hosting lavish annual dinners at the Army and Navy Club in Washington, D.C., members exchanged stories of their wartime experiences that celebrated the historical accomplishments and contributions veterans of the Indian wars had made to the country as a whole. Blending nostalgia, romanticism, and youthful adventure, these stories reduced the conquest of Indigenous peoples to a kind of stylized masquerade out of which civilization emerged on the American frontier.[11]

But the production and circulation of these reminiscences to a larger audience was also essential to the construction of a community of veterans of the Indian wars to whom the nation was indebted. Indeed, following the annual dinner meetings, reminiscences were circulated among affiliated groups and libraries throughout the United States, creating a larger network of veterans of all classes, a forum in which they could present their memories, and formal publications to record their experiences. In fact, this essential function spawned more broad-based associations such as the National Indian War Veterans, organized in 1909. The association's newspaper, *Winners of the West*, linked together all classes of veterans of the Indian wars across space and time. Edited and published by George W. Webb with significant help from his wife, Lorena Jane Webb, the newspaper consisted almost exclusively of letters to the editor, some of which ran two or three columns in length.[12]

By the beginning of the twentieth century, local and regional veterans of the Indian wars associations existed in every western state and were growing. The Indian War Veterans of the North Pacific Coast (IWVNPC), for example, began in 1885 with only sixteen members but within a few years had a thousand members.[13] Utah's Springville Comrades of the Black Hawk War began in 1893 with nine members. Within a year the leaders had identified veterans from every county in Utah. And within a decade, the Springville Comrades (reorganized as the Utah Indian War Veterans Association) had successfully lobbied for a state pension system and had turned their attentions toward obtaining federal veterans' benefits for their constituents.[14]

Even before legislation expanded benefits to include most Indian war veterans, a patchwork of legislation that historian Larry C. Skogen calls the Indian depredation claims system provided almost ten thousand Euro-American settlers and a handful of American Indians with some form of financial compensation. Intended to preserve peace by compensating individuals for property destroyed by Indians in a "relationship of amity" with the United States, the system only provided restitution for damages resulting from a period of open or declared warfare. As a result, the Indian depredation claims system transformed the systemic violence of colonialism into international warfare, defining western lands as spaces of legitimate warfare and "zones of Indian conflict."

Understaffed and beguiled by pork-barrel politics, the Indian depredation claims system provided bogus claimants with endless opportunities for fraud to the point that, according to Skogen, in some cases, "indemnity payments were supplemental income."[15] Indeed, between 1866 and 1871, more than a dozen residents of Kansas's Peketon and Saline Counties applied for and received Indian depredation claims for damages never sustained on property never owned. In the sparsely populated country around Cow Creek, rancher and trader John Prater received $16,000 for property valued at no more than $2,000 damaged during a fictitious Cheyenne raid. Oliver Hamilton, Peter Gerishe, Lenox Baxter, and Elihu Fisher similarly claimed $4,305 in damages despite the fact that they had never been attacked. While the Indian depredation claims system did provide some Euro-American settlers with an avenue for securing legitimate financial compensation, it was nonetheless riddled with fraud to the tune of nearly one million dollars a year.[16]

The Office of Indian Affairs offered one avenue for redress; direct appeal to the War Department offered another. In 1874, California and Oregon sought a special appropriation to cover the expense of "arms, ammunition, supplies, transportation, and services of volunteers" during the Modoc War. This appropriation amounted to $76,758.41 and was paid out to about four hundred separate claimants in Oregon and fifty-one in California.[17] On June 27, 1882, Congress reimbursed the states of Colorado, Oregon, Nebraska, California, Kansas, and Nevada and the territories of Washington and Idaho for expenses incurred "between April 15, 1861 and June 27, 1882, to repel invasion and Indian hostilities in those States and territories and upon their borders."[18] For Euro-American settlers and their local governments, the Indian depredation claims system offered ample opportunity to secure federal compensation.

The Indian depredation claims system also provided more than 550 Indigenous claimants from Kansas, Nebraska, Oregon, Wyoming, and the Indian Territory an opportunity to file claims for depredations experienced at the hands of Euro-American settlers. On January 23, 1867, for example, Graham Rogers and 152 other Shawnees applied for $109,746.25 resulting from collateral damages caused during the Civil War, an application Congress later approved. Congress likewise approved the claims of W. H. Shaler and 201 other Delawares and 182 Shawnees for $463,732.49 and $26,284, respectively, on January 5, 1875, and January 27, 1870. Though Congress processed many claims for depredations committed by Confederate soldiers during the Civil War, the number declined precipitously after 1865. Between 1866 and 1874, American Indians filed twenty-five claims for depredations from white settlers, of which sixteen were forwarded to Congress for a total of $8,945.[19] Despite these instances, the Indian depredation claims system was not intended to put money into the hands of American Indians. In fact, prior to 1870, legislation provided that the funds to pay for damage come out of the accused tribe's annuity funds, though Office of Indian Affairs personnel and sympathetic lawmakers often prevented the most egregious abuses.[20]

The passage of the Indian Depredation Act of 1891 (also known as the Jurisdiction Act) changed the system by giving the U.S. Court of Claims jurisdiction over Indian depredation suits and by restricting claims to U.S. citizens whose property had been destroyed by Indian tribes "in amity with the United States." If, however, the court determined that either the applicant was not a citizen or that the property had been damaged during a period of established warfare between the United Sates and the accused tribe, neither party could be found responsible. In *Montoya v. United States* (1901), the Supreme Court further clarified this exception. Writing for the court, Justice Henry Billings Brown argued that depredation "committed by an organized company of men constituting a *band* in itself, acting independently of any other band or tribe, and carrying on hostilities against the United States," would be considered acts of war, absolving the government of responsibility.[21]

The Indian Depredation Act of 1891, then, added yet another layer of confusion to an already convoluted system. Compensation from Indian annuity funds might be provided for property destroyed by American Indians if an application had been filed before 1870 and it was not obstructed by lawmakers. Compensation for property destroyed between 1870 and 1890 might come from a special congressional appropriation, but only if that property had been damaged as a result of Indian warfare. After 1891, however, compensation for that same property could be provided only if the Court of Claims determined that the tribe was at peace. Throughout the nineteenth century and into the twentieth, in other words, both Euro-American settlers and a few American Indians received financial compensation from the federal government through a patchwork of legislation. As the veterans aged, however, this Indian depredation claims system was supplanted by a new system.

Legislation providing benefits to the vast majority of veterans of the Indian wars worked its way through Congress. As late as 1892, disabled veterans of the Indian wars who served between 1832 and 1842, their widows, and their children could secure pensions of eight dollars per month.[22] Within ten years, the lobbying efforts of broad-based veterans' organizations such as the National Indian War Veterans (NIWV), IWVNPC, and Utah Indian War Veterans Association had extended this privilege to veterans of all Indian conflicts—broadly defined—before 1860 and increased payments to twelve dollars per month for widows and twenty dollars for veterans, disabled or otherwise. Veterans of the Indian Wars who served after 1860, however, remained ineligible.[23]

To rally support, veterans' organizations claimed a public debt for their service to the nation and emphasized personal suffering. "It was the Indian War Veterans of the Pacific North West who ventured to this coast . . . and, furnishing their own outfit, guns, ammunition, horses, blankets and provisions, conquered this land and added three and one-half stars to the Union flag," noted one particularly vociferous veteran in a letter to the editor. But, he warned, "if [a] bill is not passed soon, it will be too late."[24] Another veteran pointed out that "the scythe of time is fast cutting into the ranks of men who rendered valiant service in subduing the marauding bands of redskins that infested [the land]. . . . Even now, the rollcall is responded to by only a few."[25] Arguments such as these played on familiar themes and proved popular in rural western states.

Political rhetoric was instrumental in the formation of a national interest group that could unite the disparate activities of the local servicemen's organizations. In 1909, the NIWV was formed in Denver with the explicit objective of "obtain[ing] pensions for all those who, while serving the government, contributed their share to open for peaceful settlement this great western country."[26] Unlike previous national organizations, the NIWV did not limit its membership to officers and gentlemen, and over the next several years, the group published announcements in newspapers across the country calling for individuals who served in the Indian wars after 1860 to join and lobby their representatives to support legislation expanding pensions. Through these efforts, the NIWV established regional headquarters in San Francisco and St. Louis in 1912 and additional camps in Philadelphia, Washington, D.C., and Newark, New Jersey, over the next six years.[27]

Even as the NIWV grew nationally, local organizations began lobbying Washington to extend veterans' benefits to those who served after 1860. "Veterans of later Indian Wars up to 1890 . . . desire our action," wrote Cyrus Walker, president of the IWVNPC, in an open letter to his members. "I ask that your influence be thrown in their behalf [for] our comrades are fast passing away. Let us who remain crown our latest days with every possible act of generous helpfulness."[28] Larding their populist message with the potent rhetoric of obligation, the NIWV and its local collaborators built a coalition of U.S. representatives to support legislation that would extend benefits to all veterans of Indian wars.

The passage of the Keating Measure on March 4, 1917, produced an immediate flurry of applications; the guidelines for evaluating these claims as set forth by commissioner of pensions Washington Gardner, however, reveal the system's complexity and inherent contradictions. Responding to fears or allegations of fraud in the pension system, Gardner established dozens of reasons for denying these claims. One stipulation read, "If War Department report shows service but is adverse as to service against Indians," reject the application on the ground that "claimant rendered no service in any Indian war or campaign named in the Act of March 4, 1917." Another directed that if the War Department's records failed to document service, the application should automatically be rejected. Applications should also be rejected if the "signatures bear but slight resemblance" to those on the claimants' discharge certificates or if they could not provide proof of their date of birth. Widows' applications were to be rejected if they could not provide proof of marriage, a death certificate for the husband, and proof of divorce from all previous marriages by either party. Regulations initially directed the rejection of all claims from applicants who served less than thirty days, but since some engagements covered by the act lasted less than thirty days, this directive was amended.[29] Such stringent procedures may have prevented some fraud, but they also denied benefits to many legitimate claimants, especially African Americans, immigrants, and above all American Indians.

To negotiate these systems, many Euro-American veterans turned to local historical societies for help in authenticating claims. Indeed, the founders and members of the veterans' and pioneer associations and of the historical societies often had significant overlap. Portland printer and publisher George H. Himes was instrumental in founding both the Oregon Historical Society and the IWVNPC. In his role as curator of the historical society, Himes was very interested in collecting the reminiscences of the pioneer days and consequently served as secretary of several veterans' associations for many years.[30] The Native Sons and Daughters of the Golden West, a commemorative association dedicated to promoting the history of California, likewise collaborated with a number of veterans' associations in both Oregon and California.[31] In Washington, D.C., the War Department and Bureau of Pensions collected extracts and other historical material from historical society and pioneer association publications such as the *Transactions and Reports of the Nebraska State Historical Society* and the *Transactions of the Oregon Pioneer Association* and used the historical data they contained as evidence for awarding pensions.[32]

Many veterans of the Indian wars navigated the bureaucratic obstacles with the help of their local historical societies, pioneer associations, local and national veterans' organizations, and paid professionals. As more applicants began receiving pensions, pressure to expand the system mounted. The primary obstacle to authenticating the service of most veterans was the haphazard nature of frontier warfare. According to General George A. White, "Volunteer units were frequently enrolled over night and dispatched to the scene of some uprising and later disbanded, apparently without any record being made of their activities. . . . The system of record keeping during the days of Indian hostilities was about as primitive as the country in which the battles" were fought.[33] In an attempt to ameliorate the situation, Congress extended pensions in 1927 to include veterans who served "in the zone of any active Indian hostilities." This slight change in language produced an additional one thousand Indian war pension claimants and laid the responsibility for establishing a service record on state and local governments.[34]

By the 1920s, then, these veterans' and historical organizations, in conjunction with their congressional representatives and other support groups, had created an expansive benefit system capable of accommodating the heterogeneous and unwieldy category of veteran of the Indian wars. Most claimants found it challenging to navigate this complex bureaucratic system, but many organized themselves into associations to support their applications, leveraged political patronage, and satisfied often arbitrary or even contradictory requirements with assistance from lawyers or historical societies. But the veterans' pension system also created opportunities for some Indigenous veterans who served with the U.S. Army in the Indian wars to develop similar strategies. Though they were often excluded from established avenues for pensions because of the process's racialist and nationalist underpinnings and origins, they nonetheless deployed many of the same tactics as they sought to negotiate this bureaucratic marketplace of remembering, an aspect of this system captured well by the specific experiences of the Indigenous veterans and widows of the Modoc War.

■ In the fall of 1922, Republican representative Nicholas J. Sinnott received a letter of thanks from Henry Brown, Albert Jackson, Kate Smiley, and thirteen other Klamath Basin Indian residents of his district. "We, the undersigned, survivors and widows of survivors [of the Modoc War] thank you for your very great assistance . . . in securing for us pensions, which so greatly assist us in our old age. We also wish to say that we are proud to know that these pensions, evidenced by the certificates we hold and cherish, show our love and loyalty to our great nation, and this love and loyalty we hope to leave with those of our people who come after us, that they may always prove good and faithful Americans."[35] By relying on political patronage, networks of cooperation and aid, and community-developed knowledge and support, these Indigenous veterans and widows of the Modoc War navigated a complex bureaucratic system. But in so doing, they also exposed the interconnectivity of settler colonialism, American innocence, and the materiality of remembering nineteenth-century U.S.-Indian violence.

Unlike Euro-American veterans who sought assistance and found camaraderie in organizations like the NIWV and the IWVNPC, only a handful of Indigenous veterans of the Modoc War became dues-paying members of veterans' groups or participated in their functions. David Waushumps, a Warm Springs Indian, subscribed regularly to *Winners of the West* and wrote a letter to the editor in which he proclaimed himself an Indigenous person who had "fought my own people, for the liberty of the country, wives and children." In 1889, William and Donald McKay were elected honorary members of the IWVNPC, and by 1925, the organization included at least five Indigenous members: Antowine, Indian Robert, Thomas Chapman, Siwash John, and Charles Linksuilex.[36] But these were the rare exceptions. Indeed, white veterans often used the presence of Indigenous pensioners to deride the government for its unwillingness to further expand benefits. In announcing the new membership of Comrade Brave Heart of Porcupine, South Dakota, George Webb, president of the NIWV, noted, "It may not be generally known . . . but there are a great many Indians on the pension rolls. . . . We wish the government had been equally as liberal with the brave white men who no doubt served in the wars along with these friendly Indians."[37]

Indigenous veterans avoided participating for the most part in Indian war veterans' associations, a stark contrast to the experiences of Indigenous veterans who joined veterans' groups from other wars. Indeed, many American Indians, especially the Iroquois, joined the GAR in droves. When Ely S. Parker, a Tonawanda Seneca veteran, former commissioner of Indian affairs, and adjutant to General Ulysses S. Grant, died in 1895, honorary pallbearers included members of the GAR and as well as of the Iroquois community. The GAR, in conjunction with the Buffalo Historical Society, sponsored Parker's subsequent reburial in Buffalo and even paid for the headstone. Likewise, the GAR participated in the funeral of the Tuscarora lieutenant Cornelius C. Cusick at Old Fort Niagara in 1904 and provided funeral rites to other Iroquois veterans through the 1920s.[38] Following his deployment to the Philippines from 1901 to 1904, another Iroquois veteran, Clinton Rickard, returned home and joined the Army and Navy Union, the United Spanish War Veterans, and a Masonic lodge. He also spearheaded the organization of Tuscarora Post 8242 of the Veterans of Foreign Wars because he believed that such veterans' organizations might play a role similar to that of the old Iroquois warrior societies.[39]

But to receive benefits, Indigenous veterans and widows of the Indian wars often relied on their own networks of cooperation. Typically, an Indigenous veteran would begin by seeking assistance from Indian Agency personnel, who could procure applications and assist in their preparation. The Klamath Indian Mission minister R. T. Cookingham, for example, helped Peter Cholah, Albert Jackson, and Tom Skellock with their applications.[40] Superintendent Walter West took an active interest in the pension applications of several veterans and widows on the Klamath Reservation, contributing to the applications of Julia Shore, Kate Smiley, Nancy Yahooskin John, and Edmund Dufur, among others.[41] The usefulness of agency personnel, however, was limited. When the Bureau of Pensions rejected Dufur's application, Superintendent O. L. Babcock of the Warm Springs Indian Agency suggested that Dufur engage the services of Joseph Hunter, who charged twenty-five dollars and was said to have access to required governmental records.[42] Perhaps after receiving similar advice, Warm Springs Indian John Jack hired Stuart H. Elliott, a Tacoma, Washington, attorney.[43]

Government patrons, lawyers, and other professionals provided some assistance, but most Indigenous veterans relied on their former commanders for help in preparing applications and navigating the system. Oliver Applegate, captain of the Oregon Militia and former superintendent at the Klamath Reservation, helped virtually every Indigenous claimant connected to the Modoc War in some way. A tireless advocate for expanded veterans' benefits, Applegate had recommended to the commissioner of Indian affairs that former Klamath Indian scouts should receive a pension of $5 a month for their service as early as 1898. Two years later, he doubled the recommended pension, claiming that "$10 a month would certainly be generosity well bestowed and a suggestive object lesson to our younger people."[44] While Applegate portrayed his efforts as pro bono, he generally asked the veterans he helped to pay for expenses and to compensate him for his time. Sargent Brown, a prominent rancher and leader on the Klamath Reservation, brokered an agreement with Applegate whereby Solomon Lalakes, Thomas Skellock, Peter Cholah, and Albert Jackson promised to pay $50 each when their pensions were secured if Applegate would assist them. Within a year, the four men had received $1,140 in back pay from the pension fund and were receiving regular monthly payments of $20.[45]

Indigenous veterans of the Modoc War, like other veterans, also turned to their congressional representatives to help navigate Washington bureaucracy. Sinnott, whose Second District included the Klamath Reservation, wrote numerous letters checking on the status of Indian claimants' petitions and relaying information to them.[46] But Sinnott was not alone. Senators McNary and Frederick Steiwer as well as Representatives Willis C. Hawley of Oregon's First District and Robert R. Butler and Walter M. Pierce, Sinnott's successors, all wrote letters urging the Bureau of Pensions to approve their Indigenous constituents' claims or introduced bills on their behalf.[47]

But political patronage did not always help. The first obstacle many Indigenous veterans faced was matching their names to those on the official muster rolls used by the Bureau of Pensions to determine eligibility. Produced haphazardly at the best of times—and in the case of Indian scouts sometimes not at all—the names as recorded on the muster rolls often differed from those used by Indigenous applicants a half century later, when they had often adopted westernized names. The Klamaths and Modocs in particular had a regular custom of changing their names or adopting aliases without much ceremony.[48] One applicant, John Koppas, had used the name Modoc Henry when he mustered out in 1873. Another, Dufur at various times went by Ta-Hum, Luckany, and Ruffer. Jim Copperfield enlisted as Little Jim, Jack Drew as Drew Jackson, Charley Faithful as Modoc Charley, Albert Jackson as Albert Hochis, Sam Solomon as Solomon Lalakes, Rube Walker as Ruben Konoki, Peter Cholah as Jola, and Tom Skellock as Yatchose, Watchoss, or Tom, depending on which roll the Bureau of Pension chose to examine.[49]

Indigenous widows faced similar challenges. Birdie John's claim for benefits stalled when it became unclear whether she and Bertha John were the same person.[50] Mary Ann Copperfield's application was delayed when the Bureau of Pensions discovered that for a period she went by Molly or Molly Ann. And Ursula Whistler had to clarify several times that when she married John Whistler, she went by Jane.[51] The cultural expectation that Indigenous veterans and widows adhered to Euro-American naming practices meant they had to submit dozens of notarized affidavits, write letters of clarification, and produce letters of support from superintendents or other individuals.

The experience of the Warm Springs Indian scout John Jack captures well the inherent inconsistencies that arose when government officials insisted on matching names with service records. "The Indians around this portion of the country seem to know you by the name Toplash?," special examiner of the Bureau of Pensions Milford M. Brower asked Jack.

> Well, the Indians call me Toplash but the name under which I was allotted land in this reservation is Histo. Why, I have had the name Histo ever since I can remember—when I was a child. Why, it is about twenty years since they commenced to call me Toplash. Why, I commenced calling myself that. It came from seeing or thinking I could see something white on a hill or high ground. Why, that was at Warm Springs.
>
> Q. How many other names have you had? A. Well, someone one time counted my names for me and said there were seven. One was Shell. I don't know any of the others. Histo was the name I was a soldier under. . . . If the Government cannot find the name Histo on the list of soldiers, I am Histo and I am a soldier, but they might have forgotten to write my name.[52]

John Jack was comfortable with his various names, but the Bureau of Pensions saw these inconsistencies as potential evidence of fraud. Eventually it became clear that John Jack's name had been recorded as "Stow" (resulting from an elision of the "H" in Histo) on the muster roll, and he was awarded a pension.[53]

This insistence on consistency of names was further complicated by American colonial policy. Beginning in the 1890s, government officials assigned westernized names to Klamath Basin Indians as part of the reservation's assimilation efforts when annuities were issued. According to local historian Rachel Applegate Good, "It became one of the functions of the interpreter and clerk to rename the stalwart braves, who were highly delighted with such commonplace appellations as 'Joe Wilson' and 'George Brown.' 'This is your name,' he would say, writing it on a card, 'and if you forget what it is, ask anyone who can read, and he will tell you.'"[54] Allotment only further complicated the situation. Noted one observer of the Indigenous veterans of the Modoc War, in almost every case "their enlistment names were all different from their allotment names," but someone who "knew them individually" would be able to match the individuals to the names on the muster rolls.[55] Not surprisingly, many veterans languished in bureaucratic limbo. Those who did not often found ingenious ways of circumventing a system that denied their requests at every turn.

Indigenous veterans and widows of the Modoc War, like other veterans, deployed the rhetoric of personal sacrifice and honorable service to the causes of American civilization to persuade their congressional representatives to introduce bills on their behalf. "Dear Senator," wrote Harrison Brown to Steiwer in the spring of 1930, "I am a Klamath Indian [who was put] on duty to guard the government property, and to act against the hostile Modocs under captain Jack . . . for more than forty days during the war. I am now in poor health, have lost the sight of one eye, and am worthless for manual labor. Though not regularly enlisted, I rendered valuable and active service, and I am asking, through Congress, the amount of a pension granted to veterans under the Leatherwood Act, for which I would be very grateful."[56] A former Klamath Reservation superintendent echoed Brown's contentions. "To my certain knowledge Harrison Brown's service during the darkest days that ever came to Klamath County, as a result of the Modoc War, were of essential importance, and his loyalty to the Government and his leadership on the Reservation, have been most valuable."[57]

Decrepitude often provided the impetus for special consideration, and some Indigenous veterans exaggerated their age in an attempt to garner greater sympathy. In 1928, Wama Louie claimed to be ninety-one years old, though agency records placed his true age at seventy-six.[58] Cinda Checaskane exaggerated her age by more than a decade when she claimed to be seventy-five in 1918, while Ike Owhy, Daniel Katchia, and Albert Kuckup all inflated their ages when they claimed to be ninety-one, ninety-two, and one hundred, respectively, in 1929.[59] If some exaggerated, others simply claimed to be just "old." Peter Cholah was said to be "a very old Indian . . . among the older Indians of this reservation," making it impossible to determine his exact age.[60]

The requirements of the Bureau of Pensions also shaped the specific details Klamath Basin Indian veterans and widows chose to narrate. Many of their petitions insisted on the voluntary nature of their service, which they hoped would entitle them to special consideration. As Rev. Cookingham recalled, several Indigenous veterans "came to me and ask[ed] why my government [was] so slow in helping them now when they went willingly at the call of our soldiers and risked their lives to capture Captain Jack and his Modoc Braves. . . . These men," he told the commissioner of pensions, "are worthy of some consideration, and quite needy now."[61] The belief that such stories would influence the bureau's decision drove many Indigenous veterans to connect their current physical condition with their service in the Modoc War, further elevating its importance in their lives.[62]

Frustrated by the Bureau of Pensions's inflexibility, many Indigenous veterans and widows took the opportunity to educate government bureaucrats on the historical conditions that prohibited them from establishing their claims. When Warm Springs Indian scout Jacob Thomas was denied a disability pension in 1914, he wrote to the commissioner of pensions, "In regard to this matter, I wish to state that when I was out here fighting these Modoc Indians this country was a wilderness and that if you were shot the chances were that you would not see a doctor, and you got well the best way you could. Another thing the men in this War serving the United States were not thinking about getting pensions at that time. For that reason evidence of this kind is very hard to secure."[63] In the spring of 1918, Drew Jackson likewise conformed his narrative to white expectations when he explained to the commissioner of pensions that "in relation to the date of my birth, as I am an Indian, and was born long before my tribe came under the civilizing influences of white people, no record was made."[64] Supporting Jackson's explanation, Applegate wrote, "These Indians were all born before treaties were made with their tribe; hence it is impossible for them to furnish the exact date." Yet, he added, "these men were all faithful and effective soldiers and were without exception honorably discharged."[65]

Indigenous veterans and widows of the Modoc War often pointed to their lack of education, literacy, and fluency in English as a hindrance as well as a mitigating circumstance. When Ursula Whistler missed the deadline for submitting evidence in her case, she begged special consideration. "Dear sir . . . I am an uneducated Indian woman, and did not know of the receipt of the said letter at this office. I am anxious to furnish the evidence required and shall be glad to have the letter returned to my address at Chiloquin, Oregon."[66] Occasionally, lack of fluency created relationships. When Mary Chiloquin received a letter from the Bureau of Pensions requesting routine evidence to support her application, the widow approached Fred Baker, a former superintendent and the examiner of inheritance, for assistance. Writing to the commissioner of pensions, Baker reported, "As she is an old and illiterate person, and does not understand the English language, she brought her letter to me for advice and counsel."[67] Baker, versed in the bureaucratic requirements of probate, helped Chiloquin complete her application and submitted the required supporting documentation. Five months later, she received a pension of twelve dollars a month.[68]

Widows had a particularly difficult time establishing their claims. To receive veterans' benefits, a widow had to provide the Bureau of Pensions with a death certificate for her husband, a copy of the couple's marriage license, sworn statements that she had never divorced the soldier and had never remarried, and death certificates or other evidence of divorce from any previous marriages on both sides. Such documentation was difficult for Euro-American widows to provide, given the haphazard nature of record keeping in the American West; for Indigenous widows whose marriages and divorces were rarely recorded by settler governments, doing so was nearly impossible.

The experiences of Ursula Whistler (aka Jane Whistler or Jane Chiloquin) and Nancy Yahooskin illuminate well the challenges Indigenous widows often faced. When Ursula applied for widows' benefits in 1917, she claimed to be the widow of John Whistler, a Klamath Indian scout who had served as a private in Applegate's Oregon Militia along with Yahooskin John. Since the name "John Whistler" appeared on the muster roll, his status as a veteran was established. But his previous marriages to Nancy Yahooskin and Annie Whistler and Ursula's previous marriage to George Chiloquin, who also served in Applegate's militia, soon caused problems. According to a deposition from Cora Skellock and Mary Moore, John divorced his first wife without the benefit of the courts, and his second wife and their three children died sometime before or shortly after he received his allotment. Ursula had been married to George Chiloquin by "Indian custom" until his death in 1893; six years later, she married John Whistler. Ursula believed that both of her marriages provided her with claims to benefits. Nancy Yahooskin's application was likewise delayed because of her marriage to John Whistler and her subsequent marriage to Yahooskin John, both of which took place before 1864 and therefore lacked documentation. For his part, Yahooskin John had been married twice before, to Sallatus (Belwax) and to Koachax. In both cases, benefits were delayed for years before being awarded.[69]

Government policy during the early days of the Klamath Reservation made documenting legal marriages and divorces challenging. According to anthropologist Theodore Stern, the government targeted widespread legal marriage as effective tool for eradicating the practice of polygamy and further undermining the power of traditional chiefs, for whom polygamy was evidence of affluence. Following the Modoc War, the head chief gained the authority to punish polygamy as well as to consecrate marriages and perform divorces as long as the groom paid the bride's family a fee ranging from two to five dollars.[70] Mirroring the traditional Indian marriage ritual in important ways (the exchanging of gifts and public acknowledgment), this system was nonetheless undermined over time by the Methodist Church as well as by the usurpation of chieftain authority by the agents. Indeed, some of the individual petitions alluded to this period of hasty marriages and poor record keeping by the church. In one petition, the applicant blamed the lack of documentation of marriage on the Reverend Joseph L. Beatty, described as the "marry parson."[71]

The lack of documentation for marriage during Beatty's period of service created subsequent logistical problems, as the case of Mary Ann Copperfield demonstrates. "In those days, Indians came to the superintendent or agent of the reservation and asked his permission to marry, the agent would issue the necessary permit, and the Indians were then considered married," Superintendent Wade Crawford explained to the director of pensions. "Many, if not all of the older Indians, did not know the dates of their birth, nor of other events in their lives and therefore calculated the dates in relation to some important event such as a treaty or a war. . . . Our records here show that Jim and Mary Ann Copperfield were husband and wife at all times from the date of their marriage until his death in March, 1933, and that they were not separated or divorced."[72] In their haste to stamp out polygamy and destabilize the power of the traditional chiefs, government agents and church officials also undermined Indigenous veterans' and widows' claims to future benefits. The lasting affect of colonial policy often continued to influence the lived reality of American Indians in unexpected ways.

To compensate for these structural impediments, Indigenous widows relied on networks of cooperation to prove the legality of their marriages. As a result, many widows served as witnesses for each other and backed one another's claims. When Ben-John, a Klamath Indian who served as a scout with the Klamath headman Dave Hill, died in an automobile accident in July 1920, his wife, Nancy, applied for a widow's pension. Since they had been married "in the Indian fashion," she was unable to produce a marriage certificate. To satisfy the Bureau of Pensions, Nancy submitted two affidavits from two Klamath women, Millie Jack and Adeline Koppos, attesting to the "faithful continuation" of Nancy's marriage to Ben-John.[73] When Millie Jack required proof of her 1857 marriage to Link River Jack, Millie called on Nancy Ben-John and Mary Chiloquin to furnish affidavits.[74] For her part, when Mary Chiloquin needed three witnesses to attest to the legality of her deceased husband's divorce from his previous wife, Mary asked Millie Jack, Henry Brown, and another Klamath to provide witness.[75] All of these petitions proved successful.

The importance and extent of these networks of cooperation is further suggested by the fact that most successful applicants applied for benefits at the same time. On the Klamath Reservation, for example, Henry Brown, Dick Brown, Jim Copperfield, Ruben Walker, John Koppos, Charley Faithful, and Drew Jackson all filed their claims on June 28, 1917.[76] And they all received pensions. Similarly, on the Warm Springs Indian Reservation, Albert Kuckup and Jacob Thomas filed their claims together on November 28, 1917, while Tullux Holliquilla, James Winneshet, and David Washump all applied for veterans' benefits on December 13, 1917.[77] Both Birdie John and Sam Solomon applied on January 30, 1920, and swore affidavits supporting each other's claims, while Eli "Walter" Checaskane and Mary Chiloquin filed claims on January 19, 1918.[78] Apart from all other evidence, the fact that so many Native claimants applied for pensions at the same time seems to suggest that they were working together to procure veterans' benefits.

Headmen and other traditional power brokers had long dominated political and economic relationships on the Klamath Reservation. They now also emerged as influential figures in the veterans' benefits system. At one point or another, Thomas Skellock, Sam Solomon, Ben John, Frank Chilks, Nancy Ben-John, Birdie John, Mary George, Ursula Whistler, and Cinda Checaskane all sought the assistance of Charles S. Hood, a graduate of Carlisle Indian Industrial School and a leader among those Modoc who returned to Oregon in 1908.[79] Similarly, Kate Brown, Alex Wilson, John Pitt, Peter Cholah, and Albert Jackson turned to Sargent Brown for assistance.[80] Although power brokers such as Hood and Brown might not always have been the most effective advocates, they do seem to have helped these veterans, perhaps out of a sense of obligation stemming from their political support.

Kinship relations also seem to have supported Indigenous veterans and widows as they negotiated the veterans' benefits system. When forwarding his petition to Senator Steiwer and Congressman Hawley, Harrison Brown included sworn affidavits attesting to the truthfulness of his claim from his uncles, Dick Mosenkosket and Jim Cooperfield.[81] Similarly, when Anna Holliquilla sought a widow's pension following the death of her husband, Tullux, she obtained affidavits from her daughter and son, Etta Bennett and Jerry Holliquilla, who were Tullux's children from previous marriages, to corroborate her lawful marriage.[82]

These networks of cooperation often sprawled across the reservation and beyond. When Cinda Checaskane applied for a pension as the widow of Eli "Walter" Checaskane, she was forced to account for a staggering number of relationships. Checaskane had had no fewer than five wives, Moli, Millie, Missie Jim, Lizzie Checaskane, and Cinda Checaskane. To clarify these complicated relationships and prove that she was legally his widow, Cinda had to compile affidavits from Warren Skellock, Sargent Brown, O. C. Applegate, and John Shook as well as depositions from Missie Jim and Lizzie Checaskane. Drawing together evidence from individuals around Oregon and from both Indigenous and Euro-American supporters, Cinda Checaskane proved her case and was awarded a pension in the summer of 1922.[83]

As these networks of cooperation expanded, certain individuals emerged as influential nodules, people to whom several claimants turned for support of their petitions. Among the Warm Springs Indian veterans, Wasco Indian Ike Owhy swore affidavits supporting the claims of virtually every applicant who served with him. Owhy's capacity for recollecting specific details was both impressive and convenient. In supporting Jacob Thomas's application, Owhy recalled that "about the middle of June, 1873 . . . I saw his horse shot from under him. . . . The horse rolled over on him breaking his right shoulder and his left foot. . . . Three days afterwards we were sent home."[84] Another individual with a prodigious memory for recalling precise facts that aligned with the specific requirements of the pension commissioner was Klamath Indian Tom Skellock. On July 30, 1931, he swore an affidavit supporting Wama Louie's claims in which he named twenty Natives who served with them, provided accurate details of Louie's service, and even recalled specific events such as the attack on the Modoc Stronghold. Skellock concluded that "Louie was with us as a soldier during the whole winter."[85] Nonetheless, Louie's claim was never approved.

■ Questions continue to abound about the experiences of Indigenous veterans and widows of the Indian wars as they pursued pensions for their service with the U.S. Army. How representative were the experiences of the Klamath and Warm Springs Indians who served in the Modoc War? What role did kinship or geography play in the tactics applicants deployed? Did Indigenous veterans experience discrimination within their community? What other factors influenced the outcome of these applications? And given the irony of Indigenous veterans seeking pensions for their part in the colonization of their people, what did their service mean to them? I have tried to answer some of these questions here; more work remains to be done before we can truly understand the significance of this particular marketplace of remembering nineteenth-century U.S.-Indian violence.

This much, however, we can say: in pursuit of the economic and symbolic significance of veterans' benefits, Euro-American veterans organized themselves into effective lobbying groups, leveraged their political patrons, and established institutions such as historical societies and pioneer associations to support their claims. Creating a marketplace wherein remembrances of service, valor, and individual sacrifice might be exchanged for financial support, the veterans' benefits system continued the process of reimagining and negotiating the meaning of nineteenth-century U.S.-Indian violence and Americans' relationship to these conflicts. Euro-American veterans, however, were not alone. Indigenous veterans and widows of the Indian wars also navigated the complex ideological, technocratic, and racialized boundaries of the Bureau of Pensions. But they faced unique challenges. Often illiterate, forced to navigate a complex and unyielding system, and hampered by the structural and bureaucratic inequalities of settler colonialism, Indigenous veterans and widows used tactics analogous to those employed by their Euro-American settler counterparts. They sought assistance from their friends and family members, sympathetic supporters, and paid professionals. They deployed the rhetoric of service, clarified their names, and supported their claims when documentation was lacking. They strove, sometimes for decades, to secure the considerable economic value associated with establishing their identity as legitimate Indian wars veterans. Their experiences suggest the extent to which the disciplining hand of the Bureau of Pensions transformed the meaning of Indigenous soldiers' service even while reconstructing and preserving it. But the experiences of these Indigenous veterans and widows also in many ways supported claims to American innocence. Indigenous claimants had to use the same narratives of progress, civilization, and American innocence to navigate the pension system. Therefore, the United States allowed (and rewarded) only one narrative regarding the Indian wars. Nevertheless, the stories of the Indigenous veterans and widows of the Modoc War constitute an unwritten part of the history of American Indian engagement with American settler colonialism.

Chapter Six

REDEMPTIVE LANDSCAPES

On June 13, 1926, a cavalcade of more than 175 cars wound its way down the freshly constructed dirt and gravel roads connecting Klamath Falls to the newly created Lava Beds National Monument. Led by renowned Modoc War veteran Oliver Applegate, they proceeded at a leisurely pace, passing by the prosperous farms and ranches lining the shores of Tule Lake. Behind Applegate were representatives from local chapters of the Native Sons and Daughters of the Golden West, the Daughters of the American Revolution, and several chambers of commerce. Visitors and dignitaries from as far away as San Francisco and Portland had joined the crowd of more than one thousand to consecrate a new memorial to U.S.-Indian violence and to inaugurate an era of historical tourism that would assure the region's future prosperity.[1]

The commemoration began with a performance of the "Star Spangled Banner," followed by a rendition of "I Love You, California" sung by all assembled. After some opening remarks, Catherine E. Gloster of Alturas removed the draped American flag to reveal the memorial beneath. Designed by Paul D. Fair, a San Francisco sculptor, the memorial featured a bronze-cast golden bear that had been wounded by Indian arrows atop a cairn of local lava rocks (figure 20).[2] The plaque read,

TO COMMEMORATE THE HEROISM OF GENERAL EDWARD R. S. CANBY OTHER OFFICERS AND SOLDIERS AND PIONEER SETTLERS WHO SACRIFICED THEIR LIVES ON THIS BATTLEFIELD DURING THE MODOC WAR THIS MONUMENT IS ERECTED AND DEDICATED BY ALTURAS PARLOR 159 N.D.G.W. ASSISTED BY GRAND CHAPTER ROYAL

Figure 20. Dedication of the Golden Bear Monument by the Native Daughters of the Golden West, Lava Beds Monument, June 13, 1926. Courtesy of the Klamath County Museum, Klamath Falls, Ore.

ARCH MASONS OTHER FRATERNAL AND CIVIC ORGANIZATIONS AND CITIZENS 1926 A.D.

Symbol and narrative intersected in this memorial to portray the Modoc War as a significant event in California's history, a symbol of Manifest Destiny's promise of redemption through sacrifice. The performance of the "Star Spangled Banner" signaled to everyone that the event was part of the American saga of nation building, while "I Love You, California" reinforced the commemorators' claim on the Modoc War as a part of California's past. The plaque, with its homage to American sacrifice and courage, celebrated the reluctant but persistent heroism of California's soldiers and settlers. According to the *Alturas Plain-Dealer*, the memorial celebrated "the rugged characters of the brave men who broke forever the Indian dominion in Southern Oregon and Northern California, and paved the way for progress both for the white man and the Indian."[3] Innocence preserved, progress assured, the Modoc War represented a tragic but necessary episode of U.S.-Indian violence in the Klamath Basin.

The memorial, moreover, shifted the symbolic register of sacrifice in the region from individual to collective victimhood and revealed the ever-present violence in Americans' conceptions of their own innocence. The golden bear represented the state of California. Wounded as it was, the bear roared on, wrestling the land from its now-vanished Indian enemy. The only remaining evidence of the once-threatening presence of Klamath Basin Indians was a single arrow, lodged in the bear's shoulder. As a symbol of white victimhood, the bear reflected the perseverance of masculine virility in the face of frontier insecurity and served as a reminder of the sacrifices of progress and civilization. As a symbol of the nation, its wounding justified a devastating war of extermination. And when coupled with its tribute to martial sacrifice, the bear, preserved forever in ageless gold, represented a kind of masculine innocence, wounded but persistent in the prime of its life.

Monuments and memorials to settler colonial violence were key to the solidification of a public memory; they appropriated more than they represented the past, and in so doing, they became not merely evidence of power but a site for creating power in regimes of settler colonialism. This chapter tells the story of how memorials such as this one enabled Americans to imagine themselves as the innocent victims of frontier violence by representing Indians as irrational aggressors and violators of a civilized nation's just laws. As spaces of historical narrative production, hermeneutic accretion, and economic exchange, monuments and memorials to the Modoc War have reproduced claims to American innocence through the commercialization of white victimhood and Indigenous outlawry even as they purport to revise historical interpretation through shifting categories of victimhood.

Beginning in the 1870s, journalists, novelists, artists, cartographers, and commemorators embraced the colonial logic of America's nineteenth-century racialist jurisprudence by creating memorials that portrayed Modoc resistance as illegal while leaving unquestioned the legality of American settlers and their occupation of the Klamath Basin. Throughout much of the nineteenth century, Euro-Americans maintained their claims to innocence by reifying the death of General Edward R. S. Canby as a quintessential moment of white victimhood. With the rise of tourism in the 1910s and 1920s, Euro-Americans expanded the cult of victimhood to include all soldiers and settlers, as heritage groups, local business leaders and entrepreneurs, and outside investors surrounded themselves with domesticated representations of modern-day Modocs who had "forgotten" the violence of the past. Claiming American innocence through their collective victimization and selective amnesia, Progressive Era commemorators asserted an end-of-history narrative that both refused to acknowledge culpability and located the violence of colonialism thoroughly in the region's past. This chapter, then, considers how memorial sites in the Klamath Basin have for more than a century transformed historical narratives into tangible and productive if unstable elements of the region's landscape.

■ Early descriptions of the battlefields of the Modoc War reproduced extravagant and fanciful descriptions of the Lava Beds in an attempt to profit from the region's notoriety. In his dime novel based on the Modoc War, *The Squaw Spy*, Charles Howard described "a perfect honeycomb of dark passages" beneath the Lava Beds, through which "the savage can retreat from one stronghold to another—miles distant—without once showing his face above earth."[4] Despite the fact that such passages did not exist, they became a popular motif in contemporary descriptions of the region. John Boddam-Whetham repeated this fantasy when he relied on the imagination of eastern engravers to fabricate his 1874 visit to the Lava Beds: "The principal part of the Modoc camp was a large opening in the ravine . . . on all sides of which rises a wall a hundred feet in height, forming a bowl with sloping sides. . . . Huge rocks, two and three hundred feet in height, rise from the earth almost perpendicularly, and sometimes a narrow path leads to the top of them, the summit being defended by a breastwork of rock."[5] Since the Lava Beds have no hundred-foot cliffs, it seems likely that Boddam-Whetham reproduced descriptions of the region he encountered in newspaper coverage of the Modoc War.

If representations of the Lava Beds established a series of negative associations, the creation of physical memorials to the Modoc War transformed narratives of white victimhood into tangible elements on the landscape. In the days and weeks after the death of Canby and the Reverend Eleazer Thomas, soldiers of the U.S. Army erected a temporary cross made out of wood from the peace commission's tent and held in place, according to at least one account, by a base of local lava rocks covered in the general's own blood.[6] Captured in a photograph by Louis Heller and featured in *Harper's Weekly* with the caption "Scene of Canby's Death," this makeshift and macabre monument soon deteriorated. Within a year, visitors to the area failed to mention its presence. By June 1880, all that remained of the original monument was a single board sticking out of the ground with the words "This marks the spot where the Peace Tent stood April 11, 1873" scribbled across it.[7] In September 1882, Lieutenant John

S. Parke visited the Lava Beds while on leave. According to his report, Parke wanted to find "the exact locality" where General Canby died and create a memorial such that "when this historic place comes to be visited by the interested or the curious, it may not be of such uncertain location as to be a matter of speculation and discussion." Parke enlisted the help of local rancher John Fairchild and his carpenter, and together they erected a memorial cross "of lumber about six inches square, twelve feet high with arms of four feet." On the horizontal piece, Parke inscribed, "GEN. CANBY USA WAS MURDERED HERE BY THE MODOCS APRIL 11 1873" (figure 21).[8]

The narrative of U.S.-Indian violence presented by Parke's memorial marked the landscape with a combination of Christian iconography, colonial jurisprudence, and American innocence. A life-sized cross rising from the sagebrush symbolized Canby's sacrifice and evoked the Christian context of the memorial. By using the word "murdered" as opposed to "killed" or even "died," it portrayed Indigenous resistance to American settler colonialism within a western legal framework. The Modocs were murderers, criminals, and their acts of violence were unprovoked homicide. Like Christ, the lamb, who was betrayed by his followers and suffered on the cross for the sins of humanity, Canby was "betrayed," in the words of the *San Francisco Chronicle*, by a band of "Red Judas."[9] Moreover, by identifying the Modocs as murderers, the memorial argued that they fell under the legal purview of the United States, an elision that portrays Canby as the innocent victim of an injustice and the Modocs as the culpable perpetrators of an unlawful crime. In this way, "Canby's Cross," as it came to be known, transformed a narrative of American innocence into a tangible element of the landscape, tapping into an emerging national secular religion dedicated to a cult of white victimhood.

Public monuments and memorials to American innocence through redemptive violence were popular throughout the nineteenth century, and it is important to understand Canby's Cross in this context. Beginning as early as the 1820s, Americans had adopted an expansionist policy founded on the Jeffersonian belief that widespread private ownership of property would result in an independent and virtuous citizenry. Within this logic, the "empire of liberty" required the appropriation of Indigenous lands, and as a result, violent resistance by American Indians was portrayed as unjustified at best and irrational or savage at worst. Numerous monuments and memorials erected in the 1870s and 1880s reminded the American public of this fact by portraying American colonists and western army officials as the innocent victims of Indian violence. For example, between

Figure 21. "Trip to the Lava Beds: Ivan and Alice Applegate at Canby's Cross at Lava Beds." Ogle66-1394. Courtesy of the Klamath County Museum, Klamath Falls, Ore.

1861 and 1879, New England residents erected three separate monuments to Hannah Duston, a colonial New England woman who was captured by Abenaki Indians during a 1697 raid and then killed and scalped ten of her twelve captors, including six children. According to historian Barbara Cutter, the memorials to Duston proliferated because her story allowed Americans to understand U.S.-Indian violence as defensive and virtuous, feminine violence. After all, Duston was a mother whose baby had been "murdered" before her eyes. The "natural" impulse for revenge was "a perfect symbol for the virtuous violence of the outraged innocent."[10]

Virtuous violence and outraged innocence were not limited to women. Since the nineteenth century, there has been no more celebrated victim of Indian violence than Lieutenant Colonel George Armstrong Custer. Following his death in 1876 at the Battle of Greasy Grass Creek, the nation transformed this soldier, previously famous for his early morning raids on sleeping Indian villages, into the heroic victim of an Indian massacre. In 1879, Secretary of War George Washington McCary preserved the site as a U.S. national cemetery. And the same year, Captain George Sanderson, stationed at Fort Custer, erected a cordwood monument atop Last Stand Hill. Sanderson's monument was replaced two years later by an enormous obelisk made from eighteen tons of granite transported from Massachusetts to the Little Bighorn area.[11] Sites of national mourning such as Last

Stand Hill and cenotaphs for "innocent" victims of Indigenous violence such as Canby's Cross soon became popular tourist attractions, especially after the advent of automobiles.

In the late nineteenth and early twentieth centuries, curious and intrepid travelers journeyed to the Klamath Basin to see the site of Canby's death and the Lava Beds. Through their travels, they reproduced narratives of American innocence as they experienced the region's touristic landscape. Moreover, their experiences were often coupled with a simultaneous encounter with local Klamath Basin Indians employed as tour guides. Informal and temporary employment in the region's tourism industry constituted a modest source of supplemental income for Klamath Basin Indians in the half century after hostilities ended. Modoc War tourism, in other words, produced narratives and touristic landscapes in the Klamath Basin that sustained claims to American innocence even as they provided some local Indians with a means of engaging with colonialism.

Within a few years, the sites of the Modoc War began to appear on maps of the region. For many tourists, these cartographic representations anticipated and mediated their encounters with the landscape, defining it as a space associated with a history of U.S.-Indian violence and white victimhood. Rand McNally's 1883 map of railroads in California labeled three sites in the area associated with U.S.-Indian violence: "Jacks Stronghold," "Gen. Gillems Camp," and, in a reference to Parke's newly erected memorial, "Gen. Canby killed April 11, 1873." Nine years later, another map labeled the area south of Tule Lake "Modoc Rifle Pit," while Abbott Green's 1911 map of Modoc County marked the area as "Canby Monument" with a cross. With their emphasis on Canby's Cross, these cartographic representations of the region focused the attention of American and European tourists on the Klamath Basin's association with the Modoc War and its narrative of white victimhood.[12]

Once in the Klamath Basin, tourists who expected to encounter a demonic landscape wherein Indian violence was a constant danger were rarely disappointed. Such was the case when Henry Abbey and Leonard Case visited the area. They arranged for a tour of the Lava Beds during their October 1873 visit to the Klamath Basin to witness Captain Jack's execution. Traveling from Fort Klamath to the Lava Beds with Bob and Matilda Whittle as their guides, the pair became agitated and even feared for their lives when Matilda mentioned that some Modoc warriors still remained in the area, hiding among the rocks, waiting to attack. "[We spent] most of the night staring out on the black lava beds expecting every moment to hear the yell of attacking Indians," Abbey wrote in his diary.

Around 1:30 A.M., they broke camp and returned to Linkville, too scared to "mak[e] a closer examination of the lava beds."[13] Their innocent trip had become imperiled.

If Case and Abbey feared that the piled rocks of the Lava Beds might transform into flesh-and-blood Modoc Indians at any moment, an uncharacteristically morose John Muir found the area "uncanny," "forbidding," and "mysterious." Writing in the winter of 1874 for San Francisco's *Daily Evening Bulletin*, the famed naturalist described the "unnatural blackness of the rock" as enveloping the whole region in a "weird inhuman physiognomy . . . well calculated to inspire terror." While the landscape inspired terror, the Modoc Indians, both those he imagined "glid[ing] from place to place along fissures and subterranean passes, all the while maintaining a more perfect invisibility than that of modern ghosts" and those who had "come under my own observation," were "repellant," "unkempt and begrimed," "incapable of feeling any distinction between men and beasts," and "devilish." According to Muir, the region's only hope lay in the redemptive power of nature. As he observed after touring the Modocs' Stronghold, "The sun shines freely into its mouth, and graceful bunches of grasses and eriognae and sage grow around it, redeeming it from all its degrading associations, and making it lovable notwithstanding its unfinished roughness and blackness."[14] By portraying the landscape as bound up with the tragic history of U.S.-Indian violence, Muir and others experienced the sense of dread they had come to expect.

For many visitors to the Klamath Basin, historical tourism became a proxy for encountering the region's romantic and vanishing Indigenous past. When John Hamilton toured the region in 1894, he met a Modoc Indian living on the north end of Tule Lake and hired him as a guide.[15] They left the following morning and traveled south along the shoreline, visiting Canby's Cross before continuing on to the Stronghold. Once in the Lava Beds, Hamilton found physical remnants of the Modoc War still present on the landscape. He discovered "the ankle bone of a human foot" and noticed that "the whitened bones [of Modoc cattle] were lying about" and that "the ashes of the long-extinguished fires are still to be seen."[16] Amid the detritus of war, Hamilton found himself reflecting on the continuing presence of the past in the landscape. "I glanced involuntarily at my Modoc guide; he was sitting on a block of lava looking into the pit, and repeating over and over to himself, 'Cap'n Jack's stron'hold; Cap'n Jack's stron'hold.' Whether the jingle of the words had caught his ear, or whether he was meditating on the annihilation of his tribe, I do not know." The mutterings of Hamilton's guide suggest the depths of trauma experienced by those who survived. Like Coleridge's Ancient Mariner, Hamilton's nameless Modoc seems compelled to bear witness to his people's suffering, but his testimony falls on deaf or indifferent ears. Confronted with the devastating physical and psychological effects of U.S.-Indian violence, however, Hamilton discarded his experience with the Modoc guide and announced, "Though the Modocs were but savages, and of course in the nature of things must soon have given way before the relentless march of the white race, yet it seems sad that the race should have been annihilated."[17]

Hamilton's sense of imperial nostalgia can be found in other touristic encounters with the Klamath Basin's legacy of Indian violence. Writing for *Sunset Magazine* in 1913, Rufus Steele, a San Francisco author and former editor of the city's *Chronicle* and *Call*, extolled the "mystical" and "diabolical" nature of the Klamath Basin's history of U.S.-Indian violence. Recounting his experience while visiting a "great shallow cave" along the Klamath River, Steele described a place called "the cave of Captain Jack." According to Steele, this "temple of memories" was named after the Modoc chief because his unredeemable acts of violence continued to haunt the site. The cave, he believed, was the site of several Modoc slave raids on the Shasta Indian fishermen and their families who slept there during the annual trout run. Seeking slaves to trade on the Columbia River for ponies, the Modocs raided this camp a number of times until the Shasta "found a certain Spartan method of cheating the Modocs of their prizes"—dashing their children on the rocks below rather than resigning them to slavery. The specter of the Modoc War haunted Euro-American tourists' experience of the Klamath Basin's Indian past.[18]

For their part, Klamath, Modoc, and Paiute Indians maintained meaningful relationships with the area long after hostilities had ended. Throughout the 1870s and 1880s, Klamath Indian agents prohibited tribal members from leaving the reservation without signed passes and prevented many from visiting the Lava Beds because of the area's historic, spiritual, and symbolic significance. Despite their efforts, however, reservation officials found it necessary to periodically round up off-reservation Indians, usually at the request of Euro-American officials. In an example of what historian Philip Deloria has identified as American colonialism's fascination with fixing Indigenous people in confined spaces, the Klamath Falls City Council evicted Matilda Whittle from her home near Link River in 1907 despite the fact that she had lived there since before the Modoc War. Evidently, she was "strongly attached to the old house" and protested the decision, stating that "she would rather die than leave her home." But the city council declared her "a nuisance" and an obstacle to development of the riverfront and insisted on her removal to the Klamath Reservation.[19]

Beginning in the 1880s, Indigenous people themselves also began undertaking journeys into the Lava Beds. In 1886, several exiled Modocs sought permission to visit the Klamath Basin, and sixteen years later, Samuel Clinton and Charles S. Hood submitted a proposal to the Klamath tribal council requesting permission to return home.[20] As these families returned, many visited the Lava Beds, often in secret. These visits were motivated by the fact that for Klamath Basin Indians, the Lava Beds remained an important site for harvesting certain resources and a culturally significant place for certain religious ceremonies and practices. Indeed, Albert Summers remembered his grandmother returning to the Lava Beds in the early 1900s for "camp meetings" involving an array of Modoc ceremonial activities.[21]

If some returned to the region for spiritual or cultural reasons, other returned exiles may have wanted to visit for another reason; some visited the Lava Beds to dig up personal items hidden away by their family before and during the Modoc War.[22] According to Modoc historian Cheewa James, Jennie Clinton—remembered as the last survivor of the Modoc War—used to tell stories of a large cache of buried gold, saddles, and other valuables hidden away in a cave in what is now Lava Beds National Monument. One day in the mid-1940s, Clinton convinced Clyde L. James to drive her to the park in search of the cave. As they drove, the weather took a turn for the worse, and "with limited visibility and whipping wind, the decision was made to return to the reservation and try for a better day."[23] Although the location of the cave and the true nature of its contents remained a mystery, the idea that riches might have been secreted away in the area seems to parallel the material memorializing of others. The persistence of such stories suggests that just as Euro-Americans were telling tales that created space, Klamath Basin Indians were producing spaces of material significance too.

Beyond drawing Klamath Basin Indians who hoped to find lost treasure, the Lava Beds also became an important source of employment opportunities for Indians beyond their reservation-based economy around the turn of the century. The recent work of National Park anthropologist Douglas Deur suggests that members of the Klamath Tribes with strong familial ties to the Lava Beds participated in the developing sheep industry south of Tule Lake. Ted Crume's mother and aunt worked out of Sheep Camp, running the herds along the bluff to the west and southwest of Tule Lake. Charles Laird, whose ranch lay along the southwestern shores of Lower Klamath Lake, also employed several Indians in his extensive sheepherding operation. Still others found employment as day laborers on the region's numerous rye, wheat, and potato farms. Klamath Basin Indians working on these farms and ranches probably visited the Lava Beds in their free time, sharing stories about places of historical and cultural importance or otherwise enjoying the area.[24]

The Lava Beds also experienced an increase in tourism around the turn of the century, though the actual number of visitors is impossible to estimate. Milo F. Coppock, a Lost River Valley homesteader, recalled "a large book in the cave known as Captain Jack's Stronghold. Many famous people including the governors of four states had signed it."[25] Nevertheless, before the automobile came into wide use, few visitors traveled to the area, and those who did arrived on foot, by boat, or on horseback. Beginning around 1900, boating became a popular regional activity for younger, middle-class non-Indigenous settlers, and Canby's Cross and Captain Jack's Stronghold became popular destinations for Sunday picnickers and boaters on vessels with such names as the *Canby*, the *Winema*, and the *Captain Jack*.[26]

Many local Euro-American settlers and their descendants enjoyed extended visits to the scenes of the Modoc War, transforming the area into a landscape of leisure as well as a site for remembering the region's history of U.S.-Indian violence. Thirteen people from Klamath Falls spent four days in 1909 in the Lava Beds.[27] The following year, Seldon K. Ogle spent nine days camping alone in the Lava Beds, staying one night in a cave he called "Toby Riddle's Restaurant" as well as visiting "the cross monument" and Captain Jack's Stronghold.[28] Most visitors to the Lava Beds, however, required tour guides. In July 1910, Charles Whitaker of Palo Alto traveled to the Lava Beds to visit the sites of the Modoc War and hired Euro-American Modoc War veteran J. C. Rutenic and his daughter, Yaden, to serve as guides.[29]

The rise of Modoc War tourism created a second informal economy as outings that included an Indigenous guide were of particular interest to tourists who sought an authentic encounter with the region's Indian past. As historian Paige Raibmon describes this relationship, "The native tour guide allowed tourists to commune simultaneously with vanishing landscapes and their premodern inhabitants. Sightseers were afforded a rare glimpse of nature and natives as they retreated together before modernity's onslaught."[30] Prominent Klamath Basin Indian guides included Matilda Whittle, Jeff Riddle, and above all Peter Schonchin.

Sometimes also known as Peter McCarty, Schonchin was the son of Schonchin John, one of the headmen executed alongside Captain Jack. As a young man, he had observed the Modoc War from within the Lava Beds and later claimed to have witnessed the attack on the peace commission. Returning to the Klamath Reservation around 1909 after more than three decades of exile in Oklahoma, Schonchin took a job delivering mail to the subagency at Yainax and soon gained a reputation for being a good tour guide since his memory of the Modoc War remained vivid.[31] In early May 1911, Schonchin guided his first tour, showing J. Fred Goeller, John Shook, and Rutenic around the Lava Beds. "Probably the most thrilling experience was to listen on the ground to [Schonchin's] description of the defeat of Major Thomas," the three men told a local reporter a week later. "The Indian's sense of locality was wonderful to the city-bred whites, empty cartridge shells attesting to his correctness in location, though a fire had swept over the country in the thirty eight years of the Modoc's absence, changing the appearance of things." An effective and powerful speaker, Schonchin also had a knack for locating relics. Human thighbones, bullets, and other physical reminders of the Modoc War were often found as part of his tours. These relics, in turn, formed the basis for the historically themed window display at Brinker's Pharmacy, on Klamath Falls's Main Street, a popular attraction for cosmopolitan consumers in the Klamath Basin.[32] Schonchin earned additional cash by trapping coyotes during his visits to the Lava Beds. In October 1911, while conducting a tour of the area, he collected half a dozen pelts from traps he had set, for which he was paid $1.50 each.[33]

The centrality of mobility to Schonchin's livelihood is paralleled by the experiences of American Indians throughout the United States. For aboriginal workers in the Puget Sound's hop fields, for example, migratory labor offered both the ability to earn wages and the opportunity to travel to participate in religious communities such as the Shakers and regional gatherings of friends and family.[34] Mobility, however, could also be as much a political statement as an economic and social one. As historian Chantal Norrgard has found in her research on Ojibwes who worked in the postal, shipping, and railroad industries, mobility was and remains both central to Ojibwe self-determination and an important tool for resisting the disciplining and isolating influence of reservation boundaries.[35] Schonchin may well have cherished his work as a guide not only for the economic opportunities it afforded but also for the life of mobility it sustained.

Visitors to the Lava Beds region had a variety of opportunities to experience the area's legacy of U.S.-Indian violence. Throughout the 1910s,

Milo Coppock often guided large groups of visitors into the Lava Beds, taking them to Captain Jack's Stronghold and other scenes from the Modoc War.[36] J. C. Rutenic and Oliver Applegate, both of whom were Euro-American veterans of the Modoc War, served as tour guides on a number of occasions, leading visitors through the caves and regaling their guests with war stories. These tourist groups were socioeconomically diverse, including, according to one account, "men from all walks of life, professional men, business men, artisans, mechanics and laborers."[37] The advent of national Prohibition in 1920 brought new opportunities as Guy Merrill's Bearpaw Resort, a rural speakeasy, became a popular destination. Established in the summer of 1922 on land Merrill's father had acquired in 1916, the same year Oregon became a dry state, the Bearpaw seems to have offered clean beds for up to forty people, hot chicken dinners, a four-piece orchestra, a large open-air platform for dancing, and booze. The resort also had a museum showcasing the region's history, with daily tours of the Lava Beds, its caves, and the sites of the Modoc War.[38] Prohibition thus spurred Modoc War tourism by bringing more visitors to the Lava Beds for extended periods of time.

Despite these tourist activities, the Lava Beds were a marginalized landscape throughout much of the late nineteenth and early twentieth centuries. According to National Park historian Frederick Brown, "the Lava Beds had gone from being at the center of the Modoc world to being at the edge of white society."[39] Maps produced in the aftermath of the Modoc War associated specific sites in the Lava Beds with claims to American innocence, and visitors embraced the region's legacy of violence. Despite its persistence, the Klamath Basin's fledgling tourism industry remained a secondary economic activity throughout the first two decades of the twentieth century. The rise of automobile tourism in the 1910s and 1920s, however, accelerated the development of a memorial landscape that expanded American innocence to include soldiers and settlers in the cult of white victimhood at the hands of Indian outlaws.

■ On May 26, 1911, Guy Merrill packed his lunch, loaded his Buick Model 14 with supplies, and drove into the Lava Beds of Modoc County. Traveling twelve miles on a relatively well-maintained wagon road, he entered the Lava Beds from the east, negotiating his vehicle through the rough terrain. "The machine climbed rocks and squeezed through tight places where no one would believe an auto could go," the *Klamath Falls Evening Herald* reported. "No doubt a number of crack drivers will include this exciting trip in their auto repertoire."[40] Ostensibly on a trip to gather in his flock of sheep grazing in the Lava Beds, Merrill's "feat in automobile daring" generated media excitement that combined the early twentieth-century fascination with modern technology, exploits of male bravado, and excitement over encounters with a region's vanishing Indian past. Merrill's trip was accompanied by a revival of interest in commemorating the Modoc War. A week earlier, his father, Charles H. Merrill, and J. Fred Goeller had declared their intention to erect crosses in the Lava Beds to show tourists the exact locations where American soldiers had fallen during the Modoc War.[41] Drawing inspiration from the use of tombstones to mark the graves of Custer's soldiers, this memorial movement was accompanied by increased interest in the region both for its relics and for its tantalizing and mysterious caves. The touristic landscape of the Lava Beds made possible by the introduction of the automobile acquainted a new generation of Americans with the region's history and helped establish the Modoc War as the defining moment in the Klamath Basin's transition from Indigenous to Euro-American control.

Development of the region for automotive tourism began in earnest after Guy Merrill's initial trip. Following a three-day visit to the Lava Beds in the fall of 1913, a group of sixty Klamath Falls men formed the Klamath County Scenic Attraction League to build a road into the region. "Yellowstone Park would have nothing on Klamath County, once our scenic attractions w[ere] properly discovered, label[e]d, and advertised," they declared. The following year, the clamor for development received a new impetus with the outbreak of war in Europe. "The American must travel," declared one supporter in an open letter published in the *Klamath Falls Evening Herald*, "and with Europe out of the question, he will heed the slogan heard on every hand, 'See America First.'"[42] War might keep American tourists out of Europe, but good roads would bring them to the Klamath Basin.

On April 22, 1915, delegations from Modoc, Siskiyou, and Klamath Counties met at Captain Jack's Stronghold for a two-day conference to discuss the proposed road and to determine its exact route. The joint delegations voted to build a road from Lookout, California, through the Lava Beds to Klamath Falls, Oregon. Volunteer labor would be used to connect a number of existing roads, and subscriptions from local businesses would fund the project. To celebrate the agreement, Klamath County declared May 20 "Good Road Day," closing all businesses so that townsfolk might work with ranchers to improve the county's roads. The event raised several hundred dollars and was declared "the biggest and best supported cooperative movement in the history of Klamath County." The Lava Beds road project received final approval on June 20, 1915, and work began two weeks later.[43]

Aspirations for the new road were high. Following the conclusion of negotiations, the Good Road Association of Modoc County declared, "With the Pit River Canyon, Basset Hot Springs, Modoc Lava Beds, Klamath Falls and Crater Lake, we certainly have the most attractive route in the states of California and Oregon, and with good roads through this section we will surely make the people take notice."[44] During San Francisco's 1915 Panama-Pacific International Exposition, the Klamath County Chamber of Commerce invested nearly one thousand dollars on an exhibit touting the recent improvements. "Though we have had very little money to spend as compared to most of the counties represented, we feel that we have a very creditable display and one that will attract the visitors as much as some of the more pretentious and expensive exhibits."[45] As ambitious as these improvements were, large-scale investments were necessary to transform the Lava Beds into a national tourist destination.

For remote western communities in the 1920s, national parks and national monuments meant increases in federal spending on infrastructure and tourism. The Klamath Basin got its first taste of the development potential of national parks when Congress established Crater Lake National Park on May 21, 1902. The new park's remoteness and inaccessibility initially kept visitor rates down, and between 1902 and 1910, the park reported fewer than 5,275 visitors in any given year and often as few as 1,000. At the 1911 National Park Conference in Yellowstone, the park's superintendent, William Arant, complained about the need for road development: "I want a road entirely around the lake that will cost $500,000, and I want other roads and trails that will cost as much more. . . . If necessary for the good of the cause, I will come to Washington and stay there through the winter to aid in getting money from Congress to build our roads."[46] The next year, construction began on a network of roads running through the park and connecting the park with population centers to the south and west. Between 1910 and 1915, annual visitation doubled from 5,235 to 11,371, and over the next five years, visitation rates doubled again. Many of those who visited arrived by car.[47]

Inspired by the success of Crater Lake, local developers and other influential individuals advocated on behalf of national park status for the Lava Beds, arguing for their significance both as a tourist destination and as a site of heroic sacrifice. In 1918, California congressman John E. Raker mounted a spirited campaign for a greater share of federal highway dollars to expand northern California's "great empire" by exploiting the financial opportunities of the Klamath Basin's scenery and tourism potential.[48] In support of Raker's efforts, the *Siskiyou News* called the Lava Beds a "wonderland" whose cave formations "compel the attention and wonder of those who seek the strange and forceful things that nature offers," while its "individual history appeals to all." The Lava Beds were particularly significant since they were where "more than 200 soldiers and volunteers sacrificed their lives in the campaign waged against the notorious Captain Jack and his renegade band of Indians."[49] If the Lava Beds were going to be a site of national sacrifice and mourning, some believed they needed a new monument declaring it.

Working in conjunction with Raker and other political leaders in 1925, the Alturas Parlor of the Native Daughters of the Golden West initiated a campaign to erect a monument to the Modoc War. The Native Daughters, a sororal and patriotic organization whose mission was to preserve California's history by venerating its pioneering past, advanced a particular version of the state's history that valorized and legitimized Anglo-American ownership. From the group's founding in the late nineteenth century to the 1930s, the Native Daughters—along with their fraternal counterparts, the Native Sons—erected hundreds of historical monuments, statues, and plaques throughout the state.[50] The history of California's Gold Rush and pioneers' experiences with Mexicans and Indians were of particular interest to the organization as it sought to connect the history of California with that of the nation while embedding into the landscape a narrative of virtuous white ownership.[51] For the Alturas Parlor, the Modoc War had imbued the Lava Beds with a narrative of U.S.-Indian violence that valorized the civilizing aggression of westward expansion while redeeming the white pioneer as the heroic victim of Indian savagery. In the Lava Beds, "many a sturdy pioneer paid to Indian savagery the supreme sacrifice paid so oft by those in the vanguard of civilization," the Native Daughters announced in the *Alturas Plain-Dealer* under an engraving of Uncle Sam laying a wreath on a soldier's grave. From the beginning, the Native Daughters announced that the monument would be made out of "native material" and would "honor the memory of those who fell there."[52]

The emphasis on the use of native material suggests the Native Daughters' intention that the monument would claim the land's resources, naturalizing them as the property and inheritance of a settler society. Indeed, as historian Phoebe Kropp has demonstrated, early twentieth-century Anglo residents of California claimed ownership of the land through the appropriation of "native" built environments. From the preservation of

California's defunct Spanish missions to the ersatz historical restoration of Olvera Street in Los Angeles, Kropp argues, these "memory places are sites of cultural production and venues for struggles over public space, racial politics, and citizenship."[53] The Native Daughters' fetishization of the "native materials" from which their monument to white victimhood would be constructed, then, was part of a larger movement to appropriate the meaning of public spaces imbued with Hispanic or American Indian history and heritage.

The Alturas Parlor of the Native Daughters of the Golden West found abundant support for their golden bear or "Lava Beds Monument" from state and local government officials, influential businessmen, and organizations. Following the launch of the fund drive in February 1925, the Alturas Boy Scouts agreed to assist in the construction of the monument, and the county superintendent of schools supported the involvement of both teachers and students in "this memorable work."[54] In early March, they announced the goal of raising one thousand dollars and began publishing the names of donors and amounts donated in the local paper. Throughout March and April, donations poured in from individuals and businesses as well as organizations, among them the Alturas Civic Club, the Odd Fellow Lodge, the Pythian Sisters and Eagles, the Modoc Development Board, and the Native Daughters of the Golden West parlors throughout the state.[55] In early April, the *Sacramento Bee* published an extensive piece supporting both the establishment of the Lava Beds as a national monument under the supervision of the National Park Service and the fund-raising efforts of the Alturas Parlor, suggesting that the whole state would soon become involved in the effort. "Since the Alturas Native Daughters began work on the plan to mark certain spots, interest in the Modoc Lava Beds has been aroused in Sacramento, San Francisco and elsewhere and steps may be taken shortly to co-ordinate this interest in the region into some kind of an organization that will sponsor the setting aside of the Modoc Lava Beds as a national monument."[56] Following the *Sacramento Bee*'s publicity, the Alturas Parlor received generous donations from individuals, towns, and civic organizations throughout northern California.

Washington responded to the calls to preserve the Lava Beds as part of the National Park Service. Partially in response to vandalism of Canby's Cross and other sites associated with the Modoc War, Congressman Raker sponsored a bill to create the monument in February 1925 and ran an article in the *Alturas Plain-Dealer* soliciting input from his constituency. Later that year, the National Forest Service, which had managed the

Lava Beds since 1920, threw its support behind the bill by recommending that the area be set aside as a national monument as a consequence of its historic significance and unique geography. Without any clear avenues of opposition, President Calvin Coolidge signed a proclamation creating the Lava Beds National Monument on November 21, 1925, preserving the battlegrounds of the Modoc War and opening the area to increased tourism.[57]

■ On June 13, 1926, the Native Daughters of the Golden West dedicated their monument to white victimhood and American innocence. As news of the Golden Bear Monument spread across the country, it elicited a variety of responses from individuals as far afield as Wisconsin, Colorado, and North Carolina. Those with ties to the Modoc War wrote letters or journeyed to the park. One veteran, Charles Hardin of Denver, wrote to the editor of the *Alturas Plain-Dealer* after receiving news of the monument. His words reflect both the deeply felt meaning of inclusion and the significance of the historical cleansing performed by the Native Daughters. "The reading of this article, which came to me on the anniversary of one of our hardest, and, to my mind, most glorious fights of the war—the battle at Dry (or Soras) [*sic*] Lake, May 10, 1873, gave me a real thrill. I wish that the Native Daughters might know how much I, a veteran of that war, appreciates [*sic*] their work. I may never see the monument, but so long as I live, I shall remember, with gratitude, all those who have worked for it."[58] For Hardin and many other veterans, the Golden Bear Monument constituted an acknowledgment and validation of sacrifices and glorious victories.

In validating Hardin's memory, the monument also provided an opportunity for others to establish connections—or at least perceived connections—with the place. Hearing of the newly established monument, A. A. Witzel of Wisconsin, the granddaughter of Thomas Wright, a colonel in the Modoc War, thought it an opportune time to visit California and reconnect with this marker to her ancestor's past. Arriving in Sacramento in 1928, Witzel was disturbed to discover that no monument to her grandfather existed. Though he had led his troops to their death during the Modoc War, he had never been memorialized by name. Unperturbed, Witzel traveled to Klamath Falls, interviewed several white veterans of the Modoc War, and consulted park officials but never located a monument to her grandfather's memory.[59] In 1930, however, two unknown soldiers of the Modoc War were honored when their bodies were unearthed during excavation on the Southern Pacific right-of-way near the Lava Beds. The American Legion post from Stronghold, California, identified the remains as those of two Warm Springs Indian scouts

*Figure 22. "Grave of Warm Springs Scouts," 1934. Courtesy of
Lava Beds National Monument, Tulelake, Calif.*

and reburied the two "fallen heroes" with full honors, marking their grave
with a large white cross (figure 22).[60]

While the Native Daughters' Golden Bear Monument expanded the
category of victimhood to include soldiers and settlers, the participation
of Modoc County in California's Diamond Jubilee celebration promoted
the conflict as California's last Indian war. Held on Admission Day in San
Francisco, the Diamond Jubilee Parade was the centerpiece of the commemoration of the seventy-fifth anniversary of statehood. According to
the *Alturas Plain-Dealer*, it was to be "the grandest celebration ever to be
held in any State, and is to be a Pageant of the different epochs of California history."[61] The float planned and designed by a committee of the
Alturas Parlor of the Native Daughters was to be one of a dozen or so that
would "depict the history of the state." Modoc County's float was designed
to capture "the epoch of 1872, when the last Indian War was fought," and it
was believed that participating in the Diamond Jubilee would be "a splendid opportunity for Modoc [County] to participate and add her early history in this picture pageant of past events which led to the making of our
grand and glorious state of California." A vaudeville show and dance were
planned for August 28, 1925, in the Modoc Union High School Hall to
raise funds for the float.[62] The event must have been a success, for on September 9, Modoc County's float participated in the parade.

The inclusion of Klamath Basin Indians in the float's design was much heralded by the newspapers and produced a seemingly authentic portrayal of a vanishing Indian race and a romantic reminder of the state's inevitable progression toward civilization. According to the *Alturas Plain-Dealer*, the float was "gaily decorated with shrubbery and wigwams, and contained eight Indians from Modoc County, Jim Bayley, Geo. Brown and two children and wife and Geo. Fuller and wife of Likely. These Indians had prepared for themselves magnificent costumes and they were splendid figures. They were the only real Indians in the parade with the exception of an Indian 110 years old who was placed behind the Modoc float."[63] The *San Francisco Chronicle* also reported the presence of Modoc Indians in the celebrations but emphasized the nostalgia of their participation. Described as "Genuine Modoc Indian warriors," Bayley, Brown, and George Fuller reportedly sported "war bonnets, blankets, war paint, tomahawks, battle axes of the days of bison hunts and tepee councils." Greeted at the San Francisco Ferry terminal by a delegation of former Modoc County residents, Bayley, Brown, Fuller, and their families, dressed in Plains Indian regalia, were conducted to the Hotel Herald in San Francisco's Tenderloin District. For the remainder of the Diamond Jubilee celebration, the Modoc Indians enjoyed all the thrills and excitements the city had to offer, taking car rides through the crowded streets, "fully appreciative of the thrills of modern high-pressure metropolitanism."[64]

Although many observers commented on the Modocs' use and enjoyment of automobiles during their visit to the city, American expectations of Indians and technology also rendered invisible their embracing of modernity. "Things get weird," historian Philip Deloria writes, "when the symbolic systems built on cars and Indians intersect."[65] The former symbolize modernity and mobility, technology, and affluence, whereas the latter represent an ancient if noble and technologically primitive past. Flesh-and-blood Modoc Indians careening down San Francisco streets in automobiles challenged early twentieth-century Americans' expectations of Indians. How would San Franciscans resolve such a paradox? Regardless of how modern the Modoc visitors might appear when driving down Lombard Street, once placed on a papier-mâché cart and floated down Market Street, Bayley, Brown, and Fuller came to typify California's "frontier days when their race was making its last stand against the inroads of civilization."[66]

If the float's design presented the Modoc War as a symbol of the state's evolution from Indian savagery to industrialized civilization, visual representations of Klamath Basin Indians circulating around the Diamond Jubilee underscored the redemptive nature of that violence. In its Sunday Rotogravure Pictorial Section, the *San Francisco Chronicle* published a full-page collage, "Injuns in Modoc Lava Beds," that combined images with text. Emphasizing the relationship between U.S.-Indian violence and the landscape of the Klamath Basin, the collage presented a narrative of American innocence that placed forgetting at its center. Moving clockwise, the first image featured "Chief Lee Snipe," standing on a lava rock outcropping, with arms raised in the air and face looking skyward. The caption informed readers that Snipe "calls upon the spirit of those of his tribe who fought and defeated the white man in the lava beds." But below this caption, almost interjecting itself, is the statement "THEY SCALP NO-BODY," accompanied by an image of two "Injun kiddies . . . playing at war." If the infantilization and domestication of the Modoc warriors were insufficient to project a nonthreatening image, the accompanying close-up of Chief Lee Snipe noted that although he is "PROUD AS EVER," the Modoc people had "long forgotten their former enmity to the whites." Simultaneously evoking the possibility of violence and containing that threat within a past whose details had long been forgotten, the living, breathing Modoc is neither the agent nor the object of violence. He is a memory-less other, unable to recall the atrocities of the past.[67]

Scholars have commented on the duality—what Richard Flores calls the "Janus-faced" nature—of remembering and forgetting.[68] Cultural geographer Kenneth E. Foote has argued that "society's need to remember is balanced against its desire to forget, to leave memory behind and put the event out of mind."[69] Ethnologist Andrew Lass has likewise suggested that the "nation-state's concern for remembrance, or encoding, is paralleled only by its obsession with forgetting, or erasure."[70] In creating narratives of the Modoc War that sustained their claims to American innocence, then, early twentieth-century Americans had two options: they could portray the violence of American colonialism as justified and therefore fundamentally innocent, or they could forget it altogether. By suggesting that Chief Lee Snipe had forgotten his former enmity, the collage supported this second claim to American innocence.

The collage also advanced white Americans' claims to innocence through its depiction of current Indigenous-settler interactions in the Lava Beds. The image on the top right shows two "little Modoc Injuns" receiving lessons "in woodcraft" from Chief Lee Snipe. Their nakedness suggests their primitiveness, but the text reveals that they are half civilized and nearly assimilated into white society: "They'd be better Injuns if they hadn't seen the barber. Truth to tell, they are Injun only in blood—otherwise, all the same [as] white children." A barber's scissors might tame their savagery, but their openness to white visitors suggests that they have forgiven Americans for the violence of the past. "The whole family seems to be all dressed up to receive visitors," the right-middle image explains; "the guest is Captain O. C. Applegate . . . who fought 'em fifty years ago in the Modoc War." The transformation of an American soldier from enemy into guest reflects the redemptive promise of the Lava Beds. Within two generations, the violence of the Modoc War has been forgotten as the children of Modoc warriors receive their parents' enemies as guests; the troubled history of the Modoc War has been rendered safe for white tourists to encounter and consume.[71]

Through physical markers like the Lava Beds monument and performative commemorations such as the Diamond Jubilee, Euro-American settlers and their descendants produced representations of the Modoc War that contained narratives of American innocence. Where the area's focus on Canby as a Christian martyr had previously presented a narrative of victimhood, the shift in emphasis favored a contained and consumable version of history that catered to tourists. In honoring the hardships and triumph of white soldiers and settlers, Lava Beds National Monument represented the Modoc War as both a source of American innocence and evidence of white America's perseverance and modernity. For nearly half a century, Lava Beds National Monument, under the stewardship of the National Park Service, printed informational brochures and designed guided tours of the battlegrounds that legitimized the deaths of white soldiers while ignoring or eliding the deaths of Indian peoples. In many ways, the Lava Beds National Monument was a collective memorial to white victimhood and American innocence.

Coda

AN OUTLAW TO ALL MANKIND

In the crowded picnic area at the center of the community park in Malin, Oregon, stands a memorial to the victims of nineteenth-century U.S.-Indian violence in the Klamath Basin. Dedicated on May 25, 2009—Memorial Day—by the American Legion Post No. 84, the plaque reads, "In memory of our area's earliest settlers killed November 29, 1872 by Hooker Jim 'An outlaw to all Mankind,'" and lists the names of the fourteen homesteaders who died in the aftermath of the Battle of Lost River. Affixed to a cairn of rocks that originally honored the founding members of the Malin community park and recreation districts, the memorial's historical narrative is elaborated by a nearby kiosk with a detailed map of the region. Cluttered with photographs of the Indigenous and non-Indian participants, the display explains, "Historians have written that the 1873 Modoc War would rank as the most significant Indian war in America's western history, were it not for Custer's dramatic defeat at the Little Big Horn in 1876. It is the only Indian war in American history that a full ranking general, General Edwin [*sic*] Canby, has been killed, Custer being a Lieutenant Colonel at the time of the Little Big Horn." The map includes a detailed chronology of the Modoc War, with military actions highlighted in bold lettering and images juxtaposing today's landscape with historic photographs.[1]

Funded in part by Modoc War enthusiast and San Francisco philanthropist Daniel Woodhead, the dedication of the 2009 memorial in Malin accompanied efforts to increase tourism to the Klamath Basin by promoting the region's history to a wider American audience. Woodhead planned to place additional plaques and kiosks throughout the Klamath Basin, including at the Lava Beds National Monument and other sites associated with the war. He also hoped to distribute a folder-sized version of the map to schools, local historical societies, and museums as well as to promote a driving tour of the area. As part of the effort to increase general awareness of the region's legacy of U.S.-Indian violence, several community theaters have produced plays based on events from the Modoc War, and reenactors gather each year at the Lava Beds, putting on a kind of living history program geared toward school-aged children.[2]

Malin's commemorative plaque, then, reaffirms and reproduces a narrative of American innocence in the Klamath Basin strikingly similar to those of a century earlier. Dedicated on Memorial Day and bearing the homesteaders' names, Malin's commemorative plaque represents the fourteen settlers as honored veterans and tragic victims of the Indian wars. The tension between identifying these settlers as soldiers and victims—a common problem for Indian war memorials—is resolved by the memorial's unambiguous identification of the Modoc warrior Hooker Jim as "An outlaw to all Mankind." This interpretation of American Indian resistance to colonialism as technically a crime both embraces the logic of America's nineteenth-century settler colonial jurisprudence and inscribes that narrative onto the landscape, elevating Euro-Americans' deaths as evidence of American innocence in the face of uncontrollable Indigenous outlawry. The legality of American settlers' ownership of the Klamath Basin remains unquestioned, while the illegality of Modoc resistance is reaffirmed.

Underscoring the theme of victimization in this memorial, the interpretive kiosk extends the argument to make a larger claim about the importance of U.S.-Indian violence in the Klamath Basin. The historical significance of the Modoc War, we are told, derives from the tragic death of an American military leader struck down in the service of his country while defending innocent settlers from Indigenous outlaws. Were it not for Custer and his vainglorious demise, General Canby's death would have assured the Modoc War its proper place of prominence in the annals of America's western history. While such counterfactual historical statements may seem naive, they nonetheless create hierarchies of historical significance based on claims to white victimization. Canby's death is more important than Custer's because Canby outranked him. The Modoc War, then, derives its significance from the status of its white victims, not from its decisive effect on American sovereignty in the region or, for that matter, from the enormous suffering of the Klamath, Modoc, and Paiute peoples.

Such memorials construct narratives of American innocence that discursively amplify and extend U.S.-Indian violence into the present. Yet they also point to the persistent instability of the marketplace of remembering and the ultimate impossibility of true historical justice through reconciliation. History is never over, and the violence of the past will continue to haunt each present moment. In remembering the Modoc War, Klamath Basin Indians and Euro-American settlers and their descendants have and will continue to produce, commodify, and exchange their shared history of violence. The violence, long over, is made fresh on the landscape as historical narratives create touristic landscapes of American innocence through the marketplace of remembering the Modoc War.

If memorials and celebrations of pioneer heroism and sacrifice have allowed Americans to locate colonial violence in a distant past and to weave narratives of innocence into the national fabric, they nonetheless created opportunities for certain Klamath Basin Indians to become entrepreneurs in the region's memory industry, working as interpreters and guides while promoting particular versions of history that sometimes reproduce and sometimes complicate established narratives. Opportunities for inclusion and cooperation, however, fell away by midcentury, especially following the devastating termination of the Klamath Tribes' nation-to-nation relationship with the U.S. government in 1954. Indeed, relations in the Klamath Basin throughout the 1960s and 1970s were characterized by antagonism and accusations of racism. But the Klamath Tribes' restoration in 1986, together with ascendant ideas of multiculturalism and calls for national reconciliation, resulted in a new memorial to the Modoc War two years later. The new memorial—the first to include Indigenous casualties among the so-called victims of the Modoc War—sought to mend relations between the federal government and the tribes by creating an Indian-inclusive memorial to the futility of war.

Epilogue

EXCHANGING GIFTS
WITH THE DEAD

On March 28, 1988, some two hundred people gathered in Lava Beds National Monument to consecrate a new memorial to the victims of nineteenth-century U.S.-Indian violence in the Klamath Basin. Orchestrated by the National Park Service and local historical organizations, the day's events included a guided tour of the battlegrounds, a series of expert presentations, and a panel discussion with descendants of those who participated in the war. Aspirations for the event were high. The occasion was, in the words of Senator Pete Wilson, intended to "help to correct th[e] historical oversight" of previous representations of the conflict and "to establish the conflict in its proper context."[1] Despite Wilson's supposed interest in reconciliation, the 1988 memorial did little to challenge the existing narrative of the Modoc War contained in the Lava Beds National Monument's memorial landscape. Rather, it sustained dominant representations of the conflict by reproducing claims to American innocence in the conquest and colonization of the American West.

The 1988 memorial provides a stark reminder of how physical markers to the Modoc War have inscribed narratives of American innocence onto the region's landscape without reckoning with the material inequalities of the past. During the memorial's dedication, Doris Omundson, superintendent of the Lava Beds National Monument, stood above the park's now-empty graves of U.S. Army casualties and declared that the soldiers "*were all just people doing their jobs.* . . . Each one wanted the best for themselves and for their families. . . . We reach a stalemate and we don't know how to negotiate. . . . It was a time of real sorrow, and we do want to remember that. We do also want to remember the good that came out of it and also the heartbreak."[2] Addressing the causes and legacy of U.S.-Indian violence in the region, Omundson's brand of historical revisionism was also present in the federally funded memorial's text, which declared with no apparent irony, "Many wars have occurred since the Modoc War, and many more are yet to be fought. The people involved may change, but the names we call them and the reasons we fight remain the same. *There are no true winners in war. We all pay the price.*"[3]

One persistent facet of public commemorations and memorials is that they are as much an act of forgetting as an act of remembering.[4] What is now Lava Beds National Monument, a unit of the National Park Service, which, in turn, is part of the U.S. Department of the Interior, was for thousands of years the Modocs' home. But by suggesting that "we all pay the price" and that "there are no true winners," the memorial normalizes the U.S. federal government's possession of a culturally, spiritually, and materially significant place and elides the fundamentally unequal nature of nineteenth-century U.S.-Indian violence and American settler colonialism writ large. In other words, under the guise of liberal multiculturalism, the 1988 memorial asks people to imagine a kind of equality in the face of history's material inequalities.

Beyond trivializing the violence of American settler colonialism as indistinct from other historic conflicts, past or future, the memorial also absolves Americans of their guilt by magnanimously expanding the category of victimhood to include the vanquished alongside the victor—the collective "we" who must all pay the price for war. As local historian and event chair Francis Landrum declared in his dedication, "Some ninety names on this plaque are Modoc Indians, U.S. Army troops, Oregon Volunteer Militia, California Volunteer Militia, and white citizens. It includes the names of anyone who was killed during the course of the war, but does not include anyone who died a natural death. *Everyone is treated the same: civilians, soldiers, Indians.*"[5]

The incorporation of Modoc casualties in the memorial illuminates the work of remembering performed by such sites. While Landrum's assertion that this memorial *treats everyone the same* was specifically calculated to address the region's legacy of racially exclusive memorials to white victimhood, the claim to equivalency was predicated on the existence of a liberal marketplace of historical revisionism in which one narrative might be traded or exchanged for another, like so much wheat or tobacco. The memorial was to transform the Modoc War from a justified war of conquest to an unavoidable and inevitable multicultural tragedy. By providing a space for equal inclusion in Lava Beds National Monument's landscape of victimhood, it claimed to treat everyone *the same* and offered atonement for the violence of American settler colonialism by ignoring the *unequivalence* of that violence. The death of a soldier sent to the Klamath Basin by the U.S. Army to kill Indians was equal to that of an old woman burned to death in her home or an Indian prisoner pulled from the wagon transporting him to prison and slaughtered by white vigilantes. They were all *treated the same*.

Since the 1954 publication of the English version of Marcel Mauss's *Essai sur le don*, the anthropological distinction of the gift as embodying a persistent societal obligation of reciprocal exchange has engaged the imaginations of academics across disciplines and engendered, appropriately enough, an endless series of intellectual exchanges. The role, function, true nature, and even the possibility of the gift have all come under intense scrutiny, enriching, enlivening, and deepening our collective understanding of the complex social dimensions of economic exchanges.[6] But the applicability and transportability of Mauss's realization is not limited to the physical world of exchange goods. In recent decades, multicultural revisionism and historical reconciliation also have come to exist and function within a societal marketplace of exchange, obligation, debt, and reciprocity. For those who wish to correct history, the material and immaterial forms of historical justice making offer inclusion as a kind of gift to the dead, a gift in which a previously flawed narrative of the past is purportedly exchanged, wholly and fully, for another, improved version of the past.

This idealized exchange is itself an act of power that belies any attempt by the powerful to contain historical narratives of violence in the past. By offering to the dead the gift of contemporary narrative inclusion, apologists place the social obligation of a reciprocal exchange on the living—an exchange we call forgiveness. Indeed, as historian Matthew Jacobson writes, multiculturalism's desire to locate inequalities in a distant past "fossilizes racial injustice in dim national antiquity, and so glosses over more recent discriminatory practices."[7] But what happens when the living are removed from this exchange economy of historical justice? Are historical reparations possible in a liberal, progressive marketplace of remembering and forgetting in which the gift of justice is offered to the living only through the dead? To explore these questions, we must first consider the dark history of Klamath termination and restoration and the legacy of memorials to U.S.-Indian violence in the Klamath Basin.

■ "I have never seen the old battlegrounds and I never want to see them," longtime Klamath tribal chair Seldon Kirk declared in a 1968 interview with Charles Hillinger of the *Los Angeles Times*; "It stirs me up inside to think about it." Echoing a common sentiment among Klamath tribal members at the time, Kirk was responding to recent efforts by the Indian-based Klamath Memorial Association to erect a plaque in the Lava Beds honoring Captain Jack. The group, composed of a handful of Klamath Basin Indians with economic interests associated with the Lava Beds National Monument, had contacted Superintendent William J. Kennedy to discuss the project. Provisional approval had been granted on the conditions that it was done "in good taste" and that the superintendent could personally edit the plaque's wording. "We had to tone it down so it wouldn't be objectionable to a large number of people who visit the Lava Beds," Kennedy later explained. "It's a case of trying to please everyone. How would you like it if your grandfather had been killed by Modocs? A lot of good soldiers lost their lives in the battles."[8]

The result of these efforts was an insipid marker that insulted rather than honored those who had fought to preserve the Modoc way of life. Intended to "set the record straight," the edited plaque betrayed Klamath Memorial Association members' desire to honor their descendants by expunging any "objectionable" material:

> Modoc Indian War 1872–73. Within this lava fortress, under the leadership of Capt. Jack, a small band of Modoc Indians held off a much larger force of U.S. regular and volunteer troops for nearly six months.

During the plaque's dedication, Friedman Kirk delivered a fiery speech in which he lambasted the inadequacy of the monument and condemned "all the terrible things the white people did to the Modocs." As he later explained, "I just had to let everybody know what we're trying to say between the lines of this Indian historical marker."[9]

Kirk's aversion to the Lava Beds National Monument and Kennedy's ethnocentric concerns for the park's visitors in many ways capture the tensions existing between Klamath Basin Indians and the National Park Service in the decades after World War II. For many Natives, the Lava Beds National Monument had become a stigmatized site of national mourning, a feeling made even more intense by the government's decision to terminate the Klamath Tribes' federal recognition. Despite official opposition from the tribe and the Bureau of Indian Affairs, Congress adopted Public Law 587, better known as the Klamath Termination Act, on August 13, 1954, with dire social, cultural, and economic consequences for Klamath

Basin Indians. Overnight, the self-sufficient Klamath Tribes became impoverished and landless and lost their federal health and education programs. Where before they owned and managed the largest stand of ponderosa pines in the West, the government condemned their 1.8 million acres in exchange for payments of approximately forty-three thousand dollars per member. Within a few years, most of the money paid out had vanished, and the Department of Agriculture had leased former reservation lands to non-Indigenous lumber companies. "There was some really heavy duty structural discrimination within the employment market," recalled Lynn Schonchin in 2002. "Our people would apply for jobs, try to go to work and [employers would say] no, you're a rich Indian, you don't need a job."[10]

Beyond the economic hardships brought on by termination, many tribal members suffered isolation and the loss of culture as families moved apart, separating children from their parents. This upheaval severed the Modocs' ties with landscapes of historical, cultural, and spiritual significance such as the Lava Beds area. As individuals left the Klamath Basin in search of employment, an entire generation broke with certain forms of cultural and historical knowledge. Today, tribal members often say that cultural and historical knowledge "skipped a generation" for those who came of age during the termination period.[11] As Morrie Jimenez described the process, "The loss of the land base and the natural resources. All of that w[as] an inherent part of our cultural system. . . . With the loss of that natural resource, that land base . . . they take a big piece out of the culture. Really critical piece out of the culture and that's what most people who have not been a part of that experience find it very difficult to understand."[12] In short, termination alienated a generation of Klamath, Modoc, and Paiute Indians from their homelands and sites of cultural, historic, and spiritual significance. Today, many tribal members remember that their parents and grandparents "simply refused to go" to the Lava Beds. "They didn't say why, they just refused to go," saying, "That place is a graveyard and not to be messed with. . . . We shouldn't go there."[13] After three decades of cultural decay, poverty, community disintegration, and destabilization, many tribal members began to view the Modoc War as the beginning of more than a century of the U.S. assimilationist policy.[14]

Termination, however, had a significant politicizing effect on some members of the Klamath Tribes as members left the Klamath Basin and got involved in the Red Power movement and fish-ins along the Columbia River.[15] Returning home in the 1970s, some members became radicalized, a change that translated into an active engagement with the memory of

U.S.-Indian violence in the Klamath Basin. For example, Klamath tribal members declined invitations to the 1973 Tulelake-Butte Valley Fair, whose theme, "Arrows to Agriculture in 100 Years," was billed as a celebration of the 100th anniversary of the Modoc War. Similarly, some Indians boycotted the Captain Jack Centennial Medicine Show and Craft Fair in Arcata, California, and refused to participate in all activities associated with Lava Beds National Monument and the centennial.[16]

Klamath Basin Indians engaged with representations of their history in more institutional ways as well. Beginning in the mid-1970s, a group of Native parents approached the Indian Health, Education, and Welfare Office and brought a discrimination suit against the Klamath County School District for its treatment of Native students. As a result, the school district hired Lynn Schonchin in 1977 to run its Federal Indian Education Program. "I was the token Indian," he later recalled, "but it was fun." Along with a committee composed of Native parents, Schonchin developed courses in Indian history and literature and began challenging historical representations of the Modoc War and other events.[17] After the Klamath people struggled for almost thirty years to reestablish the special relationship between their tribe and the federal government, the United States re-recognized their Klamath inherent sovereignty with the Klamath Restoration Act of 1986. Two years later, the National Park Service dedicated the memorial to the Modoc War, in which *everyone was treated the same.*

Following the dedication of that memorial, a series of panel discussions were held at a community center in nearby Tulelake, California. The discussions were intended to educate the public and to expand on the historical revisionism of the new memorial. The discussion began with a panel of military historians and retired army personnel. For forty-five minutes, they debated the use of carbines, signatory flags, battle formations, and hardtack. After this macabre discussion of the accouterments of death and colonization, the clinical tone changed when the descendants of those named on the new memorial took the stage.

The descendant panel began with the usual introductions. Each descendant stated his or her lineal credentials, tying themselves to a common moment more than a century earlier. The Euro-American panelists' forbears had, by and large, left the Klamath Basin generations ago, leaving the land for which their ancestors killed, while those with roots in the Klamath and Modoc communities continued to live on or near the land for which their kin had died. The introductions were informal and brief until Lynn Schonchin, the great-great-grandson of Schonchin John, introduced himself. Speaking in an intense monotone, he said, "The Modoc War was a big game. That's all it was. It was a big game where the culture died. And that is the sad part. I've never been to the lava beds. I will never go to the lava beds. I feel it is a cemetery for my people, my culture. And with that, you know, I am bitter."[18]

But Schonchin's bitterness did not prevent him from continuing. He critiqued historical narratives of the Modoc War by rejecting the language with which society discussed the war and by challenging the terms on which it might be considered. "I see war-like people, I see books like *Modoc Renegades*, *The Modoc and Their War*," he said. "But it wasn't my people's war." Schonchin also critiqued the historical narratives of certain white scholars who identified the Klamath and Modoc peoples as enemies. Some "historical treatments of the Modoc War," identified "an incident at Modoc Point" between the Klamaths and the Modocs as the starting point of the Modoc War: "The Klamath and Modoc did not like each other, according to all of the statements and all of the textbooks written. I am here to basically refute that statement," he said.[19]

In place of the textbook version of history, Schonchin offered the audience stories from his own family history and his own experience to challenge what he considered colonial fantasies. "How did people who lived so close together, who traded, who shared the same language, who shared the same cultural patterns, the same mythology, hate each other? Our grandmother, Lizzie, was half-Klamath, and half-Modoc. . . . Yet the Klamath people and Modoc people are pitted against one another in history books. These are images that I've grown up with as an Indian—as a Klamath and as a Modoc."[20] Schonchin refused to accept stories that did not and could not account for his experience.

Schonchin also used his speech to challenge narratives of the Modoc War that presented white settlers as victims of Indian aggression. "I question the establishment of Fort Klamath," he declared. "Fort Klamath was established on the premise that the settlers needed protection from the Indians," but its location and timing suggested to Schonchin "that maybe someone was looking for a war." He also characterized the 1864 treaty between the United States and the Klamaths, Modocs, and Yahooskins as unratified until 1870. "This means the Modoc had the right to go home," he said. "They were not bound by that treaty because it was unratified."[21] According to Schonchin, the U.S. Army had no right to force Captain Jack back onto the Klamath Reservation, because until Congress ratified the treaty, the Modocs were not bound by its stipulations. He thereby challenged the legitimacy of colonial violence in the Klamath Basin.

Toward the end of his speech, Schonchin did more than reject exist-ing narratives on the basis of racial bias or factual inaccuracy. He also rejected them because he believed that these narratives failed to recognize the humanity of the Natives involved. Telling the story of his great-great-grandfather's execution, Schonchin said, "I talked a little bit about images of people. If you look at all the pictures of my people, their hair is cut off, and they wear different types of clothing. They're very stoic." But, he added, "When my great-grandfather was hung, he cried. He cried because he wondered what was going to happen to his children. Of the things we've talked about today, one is tactics, another is the terrain, type of weaponry, whether the cavalry was there, or whatever—but we've forgotten about the people. I think we need to keep that in the back of our minds. What about the people? What happened to the people? Where are the people? And where are the people going?"[22]

Through his personal testimony, Schonchin rejected the work of atone-ment that the new memorial claimed to perform. The new marker, with its narrative of inclusion, represented a reconciliation of the past that left out its continuing impact on the present and thus was insufficient. It was a past hermetically sealed off from the present. Rather than provid-ing an inclusive narrative of the war, the memorial continued to forget certain peoples—the Modoc people. According to Schonchin, "We have to . . . think about the people," he said repeatedly; "The people that were involved. My people that were sent to Oklahoma and died, my people that were killed in the war, and my people that stayed here in Klamath and lived and suffered through termination and all of this. And we're still here. And we're gonna be here for any other policy that comes along."[23] Despite the memorial's claim that it atoned for a previously flawed narrative of the past, Schonchin found the memorial and its narrative incomplete. He did not believe that this monument *treated everyone the same.*

■ In writing this book, I have sought to examine how individuals, both Indigenous and Euro-American settlers and their descendants, have re-membered the Modoc War in ways that conform to the demands of the markets within which they circulate and to explore the consequences those narratives have had in the reproduction of myths of American in-nocence. From Gilded Age newspaper accounts that emphasized white victimhood in the face of Indigenous criminality and savagery to trav-eling Indian shows that transformed the conflict into a romance, from turn-of-the-century land promotion and local histories that emphasized the inevitability of Manifest Destiny to Progressive Era petitions for veterans' benefits, war memorials, and automobile tourism in tribute to white male sacrifice, these memory markets and the individuals who have participated in them have transformed an episode of Reconstruction-era violence and ethnic cleansing into a redemptive narrative of American innocence.

But if the production of American innocence is directly linked to the circulation of historical remembrances of U.S.-Indian violence, then is historical justice through the production of new historical narratives impossible? Are all reconciliatory narratives complicit in the reproduction of American innocence? In writing about memories of U.S.-Indian violence and the possibility of true restorative justice through historical narrative truth, anthropologist Chip Colwell-Chanthaphonh suggests that "public memorials, museum exhibits, and history books can . . . become vehicles for restorative justice" but only if they "shin[e] a light on the shadows of history and [reveal] that which has remained perversely hidden."[24]

While the 1988 memorial purported to exchange a flawed, incomplete, and unjust narrative of the past for a complete, expansive, and just narrative, Lynn Schonchin found the promise of atonement to be empty. As is so often the case, the multicultural marketplace of remembering is not a neat or fair exchange economy in which the living might make a gift in the present to the dead in the past. Justice, reparation, reconciliation—these are the currency with which we make deals with the dead and seek to trade their deaths for our forgetfulness. As anthropologist Alan Klima has suggested, history is "ultimately an economics of storytelling, the narrative economy by which the past is left behind and exchanged for the future, where each may go its separate way, as when one economic man comes together with another for a single moment of exchange, when they relinquish their values completely, and then depart with no strings attached."[25] The 1988 memorial sought to dictate the price of forgiveness by offering, once and for all, a story in which the suffering of *everyone was treated the same*.

But in this sameness, multicultural narratives of inclusion reproduce the myths of American innocence. By forgetting the inequality of the past and asserting a fictive equality, the memorial's designers sought to construct a reconciliatory narrative that would allow for an exchange of remembrances in which the narrator, commemorator, historian, or mourner, in the words of Klima, may "depart with no strings attached." As with the universality of a possessive individualism that serves as the model for rational productive selfhood, the violence of multicultural equivalence is rooted in ideas of American liberal progressivism.[26] But what happens when the victims of history want to retain a version of the past that in no way resembles the one being offered? What if the gift of a new narrative, the gift of equal inclusion in the memorial landscape of Lava Beds National Monument, carries with it an immense violence, the violence of equivalence?

The 1988 memorial contained the names of Indigenous casualties of the Modoc War but refused to acknowledge those who died during removal or of illness or despair; in this way, it defined, legitimized, and described the extent and reach of American settler colonialism via the casualties incurred during a delineated period of U.S.-Indian violence. As Marita Sturken has observed, the listing of the dead on national monuments such as the Vietnam Veterans Memorial provides catharsis for the mourner while simultaneously defining who can be a legitimate mourner.[27] The legitimate mourner grieves the loss of a particular individual who died on a defined battlefield during a prescribed period of warfare. But what of those who died on the cattle cars to Oklahoma? Does the 1988 memorial atone for their deaths? Are they treated equally? And can any monument or memorial ever begin to capture the loss of culture? Through this process of providing a space for acknowledging death while also defining who might be considered the legitimately mourned dead, the new memorial created an environment unsuitable for reconciliation and forgiveness.

Born of the imperative and logic of multicultural equality, the new memorial reproduced narratives of American innocence by imagining the Indian wars as cultural rather then political conflicts and by insisting that atrocities were committed on both sides. But while Lynn Schonchin's speech suggests the limits of reconciliation through the marketplace of remembering, it may offer us a window into the possibility for true reconciliation by changing the terms of the exchange—an honest accounting with the violence of the past not through forgetting but through remembering; not by limiting the reach of the war but by acknowledging the continuing effects of violence and by allowing each individual to define his or her inclusion and explore his or her previous exclusion. The Indigenous panelists, like their ancestors, participated actively in the marketplace and used that space to articulate their own memories. Just as Schonchin refused to allow the memorial to stand alone, his nephew, Tom Ball, would not allow his uncle's narrative to stand alone. Full of emotion, pausing often, and choking back tears, Ball added, "One point I really wanted to make was that I disagree with the whole civilization and its culture is dead and dying thing. My friend, Helen, brought with her a two or three page list of Modoc words. And she taught me how to say them. And to hear those words, I want[ed] to cry. That's me. That's my people. And to hear those words is a jogging of the memory."[28] What had begun as a ceremony intended to advance a reconciliatory narrative of American innocence ended with a beautiful statement about the power of remembering to promote continuance and to repair the violence of the past.

The marketplaces of remembering through which individuals have circulated memories, remembrances, and histories of the Modoc War have certainly transformed the conflict into an ambiguous chapter of American history. Moreover, this process has resulted in an attendant reproduction of asymmetrical social, political, cultural, and economic relations between Indigenous peoples and their Euro-American settler descendant neighbors. But above all, this book demonstrates how Americans have remembered nineteenth-century U.S.-Indian violence in a way that reveals something fundamental about historical knowledge production in American society. We will never escape the material underpinnings of historical knowledge production. But by investigating the marketplaces of remembering that give shape and meaning to American cultural memory of the past, we can deconstruct the narratives with which Americans have made and remade their identity as fundamentally innocent.

Notes

ABBREVIATIONS

APD	*Alturas Plain-Dealer*
ARCIA	U.S. Department of the Interior, *Annual Report of the Commissioner of Indian Affairs*. Washington, D.C.: U.S. Government Printing Office.
IWVNPCR	Indian War Veterans of the North Pacific Coast Records, Mss 364, Oregon Historical Society Research Library, Portland
KCM	Klamath County Museum, Klamath Falls, Ore.
KE	*Klamath Echoes*
KFE	*Klamath Falls Express*
KFEH	*Klamath Falls Evening Herald*
LBNMRL	Lava Beds National Monument Research Library, Tulelake, Calif.
NARA, RG 15	National Archives and Records Administration, Washington, D.C., Records of the Bureau of Pensions and Its Predecessors, 1805–1935, Record Group 15, Records of the Department of Veterans Affairs
NYH	*New York Herald*
NYT	*New York Times*
OCAP	Oliver Cromwell Applegate Papers, Ax 005, Special Collections and University Archives, University of Oregon, Eugene
OCCWMI	U.S. House of Representatives, *Official Copies of Correspondence Relative to the War with the Modoc Indians in 1872–73*, 43rd Cong., 1st sess., Ex. Doc. 122 (Washington, D.C.: Adjutant-General Office, 1874).
OHSRL	Oregon Historical Society Research Library, Portland
SFC	*San Francisco Chronicle*
SFEB	*San Francisco Daily Evening Bulletin*
YU	*Yreka Union*

PROLOGUE

1. Throughout the text, I represent Klamath terminology as rendered in Gatschet, *Klamath Indians*. The Klamath Tribe prefers the system employed in Barker, *Klamath Dictionary* as more accurately representing all the sounds of the Klamath language. This is true. But Barker's dictionary is less extensive than Gatschet's. Where possible, I provide Barker's representations in the notes. However, for the sake of consistency, I use Gatschet's renderings throughout the text. The name "Koketat" is sometimes shortened to "Koke."

2. James, *Modoc*, 11–12.

3. Author's field notes, June 28, 2008.

4. Bancroft, *History of Oregon*, 2:636; Curtin, *Myths*, v.

5. Curtin, *Myths*, 39–45; Curtin, *Memoirs*, 331–32.

6. Deur, *In the Footprints*, 206.

7. Becker, "Mr. Wells," 642.

8. Becker, "Everyman," 235.

9. Dillon, "Costs."

10. Becker, "Everyman," 235.

INTRODUCTION

1. "Hanged: Captain Jack, Sconchin, Boston Charley, and Black Jim Expiate Their Crimes on the Gallows," *SFEB*, October 4, 1873; Abbey, Diary, October 3, 1873, KCM.

2. *OCCWMI*, 134–36.

3. "Hanged: Captain Jack, Sconchin, Boston Charley, and Black Jim Expiate Their Crimes on the Gallows," *SFEB*, October 4, 1873.

4. General Court-Martial Orders No. 34, U. S. Grant to E. D. Townsend, September 12, 1873, in *OCCWMI*, 203.

5. "Hanged: Captain Jack, Sconchin, Boston Charley, and Black Jim Expiate Their Crimes on the Gallows," *SFEB*, October 4, 1873.

6. "The Execution of Capt. Jack and Three Other Modocs," *YU*, October 11, 1873.

7. Case, Diary, 71, KCM; Abbey, Diary, October 1, 1873, KCM.

8. "Interesting Relics of the Modoc War," Transcription of Modoc War Newspaper Articles, Lieutenant George W. Kingbury's Scrapbook, LBNMRL.

9. "The Dead Warriors: Further Details of the Fort Klamath Execution," *SFC*, October 12, 1873; Angela Torretta, "Document on Captain Jack Landed by Museum," *Klamath Falls Herald and News*, November 23, 2005.

10. Abbey, Diary, October 3, 1873, KCM; "The Execution of Capt. Jack and Three Other Modocs," *YU*, October 11, 1873. "Noose, Taken from the Neck of Capt. Jack and Schonchin after They Were Hung, at Fort Klamath, Oct. 1873," Hearn's Accession and Associated Artifacts, Artifact Collection, California Indian Heritage Center, Sacramento, M.H.172 8-S.P. In a similar example, George Kingsbury evidently obtained a length of rope, which he displayed along with a printed card reading, "The Rope That Hung the Chief of the Modoc Indian, Captain Jack, Oct. 3rd, 1873." This memento is rumored to have been part of the Arizona State Museum in Tucson (Dillon, *Burnt-Out Fires*, 333).

11. "University Given Relics: Personal Effects of Captain Jack of Modoc War Fame Presented to U. of C. Museum," *Los Angeles Times*, November 11, 1929.

12. "Personal," *National Tribune*, May 12, 1892. Other examples include "A Piece of the Gallows, upon Which Captain Jack, Schonchin and Other Indians Were Hung," Hearn's Accession and Associated Artifacts, Artifact Collection, California Indian Heritage Center, Sacramento, M.H.183-8-S.P.

13. Meacham, *Wigwam and War-Path*, 649.

14. *Army and Navy Journal*, October 11, 25, 1873; John Hurst, "Indian Hero, Dead 100 Years, Awaits Final Resting Place," *Los Angeles Times*, March 21, 1977;

Lee Juillerat, "4 Modoc Skulls at Smithsonian," *Klamath Falls Herald and News*, November 18, 1979. In 1984, the heads were returned to Debbie Riddle Herrera, a descendant of Captain Jack's cousin. See also Dumont, "Politics of Scientific Objections."

15. Palmquist, "Imagemakers," 214.

16. Markovitz, *Legacies of Lynching*, xxvi–xxix; Young, "Black Body."

17. Wolfe, "Settler Colonialism"; Belich, *Replenishing the Earth*, 79–94.

18. Gatschet, *Klamath Indians*, xxxiii–xxxvi; Kroeber, *Handbook*, 318–35; Theodore Stern, "Klamath and Modoc."

19. Spier, *Klamath Ethnography*, 35–39, 107–12; Stern, *Klamath Tribe*, 24; Nash, "Place of Religious Revivalism," 380.

20. Whaley, *Oregon*, 177–82; Beckham, *Requiem*.

21. Lindsay, *Murder State*, 335–48; Madley, "American Genocide," 212–315, 326–59, 493–94.

22. Rabasa, *Writing Violence*, 22.

23. De Certeau, *Writing of History*, xxv–xxvi.

24. Thomas Jefferson to James Madison, April 27, 1809, in Jefferson, *Papers*, 1:169; Ostler, *Plains Sioux*, 14.

25. Cutter, "Female Indian Killer"; Limerick, *Legacy of Conquest*, 37.

26. Sturken, *Tourists of History*, 9, 12.

27. Frost, *Never One Nation*, 22.

28. Kammen, *Mystic Chords*, 93–100, 94; Bodnar, *Remaking America*, 78–137.

29. Slotkin, *Gunfighter Nation*, 10.

30. Ibid.; Finnegan, *Narrating the American West*, 151–57; Bold, *Frontier Club*.

31. Kerwin Lee Klein, *Frontiers*; Warren, *Buffalo Bill's America*; Elliott, *Custerology*.

32. Huhndorf, *Going Native*; Green, "Indian in Popular American Culture."

33. Meyer and Royer, *Selling the Indian*, xi–xix.

34. Castile, "Commodification."

35. Raibmon, *Authentic Indians*.

36. Bsumek, *Indian-Made*; Cattelino, *High Stakes*; Albers, "From Legend to Land."

37. Marx, "Eighteenth Brumaire," 437.

38. Halbwachs, *On Collective Memory*; Sturken, *Tangled Memories*; Kammen, *Mystic Chords*; Steve Stern, *Remembering Pinochet's Chile*.

39. Glassberg, *Sense of History*; Basso, *Wisdom Sits*; Nora, *Realms of Memory*.

40. Kerwin Klein also critiques the "new materialization of memory" in *From History to Theory*, 124–25.

CHAPTER ONE

1. "The Modoc War," *SFC*, January 21, 1873.

2. Dillon, "Costs."

3. "The Modoc War," *Boston Evening Journal*, December 28, 1872.

4. Gienapp, "'Politics,'" 41–42.

5. McGerr, *Decline*, 108–13.

6. Starr, *Creation of the Media*, 131–39.

7. Slotkin, *Fatal Environment*, xvi.

8. Barker represents Yulalóna as ?iWLaLLoˑn?a and translates it as "All-along-the-Top." Linkville later became Klamath Falls (see chapter 4).

9. *ARCIA* (1870), 54, 68.

10. J. M. True's petition to have the Modocs removed from Lost River, January 3, 1872, in *OCCWMI*, 8–15.

11. T. B. Odeneal to Frank Wheaton, November 25, 1872, in ibid., 38.

12. Isenberg, *Mining California*, 134.

13. James Jackson, "The First Blow—Jack's Expedition," and F. A. Boutelle, "Boutelle and Scar-Faced Charley," both in Brady, *Northwestern Fights*, 258–65, 266–72.

14. "The Northern Indians Rising," *San Francisco Daily Alta California*, December 2, 1872; "Fight with Indians: Fifteen Indians and Three Whites Killed and a Number Wounded," *Sacramento Daily Union*, December 2, 1872; "The Indian Trouble: Fiock Not Killed," *YU*, December 14, 1872.

15. "The Modoc Indians: The Red-Skins Taking Vengeance on Whites," *Hartford Daily Courant*, December 3, 1872.

16. "The Modoc Massacres," *New York Tribune*, December 6, 1872; "Reign of Terror in Oregon," *SFC*, December 6, 1872; "Oregon: The Modoc Indian War," *Philadelphia Inquirer*, December 12, 1872.

17. *NYT*, January 18, 1873.

18. *Gold Hill News*, January 16, 1873, reprinted in "Modoc War Notes: Rumors of the Great Campaign for the Reduction of the Lava Beds," *SFC*, January 19, 1873.

19. Sim, "Peace Policy"; Jean Edward Smith, *Grant*, 424–35, 516–41.

20. Utley, *Indian Frontier*, 127–33.

21. Jacoby, *Shadows at Dawn*, 125–27.

22. "The Modoc War: Governor Booth Called upon to Raise a Company," *SFC*, January 1, 1873.

23. "The Modoc War: A Note from Governor Booth," *SFC*, January 3, 1873; "The Modoc War: Gov. Booth Refuses to Call Out Volunteers," *YU*, January 4, 1873.

24. Extant files of the *Daily Oregon Herald* are incomplete, but other newspapers reprinted or commented on material from its pages. See "The Modoc War," *YU*, January 25, 1873.

25. "The Modoc War," *SFC*, January 1, 1873.

26. Samuel Clarke, "The Modoc Indians: Origins of Their Troubles," *NYT*, January 1, 1873.

27. Joshua Brown, *Beyond the Lines*, 29–30.

28. *New York Tribune*, March 5, 1873.

29. Elijah Steele to his brother, [ca. May 1873], in *OCCWMI*, 297–309. The name "St. Valentine's Day Treaty" may have come from Murray, *Modocs*, 36–37.

30. "Modoc War: Elijah Steele Interviewed," *SFC*, February 3, 1873. See also R. F. Bernard to Samuel Buck, January 26, 1873, Don Fisher Papers, 586–92, KCM.

31. "Modoc War: Elijah Steele Interviewed," *SFC*, February 3, 1873.

32. Genetin-Pilawa, *Crooked Paths*, 99.

33. Ibid., 99, 59–72, 99–111.

34. C. Delano to William Belknap, January 30, 1873, C. Delano to Acting Commissioner of Indian Affairs, January 30, 1873, E. D. Townsend to W. T. Sherman, January 31, 1873, all in *OCCWMI*, 65–66.

35. LaFayette Grover to Commissioners Appointed to Conclude Peace with the Modoc Indians, February 10, 1873, Letters Received of the Bureau of Indian Affairs, Oregon, in Wilkinson et al., *Klamath, Modoc, and Yahooskin Documents*, roll 1-A, frames 00826–28; *NYH*, February 17, 1873.

36. Jesse Applegate, "An Open Letter to Governor Grover," February 16, 1873, in *OCCWMI*, 252–53.

37. "A Family Job," *SFC*, February 18, 1873; "The Modoc Peace Commission," *SFC*, February 28, 1873.

38. "The Modoc War: Negotiations for Peace," *SFC*, February 27, 1873.

39. *NYH*, March 8, 1873.

40. Alfred B. Meacham to H. R. Clum, February 22, 1873, "Special File 10: Files Concerning Trouble with the Modoc Indians, 1872–1873," in *Records of the Indian Division, Office of the Secretary of the Interior: Special Files, 1848–1907*, reel 4, frames 0964–70; E. R. S. Canby to W. T. Sherman, February 7, 1873, Letters Received of the Bureau of Indian Affairs, Oregon, in Wilkinson et al., *Klamath, Modoc, and Yahooskin Documents*, roll 1, frame 0075; Jesse Applegate to H. R. Crum, February 26, 1873, in *OCCWMI*, 258.

41. "In the Modoc Camp: A Herald Correspondent's Ride into Captain Jack's Stronghold," *NYH*, February 28, 1873.

42. *NYH*, March 17, 1873.

43. Ibid., February 21, 1873.

44. "In the Modoc Camp," *NYH*, February 28, 1873.

45. Ibid.

46. "The Modoc Troubles: Visit to Captain Jack's Camp," *San Francisco Bulletin*, February 25, 1873; Deur, *In the Footprints*, 241.

47. "In the Modoc Camp," *NYH*, February 28, 1873.

48. "The Herald and Its Enterprise," *NYH*, March 19, 1873.

49. "The Herald among the Lava Beds: Chivalrous Journalism," *Trenton Gazette*, March 1, 1873.

50. "The Modoc Difficulties: The Latest from the Peace Commissioners," *YU*, March 1, 1873.

51. "Newspaper Man and Soldier," *SFC*, March 20, 1895.

52. "Peace with the Modocs," *SFC*, March 3, 1873.

53. Gatschet, *Klamath Indians*, 38–39. I have slightly altered this version for clarity.

54. Commissioners to C. Delano reprinted in "Red Wins!: Burying the Hatchet," *SFC*, March 4, 1873.

55. "Captain Jack Abdicates: The Modoc Unpleasantness Satisfactorily Settled," *NYH*, March 9, 1873; "Red Wins!: Burying the Hatchet," *SFC*, March 4, 1873.

56. "The Warriors' Council: Great War Talk at Modoc Headquarters," *NYH*, March 18, 1873.

57. Marriott and Rachlin, *American Indian Mythology*, 27–29.

58. "In Capt. Jack's Camp: The Indian Chieftain's Change of Front," *SFC*, March 11, 1873.

59. C. Delano to T. B. Odeneal, March 13, 1873, C. Delano to A. B. Meacham, March 18, 1873, E. Thomas to C. Delano, March 19, 1873, A B. Meacham to H. R. Clum, March 3, 1873, all in *OCCWMI*, 269, 273–74, 260.

60. Odeneal, *Modoc War*, 2, 3–4, 5. For the *Portland Daily Bulletin*, see Scott, *History*, 419.

61. Odeneal, *Modoc War*, 7–8.

62. Ibid., 8, 9–10.

63. Limerick, *Legacy of Conquest*, 36–46; Horner, *Oregon*, 284–85.

64. Erwin N. Thompson, *Modoc War*, 54–59.

65. A. B. Meacham to C. Delano, April 16, 1873, in *OCCWMI*, 286–87; *ARCIA* (1873), 76.

66. L. S. Dyar to H. R. Clum, April 13, 1873, in *OCCWMI*, 286.

67. William T. Sherman to John McAlister Schofield, April 13, 1873, in U.S. Adjutant-General's Office, *Letters Received*, roll 21.

68. *Army and Navy Journal*, April 19, 1873.

69. Twain, *Complete Works*, 46, 49.

CHAPTER TWO

1. "The Red Judas," *SFC*, April 13, 1873; *Yreka Journal*, April 16, 1873; "The Modoc Massacre," *Harper's Weekly*, April 26, 1873; Simpson, *Meeting the Sun*.

2. Simpson, *Meeting the Sun*, 367, 373.

3. *OCCWMI*, 134–36.

4. "Gen. Canby's Funeral," *Frank Leslie's Illustrated Newspaper*, May 24, 1873; "Funeral of General Canby," *Harper's Weekly*, May 24, 1873.

5. Samuel A. Clarke, "The Modoc Lava Beds: Voyaging on Tule Lake," *NYT*, July 1, 1873.

6. "The Policy of Massacre," *Indianapolis Sentinel*, April 13, 1873.

7. *Daily Colorado Miner* (Georgetown), April 22, 1873, quoted in Mardock, *Reformers*, 174.

8. *NYH*, April 13, 1873.

9. "Our Indian Policy," *NYT*, April 16, 1873.

10. Frost, *Never One Nation*, 1–29; "The Modoc War: Feeling in Washington—Views of President Grant, Gen. Sherman, and Other Officials," *NYT*, April 15, 1873.

11. *Boston Evening Transcript*, April 16, 1873.

12. "The Modocs," *Harper's Weekly*, May 3, 1873.

13. "The Modoc War: No Couriers from the Front Yesterday," *SFC*, April 20, 1873.

14. Simpson, *Meeting the Sun*, 365–66.

15. "Our Indian Policy," *NYT*, April 16, 1873.

16. Keith, *Colfax Massacre*, xviii.

17. Frost, *Never One Nation*, 13.

18. West, "Reconstructing Race."

19. Frank Wheaton to Edward Canby, January 25, 1873, cited in Murray, *Modocs*, 127.

20. Keith Clark and Donna Clark, introduction to Edwards, *Daring Donald McKay*; Erwin N. Thompson, *Modoc War*, 69, 155 (n. 6); *Army and Navy Journal*, April 26, 1873.

21. Erwin N. Thompson, *Modoc War*, 79–92.

22. "The Last of the Modocs," *Harper's Weekly*, June 21, 1873.

23. William T. Sherman to John McAlister Schofield, April 13, 1873, in U.S. Adjutant-General's Office, *Letters Received*, roll 21.

24. E. D. Townsend to J. C. Davis, April 14, 1873, in *OCCWMI*, 78.

25. "Modoc Maneuvering: Another Ambuscade," *Indianapolis Sentinel*, May 14, 1873.

26. *Yreka Journal*, May 24, 1873.

27. "The Dawn of Peace: Surrender of Seventy of the Modoc Tribe," *SFC*, May 24, 1873.

28. "The Modoc War: Cottonwood Captives," *San Francisco Bulletin*, May 26, 1873.

29. Nash, "Place of Religious Revivalism."

30. "The Dawn of Peace: Surrender of Seventy of the Modoc Tribe," *SFC*, May 24, 1873.

31. Jefferson C. Davis, "Official Report on the Modoc War," in *OCCWMI*, 109–10.

32. Ibid., 111.

33. Riddle, *Indian History*, 150.

34. General Court Martial Order No. 32, in *OCCWMI*, 95–97.

35. "The Modoc: What Should Be Done with Them," *YU*, June 14, 1873.

36. John McAlister Schofield to Davis, June 7, 1873, in Hagen, "Modoc War," 1075, LBNMRL.

37. "Murder of Modocs: Five Modoc Chiefs Atrociously Murdered by Oregonians," *Indianapolis Sentinel*, June 10, 1873; *Army and Navy Journal*, June 14, 1873.

38. Benjamin Coates to Ulysses S. Grant, June 11, 1873, in Hagen, "Modoc War," 1102–9, LBNMRL.

39. Unidentified Philadelphia newspaper, in ibid., 1109; emphasis added.

40. Edward P. Smith to Columbus Delano, June 19, 1873, in ibid., 1136.

41. H. P. Curtis to Gen. A. J. Schofield, June 7, 1873, in ibid., 1030–41.

42. George H. Williams to Ulysses S. Grant, June 7, 1873, "regarding the Modoc Indian Prisoners," in *OCCWMI*, 88–90. For the relationship between this attorney general's opinion and the General Orders No. 100 from the Civil War establishing the legal authority of military commissions to try violations of the laws of war, see Witt, *Lincoln's Code*, 334–35.

43. "The Modoc: What Should Be Done with Them," *YU*, June 14, 1873.

44. *Yreka Journal*, June 25, 1873.

45. Reprinted in *Yreka Journal*, July 9, 1873.

46. John Beeson, "Memorial to U. S. Grant, President of the United States," in *OCCWMI*, 313–16.

47. Alfred H. Love to Ulysses S. Grant, July 12, 1873, in *OCCWMI*, 309–11.

48. W. C. Gould to Department of the Interior, August 8, 1873, in Hagen, "Modoc War," 1293, LBNMRL.

49. "From the Modocs!: The Trial Concluded!," *YU*, July 12, 1873.

50. Foster, "Imperfect Justice."

51. "Proceedings of a Military Commission Convened at Fort Klamath, Oregon, for the Trial of Modoc Prisoners," in *OCCWMI*, 132–83.

52. H. Wallace Atwell to Columbus Delano, July 30, 1873, in *OCCWMI*, 323–24.

53. "Trial of the Modoc Prisoners," in *OCCWMI*, 154.

54. Ibid., 169–72.

55. "Capt. Jack's Story: His Interview with Gen, Davis," *NYT*, June 11, 1873; "The Last of the Modoc," *Boston Globe*, reprinted in *SFC*, October 14, 1873.

56. Murray, *Modocs*, 291.

57. "Trial of the Modoc Prisoners," in *OCCWMI*, 174.

58. Ibid., 175.

59. Ibid., 176–77, 178.

60. J. Holt to W. W. Belknap, August 12, 1873, in *OCCWMI*, 194.

61. "Trial of the Modoc Prisoners," in ibid., 183.

62. "The Modocs," *YU*, July 12, 1873; "Modoc News!," *YU*, July 19, 1873.

63. "Indian Affairs: Notice from the American Indian Aid Association," *New York Star*, July 23, 1873.

64. Elijah Steele et al. to Columbus Delano, July 30, 1873, in *OCCWMI*, 322–23.

65. H. P. Curtis to unknown, n.d., in *OCCWMI*, 190.

66. General Court Martial Orders, No. 34, September 12, 1873, in *OCCWMI*, 203.

67. Murray, *The Modocs*, 296–99.

68. "Hanged," *SFEB*, October 4, 1873.

69. Ibid.

70. Ibid.

71. James Williams, *Life and Adventures*, 4th ed., 102.

72. Ibid., 5th ed., 115–22.

73. Coward, *Newspaper Indian*, 11–12.

74. "The Modocs: Lecture on the Modoc Troubles by Hon. A. B. Meacham," *San Francisco Daily Alta California*, October 3, 1873.

CODA: AMERICAN INNOCENCE IN MY INBOX

1. "A Guide to the Memos on Torture," *NYT*, http://www.nytimes.com/ref/international/24MEMO-GUIDE.html. See also Tim Golden, "A Junior Aide Had a Big Role in Terror Policy," *NYT*, December 23, 2005; Jaffer and Singh, *Administration of Torture*.

2. George H. Williams to Ulysses S. Grant, June 7, 1873, "regarding the Modoc Indian Prisoners," in OCCWMI, 88–90. According to John Fabian Witt, U.S. attorney general George Henry Williams was a key member of the Radical Republicans and one of the authors of the 1867 Reconstruction Act, which reauthorized military commissions. He had also been a advocate for the impeachment of President Andrew Johnson (Witt, *Lincoln's Code*, 334).

3. My understanding of Williams's opinion is deeply indebted to Jodi A. Byrd's insightful analysis of it. See Byrd, *Transit of Empire*, 227.

4. John C. Yoo to William J. Haynes II, General Counsel of the Department of Defense, "Memorandum Re: Military Interrogation of Alien Unlawful Combatants Held Outside the United States," March 14, 2003. This memorandum was released to the ACLU in April 2008 and is available at http://www.aclu.org/national-security/secret-bush-administration-torture-memo-released-today-response-aclu-lawsuit.

5. George H. Williams to Ulysses S. Grant, June 7, 1873, "regarding the Modoc Indian Prisoners," in *OCCWMI*, 249–52.

6. Byrd, *Transit of Empire*, 227.

CHAPTER THREE

1. The bill went through several iterations beginning as early as 1888. Final passage appears to have occurred on October 3, 1890. See "A Friend to the Whites: Why a Pension was Granted to an Indian Woman," *SFC*, October 5, 1890. The pension received final approval from the Bureau of Pensions on February 25, 1891. See Pension Certificate No. 565101, Winemah Riddle Pension File, 12339, NARA, RG 15; Winemah Riddle, HR 2147, 51st Cong., 1st sess., 6–7.

2. "Pension for an Indian Squaw," *Chicago Daily Inter Ocean*, February 18, 1888.

3. John B. Horner, "Wi-ne-ma, Modoc Princess, Heroine of the Early Oregon Days," *Sunday Oregonian*, January 31, 1926; Dee B. Brown, *Bury My Heart*, 227–38.

4. Green, "Pocahontas Perplex."

5. "The Modocs," *San Francisco Daily Alta California*, October 3, 1873. See also Meacham, *Wigwam and War-Path*, iii–iv.

6. "Trial of the Modoc Prisoners," in *OCCWMI*, 169.

7. Hall, *Performing the American Frontier*, 85–86; Banvard's Museum, "Wood Museum's Playbill for Donald McKay: Hero of the Modoc War" (New York: Cameron, 1875), *American Broadsides and Ephemera*, series 1, no. 23633; "About the Modoc," *Zion's Herald*, December 4, 1873.

8. William McKay to Oliver Applegate, August 30, 1873, OCAP, box 5, folder 2; F. F. Victor to O. C. Applegate, March 28, 1874, OCAP, box 5, folder 4; "The Warm Spring Indians: Arrival of a Delegation of Our Red-Skinned Allies," *SFC*, May 6, 1874.

9. Classified Advertisements, *SFEB*, May 7, 1874.

10. F. F. Victor to O. C. Applegate, April 23, 1874, OCAP, box 5, folder 1; A. B. Meacham to O. C. Applegate, October 8, 1874, OCAP, box 5, folder 4; "Warm Springs Indians in Trouble," *SFC*, June 19, 1875.

11. Moses, *Wild West Shows*, 12, 19, 287 (n. 38).

12. A. B. Meacham to Oliver Applegate, August 9, 1873, OCAP, box 5, folder 2; Phinney, "Alfred B. Meacham," 222.

13. Meacham, *Wigwam and War-Path*, 665–66.

14. Alfred B. Meacham, "The Tragedy of the Lava Beds," in Bland, *Life*, following p. 30.

15. A. B. Meacham to Oliver Applegate, October 8, 1874, OCAP, box 5, folder 4.

16. Hurtado, "Modocs and the Jones Family," 86–107.

17. Patricia Scruggs Trolinger, *The History of the Modoc Tribe of Oklahoma*, 2009, http://www.modoctribe.net/history.html.

18. Phinney, "Alfred B. Meacham," 224; "Permit to Employ Indians," quoted in Meacham, *Wi-ne-ma*, 13.

19. Hill's influence is suggested by the fact that on returning to the reservation, he was chosen as second chief to Henry Blow; within a year, his followers outnumbered those of the head chief (Gatschet, *Klamath Indians*, 50; Theodore Stern, *Klamath Tribe*, 85–86).

20. Handwritten letter from the principal Klamath subchiefs to David Hill, [1875], Lindsey Applegate Papers, box 2, folder 4, University of Oregon Special Collections and Archives, reproduced in Theodore Stern, *Klamath Tribe*, appendix, 268–71.

21. Ibid.

22. Ibid., Lindsey Applegate Papers, box 24, folder 7, "Indian miscellaneous."

23. Moses, *Wild West Shows*, 44–46.

24. Meacham, *Wi-ne-ma*, 92–94; O. C. Applegate to Alfred H. Love, April 19, 1876, OCAP, box 5, folder 6; "Dramatic: Union Square Theatre," *NYT*, March 28, 1875; *New Northwest*, February 19, 1875.

25. Meacham, *Wi-ne-ma*, 89–91.

26. "A Stolen Indian: The Curious Story of an Adult, Red-Skinned Modoc Charley Boss," *Chicago Daily Inter Ocean*, September 17, 1875; *Sacramento Record*, February 3, 1875.

27. McKivigan, *Forgotten Firebrand*, 132–33.

28. David Hill's Speech at Independence Hall, Philadelphia, March 24, 1875, in Meacham, *Wi-ne-ma*, 103–7.

29. *SFEB*, August 18, 1875.

30. "The Kidnapped Klamath," *NYT*, September 14, 1875; Meacham, *Wi-ne-ma*, 100–102.

31. A. B. Meacham to O. C. Applegate, December 7, 1875, OCAP, box 5, folder 5.

32. Shaver et al., *Illustrated History*, 1092–94; Elinor F. Meacham, "Redbird of Meacham," in *Memorandum Book*, 102–4, University of Oregon Special Collections and Archives.

33. "Meacham's Indians: Their Return to Yreka," *Chicago Daily Inter Ocean*, June 23, 1875.

34. Meacham, *Wi-ne-ma*, 93.

35. Jeff C. Riddle to Ruth E. King, January 15, 1934, Vertical File: Modoc War, Jack's Head—Riddle, LBNMRL.

36. Frank Riddle to O. C. Applegate, September 17, 1875, OCAP, box 5, folder 5.

37. Jeff Riddle to O. C. Applegate, February 21, 1876, OCAP, box 5, folder 6.

38. Frank Riddle to O. C. Applegate, June 6, 1876, OCAP, box 5, folder 7.

39. Meacham, *Wi-ne-ma*, 20; hereafter cited in the text.

40. Allen, *Wi-ne-ma*; William S. Brown, *California Northeast*; Wilson, *Causes and Significance*; Quinn, *Hell*; Solnit, *River of Shadows*.

41. For an account of Bacon's examination of Toby Riddle, see Bacon, "Tobey Riddle (Winemah)."

42. Reep, *Rescue and Romance*, 89–108

43. Sedgwick, *Hope Leslie*, 92–93.

44. Tilton, *Pocahontas*, 72, 77–92.

45. Sayre, *Indian Chief*, 1–41.

46. Hardinge, *Modoc Jack*.

47. Ibid., 14, 92–100.

48. Howard, *Squaw Spy*.

49. Miller, *Life amongst the Modocs*, 5, 397–98.

50. Ibid., 7.

51. Miller, *My Own Story*, vi. Miller republished *Life amongst the Modocs* under a variety of titles, including *Unwritten History* (1874), *Paquita, the Indian Heroine* (1881), and *My Life among the Indians* (1892).

52. Miller, *Life amongst the Modocs*, 62, 106.

53. Ibid., 228.

54. Lawson, "Joaquin Miller (Cincinnatus Hiner)," 301–2.

55. Miller, *Songs of the Sierras*, 151.

56. Ibid., 147.

57. Ibid., 150.

58. Ibid., 152.

59. Joaquin Miller to Editor of the *New York Tribune*, "A Card from Joaquin Miller," October 7, 1871, cited in Peterson, *Joaquin Miller*, 69–70.

60. Frather, "Fourth of July," 121–23.

61. "The Story of Wi-Ne-Ma: She Risked Her Life to Avert War and Prevent Murder," *NYT*, October 27, 1895.

62. See LaVonne Brown Ruoff, "Editor's Introduction," in Callahan, *Wynema*, xiii–xlviii, esp. xliii–xliv (n. 1). I thank LaVonne Brown Ruoff for sharing valuable information regarding this connection as well as research relating to the name "Winema" among Oklahoma Indians in the late nineteenth century.

63. "A Famous Indian Scout, Death of Donald M'Kay near Pendleton," *Morning Oregonian*, April 21, 1880; *Idaho Daily Avalanche*, November 30, 1875.

64. Edwards, *Daring Donald McKay*, xiii.

65. Edwards, *Luk-cay-oti, Spotted Wolf*, 30.

66. "Her Name Is Wi-ne-ma: Mrs. F. W. Jennings Won Honors by Suggesting Name of Indian Heroine of the Modoc War," *Klamath Republican*, January 26, 1905; Drew, *Pages*, 11.

67. *Surprise Valley Record*, March 17, 1920.

CODA: A DRIVE THROUGH SETTLER COLONIAL HISTORY

1. The marker was erected in 1932 by the Corvallis-based Winema Chapter of the Daughters of the American Revolution. The chapter was extremely active in gathering information about Toby Riddle and her life. See Clara R. Jones to O. C. Applegate, April 30, 1923, OCAP, box 9, folder 6. Fifty-two years later, the Klamath Falls Historical Society placed a new marker beside this one "In memory of Frank Tazewell Riddle . . . Beloved Husband of Winema."

2. Sierra Design advertisement, in possession of author; A. Mosley et al., *WINEMA* (*ND02438-6R*), in possession of author.

3. Moses, *Wild West Shows*, 7–8, 284 (n. 22).

4. Albers, "From Legend to Land."

5. Debbie Herrera and Christine Allen, interview.

6. Konkle, *Writing Indian Nations*, 290; Deloria, *Custer Died for Your Sins*, 83–84.

7. Deloria, *Indians*.

8. Konkle, *Writing Indian Nations*; Silva, *Aloha Betrayed*, Linda Tuhiwai Smith, *Decolonizing Methodologies*.

CHAPTER FOUR

1. "In War Paint and Feathers: A Reproduction of Pioneer Scenes on the Klamath," *San Francisco Examiner*, July 9, 1893; "In the Jaws of Death," *KFE*, July 6, 1893.

2. Ibid.

3. Ibid.

4. Wrobel, *Promised Lands*, 19–49.

5. Oregon State Board of Immigration, *Oregon as It Is: Solid Facts and Actual Results* (Portland, Ore.: McCoy, 1885), 63, quoted in Wrobel, *Promised Lands*, 27.

6. Strahorn, *Where Rolls the Oregon*, 20.

7. Southern Pacific Company, *Oregon for the Settler: A Great Area with Rich Valleys, Mild and Healthful Climate, and Wide Range of Products* (San Francisco: Southern Pacific Company, 1922), 7, 60, quoted in Wrobel, *Promised Lands*, 60.

8. Klamath County Board of Immigration, *Great Klamath Basin*.

9. Wells, *History*, 29, 121.

10. Ibid., 126, 28, 129–30; Wells, "Massacre," 724.

11. Leavitt, "Reflections and Recollections," 55; "Klamath Neighbors Didn't Boost in 1884," *Klamath News*, May 10, 1928, reprinted in *KE* 13 (1975): 61–66; Werner, *On the Western Frontier*, 13–14; R. W. Hill, "Mount Shasta," *New York Evangelist*, July 27, 1882.

12. "A Relic of the Modoc War," *Cincinnati Daily Gazette*, May 5, 1874; Lemann, *Redemption*, 159–60; "A New Modoc War," *NYT*, February 6, 1876; "The Modocs: The Lumber-Yard Lava Beds and Their Occupants," *San Francisco Daily Morning Call*, July 30, 1873.

13. L. S. Dyar to W. Vandever, September 23, 1874, in Lane, *Klamath Indian Reservation*, 5.

14. O'Callaghan, "Klamath Indians"; "Unblushing Land Frauds: The President Sends Information to Congress," *NYT*, March 21, 1888.

15. L. S. Dyar to E. P. Smith, October 16, 1873, L. F. Grover to Secretary of the Interior, October 22, 1875, William Irwin to Zachariah Chandler, Secretary of the Interior, January 28, 1876, all in Lane, *Klamath Indian Reservation*, 4, 2–3; Theodore Stern, *Klamath Tribe*, 89.

16. J. R. Roork to Commissioner of Indian Affairs, September 7, 1877, in U.S. Senate, Committee on Indian Affairs, *Memorial*, 2.

17. J. R. Roork to Commissioner of Indian Affairs, August 21, 1877, in U.S. Department of the Interior, *In the Senate*, 6; J. R. Roork to Commissioner of Indian Affairs, February 12, 1878, in U.S. Senate, Committee on Indian Affairs, *Memorial*, 4.

18. C. Schurz to Commissioner of Indian Affairs, September 12, 1878, in U.S. Senate, Committee on Indian Affairs, *Memorial*, 8–9.

19. Curtin, *Memoirs*, 366–71; William M. Leeds to Secretary of the Interior, July 15, 1878, in U.S. Senate, Committee on Indian Affairs, *Memorial*, 7–8.

20. Stone, *Fort Klamath*, 53–61; *ARCIA* (1886), 215, (1887), 188; "Munz Biography," *KE* 12 (1974): 22–24.

21. Harrison, *Latest Studies*, 120–21.

22. G. W. Smith et al., "Resolutions Adopted by the Citizens of Linkville, September 28, 1886," in Shaver et al., *Illustrated History*, 934; Stone, *Fort Klamath*, 68–70.

23. G. S. Carpenter to Assistant Adjutant General, December 1, 1886, J. D. C. Atkins to Joseph Emery, January 11, 1887, both in U.S. Department of the Interior, *In the Senate*, 20–22; Testimony of O. C. Applegate, June 2, 1887, Mo-Ghen-Kas-Kit, June 10, 1887, Joseph Emery, Report on the Eastern Boundary, June 16, 1887, all in in U.S. Senate, Committee on Indian Affairs, *Memorial*, 14–15, 10–17; A. B. Upshaw to Secretary of the Interior, August 3, 1887, in U.S. Department of the Interior, *In the Senate*, 26–28.

24. Klamath Development Company, *Klamath Falls, Oregon*, 4, 6–7; Klamath Chamber of Commerce, *Klamath County, Oregon*.

25. *ARCIA* (1879), 125–27.

26. Bowden, "Land, Lumber Companies, and Mills," 10–12; Theodore Stern, *Klamath Tribe*, 61–63.

27. Southern, "Hard Winter"; Charles I. Roberts, "Notes on the Fire of 1889," *Klamath News*, February 20, 1931, reprinted in *KE* 13 (1975): 66.

28. *Klamath County Star*, April 10, 1891, reprinted in Shaver et al., *Illustrated History*, 979; Leavitt, "Reflections and Recollections."

29. George, *Enterprising Minnesotans*, 19–22; Good et al., *History*, 119.

30. "O. C. & E. Railroad," *KE* 12 (1974): 83–92; Ganoe, "History"; Ganoe, "History—II"; Hidy, Hill, and Nevins, *Timber and Men*, 239–40; Bowden, "Land, Lumber Companies, and Mills," 13–16, 38 (n. 48).

31. Chang, *Color of the Land*, 76–81.

32. Theodore Stern, *Klamath Tribe*, 126–27, 141–43, 132.

33. Ibid., 167.

34. *United States v. California & Oregon Land Company*, 148 U.S. 31, 13 S.Ct. 458, 37 L.Ed. 354.

35. *United States v. California & Oregon Land Co.*, 192 U.S. 355, 24 S.Ct. 266, 48 L.Ed. 476; Theodore Stern, *Klamath Tribe*, 132–33.

36. Zakoji, *Termination*; "Booth-Kelley Deal," *KFE*, January 31, 1907; "Indian Affairs: Many Improvements for the Klamath Reservation This Year," *KFE*, March 7, 1907; O'Callaghan, "Klamath Indians," 25.

37. O'Callaghan, "Klamath Indians," 26–28.

38. Good et al., *History*, 103–9; "Before Merrill," *KE* 7 (1969): 1–12; "Battle Ground to Be Garden: Scene of Modoc Outbreak in the North to Be Made a Rich Region by Irrigation," *San Francisco Call*, June 1, 1905; "Tule Lake Land Opened Next Spring," *KFEH*, January 5, 1917; Robbins, *Landscapes of Promise*, 250–54.

39. Good et al., *History*, 73–75.

40. Devere Helfrich, "Klamath Boating," *KE* 1(2) (1965): 27–33, 33–63.

41. "Greatest Building Boom in History of the Town," *Klamath Republican*, October 19, 1905; Bowden, "Land, Lumber Companies, and Mills," 11–12, 16.

42. "Merrill the Flour City," *KFE*, December 1909, in Turner, *Years of Harvest*, 118.

43. "Lakeside Land Company," *KE* 8 (1970): 20–24; Good et al., *History*, 137–39.

44. Devere Helfrich, "White Lake City," *KE* 15 (1977): 25–34.

45. Robbins, *Landscapes of Promise*, 254.

46. Klamath County: A Rich Domain That Awaits Settlement," *KFE*, January 10, 1895.

47. "The Initial Shot: Description of the First Battle of the Modoc War," in *KFE*, January 10, 1895.

48. *Klamath County*, 2, 10–11.

49. Bate, *Frontier Legend*, 27–30, 32–34, 47–54.

50. Drannan, *Thirty-One Years*, 232, 545, 543, 544.

51. Ibid., 549–50, 585, 555, 559–61.

52. Theodore Stern, *Klamath Tribe*, 160–81; Theodore Stern, "Klamath Indians," 271.

53. Zakoji, "Klamath Culture Change," 250, 96–97, 99, 170–71.

54. Ibid., 197.

55. *KFEH*, July 10, 1916, quoted in Devere Helfrich, "The Big July Time," *KE* 6 (1968): 53.

56. Riddle, *Indian History*, 3.

57. Ibid., 19, 47, 54–56.

58. Ibid., 200.

59. "Indian Writes History," *Minneapolis Morning Tribune*, May 17, 1914.

60. Libby, "Review," 136.

61. Warrior, *People and the Word*; Konkle, *Writing Indian Nations*.

CHAPTER FIVE

1. A. W. McGowan to O. C. Applegate, April 22, 1917, OCAP, box 21, folder 14.

2. Ibid., April 3, 1914.

3. C. M. Lane to Commissioner of Pensions, December 10, 1928, Wama-Louie Pension File, 18373, NARA, RG 15.

4. Ibid.; Winfield Scott to Joseph Hunter, January 14, 1929, Wama-Louie Pension File, 18373, NARA, RG 15.

5. Oliver C. Applegate, Affidavit, January 5, 1933, OCAP, box 21, folder 14.

6. "Indian Pension Cases Carried to Completion or Yet in the Hands of Captain O. C. Applegate," September 4, 1922, OCAP, box 19, folder 2.

7. Meriam, *Problem*, 451, 452–53, 454, 463.

8. O. C. Applegate to Charles L. McNary, May 28, 1918, OCAP, box 19, folder 1.

9. MacConnell, *Glorious Contentment*; Skocpol, *Protecting Soldiers and Mothers*, 102–59.

10. Little has been published about these veterans' associations. See Greene, *Indian War Veterans*, xv–xlii; John M. Carroll and Pappas, *Papers*; Gray, "'Winners of the West'"; Order of Indian Wars, "Constitution and By-Laws of the Order of Indian Wars of the United States" (Chicago, June 10, 1896), 16–17, IWVNPCR.

11. Carroll, *Unpublished Papers of the Order of Indian Wars*, 2–3.

12. *Winners of the West*, May, October, December 1924, June 1925.

13. Otto Kleeman, "History of the Indian War Veterans of North Pacific Coast," IWVNPCR, box 1, folder 1.

14. *Secretary of State Indian War Veteran Medal Records*, Utah State Archives and Records Service, Salt Lake City, Microfilm series 2220, reels 1–16.

15. Skogen, *Indian Depredation Claims*, xv–xvi.

16. Ibid., 159–66, 167–68, 93–94, 96–97.

17. U.S. Department of War, *Modoc War Claims*, 1–15.

18. Records Supporting Claims for Service during the Indian Wars, 1892–1931, NARA, RG 15, Entry A1(61), box 9, folder "Oregon."

19. U.S. Department of the Interior, *Indian Depredation Claims*, 59; Skogen, *Indian Depredation Claims*, 234 (n. 11).

20. "Indian Depredation Claims," *NYT*, July 12, 1892; Skogen, *Indian Depredation Claims*, 98, 186–88, 208–9.

21. *Montoya v. United States*, 280 U.S. 261, 21 S.Ct. 358, 45 L.Ed. 521 (1901).

22. Glasson, *Federal Military Pensions*, 115.

23. Arthur W. Dunn, "Indian Veterans Worked: Oregon Delegation to Washington Did Its Best," February 28, 1901, Scrapbook 48, p. 90, OHSRL.

24. "Indian War Pension Bill: Oregon Congressmen Are Anxious to Have It Pass at an Early Date," n.d., unidentified newspaper clipping, Scrapbook 35, p. 145, OHSRL.

25. "Indian War Veterans: Sons Organize to Perpetuate the Deeds of Their Sires," *Desert News*, July 10, 1908.

26. "Indian War Veterans: Association Which Seeks for Its Members Recognition of Government," *Desert News*, August 11, 1909.

27. Greene, *Indian War Veterans*, xxii.

28. Open Letter from Cyrus H. Walker to Comrades of the Indian Wars North Pacific Coast, June 18, 1913, OCAP, box 19, folder 1.

29. "Guideline for the Wars and Campaigns of the Indian Wars under the Act of March 4, 1917," Records Supporting Claims for Service during the Indian Wars, 1892–1931, NARA, RG 15, Entry A1(61), box 28, folder "Indian War—General."

30. IWVNPCR, box 1, folder 3.

31. Otto Kleeman, "History of the Indian War Veterans of North Pacific Coast," IWVNPCR, box 1, folder 1.

32. "Various Documents Organized as Report on Indian War Pensioners, State Organizations, March 4, 1924," Records Supporting Claims for Service during the Indian Wars, 1892–1931, RG 15, Entry A1 61, box 28, folder "Indian War Pensioners State Orgs—3/4/24."

33. George A. White to Commissioner of Pensions, October 16, 1931, Records Supporting Claims for Service during the Indian Wars, 1892–1931, NARA, RG 15, Entry A1(61), box 9, folder "Oregon."

34. Greene, *Indian War Veterans*, xxxiv.

35. Brown Mosenkoskit et al., "Indian Pensioners to N. J. Sinnott," November 1922, OCAP, box 19, folder 2.

36. "An Indian Who Fought His Own People," *Winners of the West*, March 1925; "Records of the Annual Encampment," 27–31, IWVNPCR, box 1, folder 3; "List of Claimants," n.d., IWVNPCR, box 1, folder 6.

37. "An Indian Pensioner," *Winners of the West*, February 1924.

38. Hauptman, *Iroquois*, 146–47.

39. Al Carroll, *Medicine Bags*, 100.

40. R. T. Cookingham to Commissioner Washington Gardner, June 12, 1921, Cholah Peter Pension File, 17127, NARA, RG 15.

41. Walter West to I. D. Lafferty, March 4, 1922, OCAP, box 19, folder 2.

42. O. L. Babcock to O. C. Applegate, February 11, 1921, May 30, 1922, OCAP, box 20, folder 17.

43. Stuart H. Elliot to Commissioner of Pensions, January 10, 1925, Histo Pension File, 15714, NARA, RG 15.

44. *ARCIA* (1900), 357; O. C. Applegate to W. C. Hawley, March 9, 1908, OCAP, box 22, folder 4.

45. O. C. Applegate to Miss Sauber, January 9, 1921, OCAP, box 19, folder 2; Acting Commissioner to N. J. Sinnott, December 11, 1920, January 6, 1921, Peter Cholah Pension File, 17127, NARA, RG 15.

46. O. C. Applegate to N. J. Sinnott, February 20, 1922, OCAP, box 22, folder 19.

47. O. C. Applegate to Walter M. Pierce, Charles Martin, Frederick Steiwer, and Charles L. McNary, May 22 [24], 1934, OCAP, box 19, folder 3. For a complete list, see "Senate Bills," OCAP, box 19, folder 4. See also Simpson, Wilson, OCAP, box 23, folder 11; Walker, Jesse, OCAP, box 23, folder 9; Kate Brown, OCAP, box 20, folder 3.

48. Theodore Stern, *Klamath Tribe*, 53–54; Spier, *Klamath Ethnography*, 59–61.

49. "Indian Pension Cases Carried to Completion," OCAP, box 19, folder 2; Commissioner to Cinda Checaskane, July 5, 1918, OCAP, box 20, folder 5.

50. Birdie John's Affidavit, Birdie John Pension File, 14878, NARA, RG 15.

51. E. W. Morgan to Mary A. Copperfield, August 12, 1933, Wade Crawford to E. W. Morgan, October 3, 1933, both in Jim Copperfield Pension File, 14018, NARA, RG 15. Also see Jane [Ursula] Whistler Pension File, 10778, NARA, RG 15.

52. Deposition of Histo or Toplash or John Jack, September 8, 1920, Histo Pension File, 15714, NARA, RG 15.

53. Stuart H. Elliot to Commissioner of Pensions, October 18, 1924, Histo Pension File, NARA, RG 15.

54. Quoted in Theodore Stern, *Klamath Tribe*, 54.

55. O. C. Applegate to N. J. Sinnott, February 24, 1921, OCAP, box 19, folder 3.

56. Harrison Brown to Frederick Steiwer, March 1930, OCAP, box 20, folder 4.

57. O. C. Applegate to Frederick Steiwer, May 28, 1930, OCAP, box 20, folder 4.

58. Deposition and Certificate of Search, December 8, 1928, Wama-Louie Pension File, 18373, NARA, RG 15.

59. Claimant Declaration, January 21, 1918, Deposition of Cinda Chekaskane, April 19, 1922, both in Eli Chick-kas-ka-ne Pension File, 13851, NARA, RG 15; Depositions of Ike Owhy, Albert Kuckup, and Danial Katchia on October 7 and 8, 1929, Martha Sidwaller Pension File, 1630337, NARA, RG 15.

60. Walter West to Commissioner of Indian Affairs, June 29, 1921, Peter Cholah Pension File, 17127, NARA, RG 15.

61. R. T. Cookingham to Commissioner Washington Gardner, June 12, 1921, Peter Cholah Pension File, 17127, NARA, RG 15.

62. Glasson, "National Pension System," 43–45.

63. Jacob Thomas to Commissioner of Pensions, October 30, 1914, Jacob Thomas Pension File, 15418, NARA, RG 15.

64. Drew Jackson to Commissioner of Pensions, May 1918, OCAP, box 21, folder 6.

65. O. C. Applegate to Commissioner of Pensions, May 1, 1918, Wama-Louie Pension File, 18373, NARA, RG 15.

66. Ursula Whistler to Commissioner of Pensions, January 1921, OCAP, box 23, folder 10.

67. F. A. Baker to G. M. Saltzgaber, December 18, 1918, Mary Chiloquin Pension File, 13850, NARA, RG 15.

68. G. M. Saltzgaber to N. J. Sinnott, July 2, 1919, in ibid.

69. Jane [Ursula] Whistler Pension File, 10778, Nancy Yahooskin Pension File, 15375, both in NARA, RG 15.

70. Theodore Stern, *Klamath Tribe*, 96–99, 103–4.

71. O. C. Applegate to F. A. Baker, November 19, 1917, OCAP, box 23, folder 10.

72. Wade Crawford to E. W. Morgan, October 3, 1933, Jim Copperfield Pension File, 14018, NARA, RG 15.

73. Nancy Ben-John to Commissioner of Pensions, November 29, 1921, OCAP, box 20, folder 2; Affidavits of Nancy Ben-John and Mary Chiloquin in Connection with I.W.O. 14921, December 6, 1921, OCAP, box 22, folder 16.

74. Affidavits of Nancy Ben-John and Mary Chiloquin in Connection with I.W.O. 14921, December 6, 1921, OCAP, box 22, folder 16.

75. Sworn Testimony before the Examiner of Inheritance, January 4, 1918, OCAP, box 20, folder 6.

76. Brown Mosenkosket Pension File, 14029, Jim Copperfield Pension File, 14018, Reuben Konoki Pension File, 14019, John Koppos Pension File, 14020, Modoc-Charley Pension File, 13994, Drew Jackson Pension File, 14017, all in NARA, RG 15.

77. Albert Pension File, 15393, Jacob Thomas Pension File, 15418, Tul-Lux Holliquilla Pension File, 15473, James Win-ne-shet Pension File, 15530, David Washump Pension File, 15477, all in NARA, RG 15.

78. Birdie John Pension File, 14878, Solomon Lalakes Pension File, 17107, Eli Chickkas-ka-ne Pension File, 13851, Mary Chiloquin Pension File, 13850, all in NARA, RG 15.

79. Charles S. Hood to Commissioner of Pensions, January 20, 1920, Peter Cholah Pension File, 17127, NARA, RG 15.

80. N. J. Sinnott to Sargent K. Brown, June 29, 1927, OCAP, box 19, folder 3.

81. Affidavits of Dick Brown and Jim Copperfield, March 1930, OCAP, box 20, folder 4.

82. J. B. Mortsolf to Commissioner of Pensions, December 10, 1926, Anna Holliquilla Pension File, 1537132, NARA, RG 15.

83. Special Examiner's Report, Cinda Checaskane, June 29, 1922, Eli Chick-kas-ka-ne Pension File, 13851, NARA, RG 15.

84. Deposition of Ike Owhy, May 27, 1914, Jacob Thomas Pension File, 15418, NARA, RG 15. For additional depositions made by Ike Owhy, see Tul-Luk Holliquilla Pension File, 15473, Albert Pension File, 15393, both in NARA, RG 15.

85. Affidavit of Tom Skellock, July 30, 1931, Wama-Louie Pension File, 18373, NARA, RG 15.

CHAPTER SIX

1. "Monument to Be Dedicated in Lava Beds," *KFEH*, June 12, 1926; "Caravan to Lava Beds Starts at 7:00 Sharp," *APD*, June 11, 1926.

2. "Veterans of '72 Recall War Memories and History," *APD*, June 18, 1926; "Many Historic Spots in Lava Beds Can Be Marked," *APD*, May 29, 1925.

3. "Soldier's Monument Site Located in Modoc Lava Beds," *APD*, September 4, 1925.

4. Howard, *Squaw Spy*, 31.

5. Boddam-Whetham, *Western Wanderings*, 248.

6. J. D. Howard interview, LBNMRL, transcribed by the author.

7. John S. Parke to Assistant Adjutant General, October 10, 1882, Parke Papers, LBNMRL.

8. John S. Parke, "A Visit to the Lava Beds and a Brief Account of the Modoc War of 1873," 1–18, in ibid.

9. *SFC*, April 13, 1873.

10. Cutter, "Female Indian Killer," 21–22.

11. Elliott, *Custerology*, 105–6.

12. Frederick Brown, *Lava Beds National Monument*, 96.

13. Abbey, Diary, October 6, 1873, KCM.

14. John Muir, "Modoc Memories," *SFEB*, December 28, 1874.

15. Hamilton, "In the Lava Beds," 98.

16. Ibid., 99.

17. Ibid., 100.

18. Steele, "Cave of Captain Jack."

19. "Matilda Must Move," *KFE*, March 21, 1907.

20. "Returning Modocs," *KFE*, July 2, 1903.

21. Deur, *In the Footprints*, 212.

22. Ibid., 210.

23. James, *Modoc*, 244–46.

24. Deur, *In the Footprints*, 210–14; Shawn Dumont, interview.

25. *Klamath Falls Herald and News*, October 8, 1947.

26. Devere Helfrich, "Klamath Boating," *KE* 1(1) (1965): 37, 38–44, 63.

27. "Big Cave in Lava Beds," *New York Sun*, July 15, 1909.

28. Unidentified newspaper clipping, November 4, 1956, file 214, KCM.

29. "Go to Lava Beds," *KFEH*, July 14, 1910.

30. Raibmon, *Authentic Indians*, 126.

31. "Peter Schonchin, Aged Indian Chief Passes at K. Falls," [*SFC*], April 28, [no year], in "Manuscript, Notes, and Clippings Relating to the Modoc Indians and the Modoc War," folder [Newspaper Clippings Relating to the Modoc County and Modoc War], Bancroft Library; "Widow of Modoc War Scout Dies: Lizzie Schonchin's Life Ends," IWVNPCR, box 2, folder 7.

32. "Return from the Lava Beds," *KFEH*, May 22, 1911; "Interesting Relics of the Modoc War," *KFEH*, July 25, 1910.

33. "Coyote Pelts Get Bounty," *KFEH*, October 13, 1911.

34. Raibmon, *Authentic Indians*, 103–13.

35. Norrgard, "Seasons of Change," 93.

36. Frederick Brown, *Lava Beds National Monument*, 128.

37. "The Devil's Dooryard: The Land That God Did Not Make, but Neglected," *KFEH*, October 2, 1913; "Party Will Explore the Modoc Lava Beds," *KFEH*, September 14, 1914.

38. "Ad for Bearfoot Ice Cave," *KFEH*, May 21, 1922; Guy Merrill, interview, KCM; Frederick Brown, *Lava Beds National Monument*, 163–66.

39. Frederick Brown, *Lava Beds National Monument*, 91.

40. "Guy Merrill Journeys into the Lava Beds in His Buck Car," *KFEH*, May 27, 1911.

41. "Return from the Lava Beds," *KFEH*, May 22, 1911.

42. "Let's Get Busy," *KFEH*, October 6, 1914.

43. "Five Months of Active Work by Local Chamber," *KFEH*, June 22, 1915; "Committee Leaves to Outline Scenic Road," *KFEH*, April 22, 1915; "Volunteer Road Work May Be Done in May," *KFEH*, April 24, 1915; "Road through Lava Beds Is Certain," *KFEH*, April 26, 1915; "Lava Beds Road Project Now Assured Fact," *KFEH*, June 21, 1915; "Lava Bed Road Nearly Finished," *KFEH*, July 10, 1915.

44. "Modoc County after the Lava Beds Road," *KFEH*, June 29, 1915.

45. "Five Months of Active Work by Local Chamber," *KFEH*, June 22, 1915.

46. U.S. Department of the Interior, *Proceedings*, 38–39.

47. "Crater Lake National Park Annual Visitation," in Unrau, *Crater Lake*, appendix C.

48. Frederick Brown, *Lava Beds National Monument*, 192–95.

49. *Klamath Record*, May 14, 1920; *Siskiyou News*, April 30, 1925.

50. Gendzel, "Pioneers and Padres."

51. Glassberg, *Sense of History*, 167–202, esp. 175–83; Deverell, *Whitewashed Adobe*, esp. 6–7.

52. "Native Daughters Launch Drive for Monument Fund," *APD*, February 20, 1925.

53. Kropp, *California Vieja*, 15.

54. "Native Daughters Get Valuable Allies," *APD*, February 27, 1925.

55. "Monument Ball Starts Rolling," *APD*, March 13, 1925; "Native Daughters Monument Fund Growing," *APD*, March 27, 1925.

56. *Sacramento Bee*, April 1, 1925; "Sacramento Bee Boosts Modoc Project," *APD*, April 10, 1925.

57. Within the Department of the Interior, national parks and national monuments have equal standing. The only difference is that national parks are created by act of Congress, while national monuments are created by presidential order. See Frederick Brown, *Lava Beds National Monument*, 192–95; *APD*, February 6, April 10, October 9, 1925.

58. Charles Hardin to Editor of the *APD*, May 10, 1926, Lava Beds National Monument Museum, Historical Documents and Photographs, box 1, LABE 7854, LBNMRL.

59. "Search for Historic Monument Leads Woman across Continent," *Sacramento Bee*, March 24, 1928. See also various newspaper clippings in Brown Clippings, 1925–40, LABE 10102, LBNMRL.

60. "Pictorial Follow-Up on News and Features from Four Quarters of Globe," *Los Angeles Times*, June 4, 1930.

61. "Modoc N.D.G.W. Plan Float Float [*sic*] to Represent Period of 1872 in Pageant," *APD*, August 14, 1925.

62. "Modoc Native Daughters to Have Float in Diamond Jubilee Parade," *APD*, August 21, 1925; "Modoc N.D.G.W. Plan Float Float [*sic*] to Represent Period of 1872 in Pageant," *APD*, August 14, 1925; "Vaudeville and Dance Tonight under Auspices N.D.G.W.," August 28, 1925.

63. "Modoc Float a Credit to County at Diamond Jubilee," *APD*, September 18, 1925.

64. "Modoc Indians Enjoying Visit," *SFC*, September 9, 1925.

65. Deloria, *Indians*, 146.

66. "Modoc Indians Enjoying Visit," *SFC*, September 9, 1925.

67. "Injuns in Modoc Lava Beds," *SFC*, Rotogravure Pictorial Section, September 13, 1925.

68. Flores, *Remembering the Alamo*, xvi.

69. Foote, "To Remember and Forget," 385.

70. Lass, "Romantic Documents," 467.

71. "Injuns in Modoc Lava Beds," *SFC*, Rotogravure Pictorial Section, September 13, 1925.

CODA: AN OUTLAW TO ALL MANKIND

1. Lee Juillerat, "Remembering the Modoc War: New Plaque Remembers 14 Homesteaders Killed," *Klamath Falls Herald and News*, May 24, 2009.

2. Lee Juillerat, personal communication; Kevin Fields, interview.

EPILOGUE

1. Pete Wilson to Doris Omundson, n.d., Wally Herger to Doris Omundson, n.d., "1988 Symposium on the Modoc War," both in Vertical File, LBNMRL.

2. "Addenda," *Journal of the Shaw Historical Library* 3 (Fall 1988): 62–63; emphasis added.

3. Ibid., 63; emphasis added.

4. Trouillot, *Silencing the Past*, 1–30, esp. 26–27.

5. "Addenda," *Journal of the Shaw Historical Library* 3 (Fall 1988): 63; emphasis added.

6. Bataille, *Accursed Share*; Derrida, *Given Time*; Parry, "Gift"; Taussig, "Sun Gives."

7. Jacobson, *Roots Too*, 22.

8. Charles Hillinger, "Modoc Indians, Exiled from California, Honor Famed Chief," *Los Angeles Times*, November 17, 1968.

9. Ibid.

10. Lynn Schonchin, interview, 11, 38, http://indigenousfoundations.arts.ubc.ca/fileadmin/user_upload/FNSP/indigenous_foundations/IVT-Klamath/IVT.html.

11. I heard this comment several times from members of the Klamath Tribes. Tom Ball emphasized this idea during our first meeting at the University of Oregon in 2009. Deur, *In the Footprints*, 271 (n. 3).

12. Morrie Jimenez, interview, 3, 103, http://indigenousfoundations.arts.ubc.ca/fileadmin/user_upload/FNSP/indigenous_foundations/IVT-Klamath/IVT.html.

13. Orin Kirk and Lynn Schonchin in Deur, *In the Footprints*, 210.

14. Foster, "Imperfect Justice."

15. Charles Wilkinson, *Blood Struggle*, 75–84, 129–73.

16. "Modoc Indians Snub Observance of Their Defeat," *Sarasota Journal*, September 12, 1972.

17. Lynn Schonchin, conversation. Quotations are from Lynn Schonchin, interview, 11, 45, http://indigenousfoundations.arts.ubc.ca/fileadmin/user_upload/FNSP/indigenous_foundations/IVT-Klamath/IVT.html.

18. "Panel Discussion," 47.

19. Ibid..

20. Ibid., 47–48.

21. Ibid., 48.

22. Ibid., 48. In quoting from "Panel Discussion," I also consulted the videotape recordings of the symposium to check the accuracy of the published transcript. In this quotation, meaningful discrepancies existed between the published transcript and the recording, and I have edited slightly the published transcript.

23. Ibid., 48–49.

24. Colwell-Chanthaphonh, *Massacre*, 110.

25. Klima, *Funeral Casino*, 12–13.

26. Hong, *Ruptures*.

27. Sturken, *Tangled Memories*, 44–84; Yoneyama, *Hiroshima Traces*, 71.

28. "Panel Discussion," 49.

Bibliography

ARCHIVAL RECORDS

American Antiquarian Society, Worcester, Mass.
  American Broadsides and Ephemera, series 1 (1749–1900)
Bancroft Library, University of California, Berkeley
  Rollin A. Fairchild Reminiscences, BANC MSS 73/122 c:200
  "Mary H. Farbae Letter," BANC MSS 2004/12c
  "The Lava Beds Exploration," BANC MSS C-D 5146
  Georgia Lee Pictorial Collection
  "Manuscript, Notes, and Clippings Relating to the Modoc Indians and the Modoc
    War," BANC MSS C-R 52, box 1
  Pearl Brown Smith Papers
California Indian Heritage Center, Sacramento
  Hearn's Accession and Associated Artifacts, Artifact Collection
Klamath County Museum, Klamath Falls, Ore.
  Diary of Henry G. Abbey of Cleveland, Vault Collection, 0041.2010.040.0002 and
    0041.2010.040.0003
  Diary of Leonard Case, Vault Collection, 0041.2010.040.0001
  Don Fisher Papers
  Guy Merrill Interview, 1976
  Modoc War Files
  Photographic Albums
  Vertical Files
Lava Beds National Monument Research Library, Tulelake, Calif.
  Brown Clippings, 1925–40
  Mary Case History Files
  Olaf T. Hagen, "Modoc War: Official Correspondence of Documents, 1865–1878"
  Historical Documents and Photographs
  J. D. Howard Interview, May 15, 1961
  Lieutenant George W. Kingbury's Scrapbook
  John S. Parke Papers, 973.82 PAR, Acc. No. 1381
  1988 Symposium on the Modoc War, Vertical File
Library of Congress, Washington, D.C.
  Photograph Collection
National Archives and Records Administration, Washington D.C.
  Records of the Bureau of Pensions and Its Predecessors, 1805–1935, Record Group
    15, Records of the Department of Veterans Affairs
    Albert Pension File, 15393

Eli Chick-kas-ka-ne Pension File, 13851

Mary Chiloquin Pension File, 13850

Peter Cholah Pension File, 17127

Jim Copperfield Pension File, 14018

Histo Pension File, 15714

Anna Holliquilla Pension File, 1537132

Tul-Lux Holliquilla Pension File, 15473

Drew Jackson Pension File, 14017

Birdie John Pension File, 14878

Reuben Konoki Pension File, 14019

John Koppos Pension File, 14020

Solomon Lalakes Pension File, 17107

Modoc-Charley Pension File, 13994

Brown Mosenkosket Pension Files, 14028, 14029

Cholah Peter Pension File, 17127

Winemah Riddle Pension File, 12339

Martha Sidwaller Pension File, 1630337

Jacob Thomas Pension File, 15418

Wama-Louie Pension File, 18373

David Washump Pension File, 15477

Jane [Ursula] Whistler Pension File, 10778

James Win-ne-shet Pension File, 15530

Nancy Yahooskin Pension File, 15375

Records Relating to the Montana, Dakota, and Modoc War Claims, 1875–76, RG 159, Entry 30

Newberry Research Library, Chicago

Ayer Collection

Map Collection

Jeff Riddle, "History of the Modoc War," VAULT Ayer MS 760

Elmo Scott Watson Papers, 1816–1951

Erminie Wheeler-Voegelin Papers, 1934–85

Oregon Historical Society Research Library, Portland, Ore.

George Himes Papers

Indian War Veterans of the North Pacific Coast Records, Mss 364

Ezra Meeker Vertical Files

Proceedings of the Oregon Historical Society

Scrapbook Collections 35, 38, 48, 49

Transactions of the Oregon Pioneer Association

Shaw Historical Library, Oregon Institute of Technology, Klamath Falls

Don Fisher Collection, Modoc War Correspondence

Helfrich Collection

J. D. Howard Collection

Francis Landrum Collection

Modoc War Master Photo File 4.07

Transactions of the Oregon Pioneer Association, 1888–1921

University of Oregon, Special Collections and University Archives, Eugene
  Lindsey Applegate Papers, Ax 004
  Oliver Cromwell Applegate Papers, Ax 005
  Elinor F. Meacham, *Memorandum Book of Nellie F. Meacham, Salem, Oregon,*
    October 21, 1878–May 11, 1879, and Manuscript of Autobiographical Novel,
    MICROFILM F884.M38 M43 1959
  WPA Oregon Historical Records Survey Records, box 066

INTERVIEWS

Bowan, Doris Omundson, and John William Quinn. Interview with author. July 1,
  2008.
Dorman, Craig. Interview with author. July 1, 2008.
Dumont, Shawn. Interview with author. July 10, 2010.
Fields, Kevin. Interview with author. July 10, 2010.
Herrera, Debbie, and Christine Allen. Interview with author. July 13, 2010.
James, Cheewa. Interview with author. June 28, 2008.
Jimenez, Morrie. Interview with Linc Kesler. September 3, 2002, in *Oral Narratives*
  of the Klamath Termination, ed. Linc Kesler, First Nations Studies Program
  (University of British Columbia, 2005), http://fnsp.arts.ubc.ca/klamath/.
Juillerat, Lee. Conversation with author. June 25, 2010.
Schonchin, Lynn. Interview with Linc Kesler. October 19, 2002, in *Oral Narratives*
  of the Klamath Termination, ed. Linc Kesler, First Nations Studies Program
  (University of British Columbia, 2005), http://fnsp.arts.ubc.ca/klamath/.
Schonchin, Lynn. Conversation with author. August 30, 2010.

SELECTED NEWSPAPERS AND WEEKLY MAGAZINES

Alturas (Calif.) Plain-Dealer
Army and Navy Journal (New York)
Boston Evening Journal
Boston Evening Transcript
Chicago Daily Inter Ocean
Chicago Tribune
Cincinnati Daily Gazette
The Congregationalist (Boston)
Desert News (Salt Lake City, Utah)
Frank Leslie's Illustrated Newspaper
  (New York)
Harper's Weekly (New York)
Hartford (Conn.) Daily Courant
Idaho Daily Avalanche (Silver City,
  Idaho)
Indianapolis Sentinel
Klamath (Ore.) Record

Klamath (Ore.) Republican
Klamath Falls (Ore.) Evening Herald
Klamath Falls (Ore.) Express
Klamath Falls (Ore.) Herald and News
Los Angeles Times
Minneapolis Morning Tribune
National Tribune (Washington, D.C.)
New Northwest (Portland, Ore.)
New York Evangelist
New York Herald
New York Star
New York Sun
New York Times
New York Tribune
Oregonian (Portland, Ore.)
Philadelphia Inquirer
Sacramento Daily Union

Sacramento Record
San Francisco Bulletin
San Francisco Call
San Francisco Chronicle
San Francisco Daily Alta California
San Francisco Daily Evening Bulletin
San Francisco Examiner
Sarasota (Fla.) Journal

Siskiyou News (Yreka, Calif.)
Surprise Valley Record (Cedarville, Calif.)
Trenton (N.J.) Gazette
Washington Bee
Winners of the West (St. Joseph, Mo.)
Yreka (Calif.) Journal
Yreka (Calif.) Union

GOVERNMENT DOCUMENTS

Brown, Frederick. *Lava Beds National Monument Resource Study.* [Seattle]: Pacific West Region, National Park Service, 2008.

Deur, Douglas. *In the Footprints of Gmukamps: A Traditional Use Study of Crater Lake National Park and Lava Beds National Monument.* [Seattle]: Pacific West Region, National Park Service, 2008.

Gatschet, Albert Samuel. *Klamath Indians of Southwestern Oregon.* Washington, D.C.: U.S. Department of the Interior, 1890.

Lane, Lafayette. *Klamath Indian Reservation.* 44th Cong., 1st sess., Report 183, Serial 1708. Washington, D.C.: U.S. Government Printing Office, 1876.

Meriam, Lewis, comp. *The Problem of Indian Administration: Report of a Survey Made at the Request of Honorable Hubert Work, Secretary of the Interior, and Submitted to Him, February 21, 1928.* Baltimore: Johns Hopkins Press, 1928.

Odeneal, Thomas B. *The Modoc War: Statement of Its Origin and Causes Containing an Account of the Treaty, Copies of Petitions, and Official Correspondence.* Portland, Ore.: "Bulletin" Steam Book and Job Printing Office, 1873.

Unrau, Harlan. *Crater Lake: Administrative History.* [Denver]: U.S. Department of the Interior, 1988.

U.S. Adjutant-General's Office. *Letters Received by the Office of the Adjutant General (Main Series), 1871–1880.* M-666. Washington, D.C.: National Archives and Records Service, General Services Administration, 1971.

U.S. Bureau of Indian Affairs. *Records of the Oregon Superintendency of Indian Affairs, 1848–1873.* M-2, rolls 2–30.

U.S. Department of the Interior. *Annual Report of the Commissioner of Indian Affairs.* Washington, D.C.: U.S. Government Printing Office, 1870, 1873, 1879, 1886, 1887, 1900.

———. *In the Senate of the United States: Letter from the Secretary of the Interior in Response to the Senate Resolution of May 31, 1894.* 53rd Cong., 2nd sess., S. Doc. 129. Washington, D.C.: U.S. Government Printing Office, 1894.

———. *Indian Depredation Claims: Letter from the Secretary of the Interior, Transmitting a List of Claims for Depredations Committed by Indians, &c., Called for by House Resolution of April 30, 1874.* 43rd Cong., 2nd sess., Ex. Doc. 65, Serial 1645. Washington, D.C.: U.S. Government Printing Office, 1875.

———. *Proceedings of the National Park Conference Held at Yellowstone, 1911.* Washington, D.C.: U.S. Government Printing Office, 1911.

———. *Records of the Indian Division, Office of the Secretary of the Interior: Special Files, 1848–1907,* rolls 4–5.

U.S. Department of War. *Modoc War Claims: Letter from the Secretary of War, Transmitting the Claims of the States of California and Oregon, and Citizens Thereof, on Account of the Modoc War.* 43rd Cong., 2nd sess., Ex. Doc. 45, Serial 1645. Washington, D.C.: U.S. Government Printing Office, 1874.

U.S. House of Representatives. *Official Copies of Correspondence Relative to the War with the Modoc Indians in 1872–73.* 43rd Cong., 1st sess., Ex. Doc. 122. Washington, D.C.: Adjutant-General Office, 1874.

U.S. Senate. Committee on Indian Affairs. *Memorial on Behalf of the Klamath and Modoc Tribes and the Yahooskin Band of Snake Indians Occupying the Klamath Indian Reservation.* 54th Cong., 1st sess., S. Doc. 131. Washington, D.C.: U.S. Government Printing Office, 1896.

Wilkinson, Boyden, Cragun, and Barker. *Klamath, Modoc, and Yahooskin Documents in Connection with Litigation before the Indian Claims Commission Dkt. no. 100.* Washington, D.C.: National Archives, [196?].

Zakoji, Hiroto. *Termination and the Klamath Indian Education Program, 1955–1961.* Salem: Oregon State Department of Education, 1961.

BOOKS, ESSAYS, AND ARTICLES

Albers, Patricia C. "From Legend to Land to Labor: Changing Perspectives on Native American Work." In *Native Americans and Wage Labor: Ethnohistorical Perspectives,* ed. Alice Littlefield and Martha C. Knack, 245–73. Norman: University of Oklahoma Press, 1996.

Allen, James Michael. *Wi-ne-ma.* New York: Vantage, 1956.

Bacon, Edwin F. "Tobey Riddle (Winemah): The Heroine of the Modoc War." *Phrenological Journal and Life Illustrated* 62 (February 1876): 130–38.

Bancroft, Hubert Howe. *California Inter Pocula.* Vol. 35. San Francisco: History Company, 1888.

———. *History of California.* Vol. 7. San Francisco: History Company, 1884.

———. *History of Oregon.* Vols. 24, 25. San Francisco: History Company, 1888.

———. *The Native Races of the Pacific States of North America.* San Francisco: Bancroft, 1883.

Barker, Muhammad Abd-al-Rahman. *Klamath Dictionary.* Berkeley: University of California Press, 1963.

Basso, Keith H. *Wisdom Sits in Places: Landscape and Language among the Western Apache.* Albuquerque: University of New Mexico Press, 1996.

Bataille, Georges. *The Accursed Share: An Essay on General Economy.* New York: Zone, 1988.

Bate, Walter Nathaniel. *Frontier Legend: Texas Finale of Capt. William F. Drannan, Pseudo Frontier Comrade of Kit Carson.* New Bern, N.C.: Dunn, 1954.

Becker, Carl. "Everyman His Own Historian." *American Historical Review* 37 (January 1932): 221–36.

———. "Mr. Wells and the New History." *American Historical Review* 26 (July 1921): 644–56.

Beckham, Stephen. *Requiem for a People: The Rogue Indians and the Frontiersmen.* Norman: University of Oklahoma Press, 1971.

Belich, James. *Replenishing the Earth: The Settler Revolution and the Rise of the Angloworld.* London: Oxford University Press, 2009.

Bland, Thomas Augustus. *The Life of Alfred B. Meacham.* Washington, D.C.: Bland, 1883.

Boddam-Whetham, J. W. *Western Wanderings: A Record of Travel in the Evening Land.* London: Bentley, 1874.

Bodnar, John. *Remaking America: Public Memory, Commemoration, and Patriotism in the Twentieth Century.* Princeton: Princeton University Press, 1993.

Bold, Christine. *The Frontier Club: Popular Westerns and Cultural Power, 1880–1924.* New York: Oxford University Press, 2013.

Bowden, Jack. "Land, Lumber Companies, and Mills in the Klamath Basin, 1864–1950." In *The Timber Industry in the Klamath Basin,* special issue of *Journal of the Shaw Historical Library* 16 (2002): 5–41.

Boyd, Robert. *The Coming of the Spirit of Pestilence: Introduced Infectious Diseases and Population Decline among Northwest Coast Indians, 1774–1874.* Seattle: University of Washington Press, 1999.

Brady, Cyrus Townsend, ed. *Northwestern Fights and Fighters.* New York: Doubleday, Page, 1909.

Brown, Dee B. *Bury My Heart at Wounded Knee: An Indian History of the American West.* New York: Holt, 1970.

Brown, Joshua. *Beyond the Lines: Pictorial Reporting, Everyday Life, and the Crisis of Gilded-Age America.* Berkeley: University of California Press, 2002.

Brown, William S. *California Northeast: The Bloody Ground.* Oakland: Biobooks, 1951.

Bsumek, Erika Marie. *Indian-Made: Navajo Culture in the Marketplace, 1868–1940.* Lawrence: University Press of Kansas, 2008.

Byrd, Jodi A. *The Transit of Empire: Indigenous Critiques of Colonialism.* Minneapolis: University of Minnesota Press, 2011.

Callahan, S. Alice. *Wynema: A Child of the Forest.* Ed. A. LaVonne Brown Ruoff. Lincoln: University of Nebraska Press, 1997.

Carroll, Al. *Medicine Bags and Dog Tags: American Indian Veterans from Colonial Times to the Second Iraq War.* Lincoln: University of Nebraska Press, 2008.

Carroll, John. *Unpublished Papers of the Order of Indian Wars.* New Brunswick, N.J.: n.p., 1977.

Carroll, John M., and George S. Pappas. *The Papers of the Order of Indian Wars.* Fort Collins, Colo.: Old Army, 1975.

Castile, George Pierre. "The Commodification of Indian Identity." *American Anthropologist* 98 (December 1996): 743–49.

Cattelino, Jessica R. *High Stakes: Florida Seminole Gaming and Sovereignty.* Durham: Duke University Press, 2008.

Chang, David A. *The Color of the Land: Race, Nation, and the Politics of Landownership in Oklahoma, 1832–1929.* Chapel Hill: University of North Carolina Press, 2010.

Chase, J. A. *Rogue River Valley, Southern Oregon: Its Resources and Attraction, Opportunities It Offers to Intending Settlers.* Ashland, Ore.: Tiding, 1888.

Colwell-Chanthaphonh, Chip. *Massacre at Camp Grant: Forgetting and Remembering Apache History.* Tucson: University of Arizona Press, 2007.

The Covered Wagon. Redding, Calif.: Shasta Historical Society, 1966.

Coward, John. *The Newspaper Indian: Native American Identity in the Press, 1820–90.* Urbana: University of Illinois Press, 1999.

Curtin, Jeremiah. *Memoirs of Jeremiah Curtin.* Madison: State Historical Society of Wisconsin, 1940.

———. *Myths of the Modocs.* Boston: Little, Brown, 1912.

Cutter, Barbara. "The Female Indian Killer Memorialized: Hannah Duston and the Nineteenth-Century Feminization of American Violence." *Journal of Women's History* 20 (Summer 2008): 10–33.

De Certeau, Michel. *The Writing of History.* Trans. Thomas Conley. New York: Columbia University Press, 1988.

Deloria, Philip J. *Indians in Unexpected Places.* Lawrence: University Press of Kansas, 2004.

Deloria, Vine, Jr. *Custer Died for Your Sins: An Indian Manifesto.* Austin: University of Texas Press, 1988.

Derrida, Jacques. *Given Time: 1. Counterfeit Money.* Trans. Peggy Kamuf. Chicago: University of Chicago Press, 1992.

Deverell, William. *Whitewashed Adobe: The Rise of Los Angeles and the Remaking of Its Mexican Past.* Berkeley: University of California Press, 2005.

Dillon, Richard H. *Burnt-Out Fires.* Englewood Cliffs, N.J.: Prentice-Hall, 1973.

———. "Costs of the Modoc War." *California Historical Society Quarterly* 28 (June 1949): 161–64.

Drannan, William F. *Thirty-One Years on the Plains and in the Mountains; or, The Last Voice from the Plains: An Authentic Record of a Life Time of Hunting, Trapping, Scouting, and Indian Fighting in the Far West.* Chicago: Rhodes and McClure, 1900.

Drew, Harry J. *Pages from the Past.* Klamath Falls, Ore.: Klamath County Museum, 1979.

Dumont, Clayton. "The Politics of Scientific Objections to Repatriation." *Wicazo Sa Review* 18 (Spring 2003): 109–28.

Edwards, Thomas Augustus. *Daring Donald McKay; or, The Last War Trail of the Modocs.* Erie, Pa.: Herald, 1884.

———. *Luk-cay-oti, Spotted Wolf.* Corry, Pa.: Oregon Indian Medicine, [1885].

Elliott, Michael A. *Custerology: The Enduring Legacy of the Indian Wars and George Armstrong Custer.* Chicago: University of Chicago Press, 2007.

Finnegan, Jordana. *Narrating the American West: New Forms of Historical Memory.* New York: Cambia, 2008.

Flores, Richard. *Remembering the Alamo: Memory, Modernity, and the Master Symbol.* Austin: University of Texas Press, 2002.

Foote, Kenneth E. "To Remember and Forget: Archives, Memory, and Culture." *American Archivist* 53 (Summer 1990): 378–92.

Foster, Doug. "Imperfect Justice: The Modoc War Crimes Trial of 1873." *Oregon Historical Quarterly* 100 (Fall 1999): 246–87.

Frather, Julia F. A. "Fourth of July at the Klamath Reservation." *Overland Monthly,* December 1903, 116–23.

Frost, Linda. *Never One Nation: Freaks, Savages, and Whiteness in U.S. Popular Culture, 1850–1877.* Minneapolis: University of Minnesota Press, 2005.

Ganoe, John Tilson. "The History of the Oregon and California Railroad." *Oregon Historical Quarterly* 25 (September 1924): 236–83.

———. "The History of the Oregon and California Railroad—II." *Oregon Historical Quarterly* 25 (December 1924): 330–52.

Gaston, Joseph, and George H. Himes. *The Centennial History of Oregon, 1811–1912.* Chicago: Clarke, 1912.

Gendzel, Glen. "Pioneers and Padres: Competing Mythologies in Northern and Southern California, 1850–1930." *Western Historical Quarterly* 32 (Spring 2001): 55–81.

Genetin-Pilawa, C. Joseph. *Crooked Paths to Allotment: The Fight over Federal Indian Policy after the Civil War.* Chapel Hill: University of North Carolina Press, 2012.

George, Stephen. *Enterprising Minnesotans: 150 Years of Business Pioneers.* Minneapolis: University of Minnesota Press, 2005.

Gienapp, William E. "'Politics Seem to Enter into Everything': Political Culture in the North, 1840–1860." In *Essays on American Antebellum Politics, 1840–1860,* ed. Stephen E. Maizlish and John J. Kushma, 14–69. College Station: Texas A&M University Press for the University of Texas at Arlington, 1982.

Glassberg, David. *Sense of History: The Place of the Past in American Life.* Amherst: University of Massachusetts Press, 2001.

Glasson, William H. *Federal Military Pensions in the United States.* New York: Oxford University Press, 1918.

———. "The National Pension System as Applied to the Civil War and the War with Spain." *Annals of the American Academy of Political and Social Science* 19 (March 1902): 40–62.

Good, Rachel Applegate, Linsy Sisemore, Harry B. Schultz, and Howard I. Schuyler. *History of Klamath County, Oregon.* Klamath Falls, Ore.: n.p., 1941.

Gray, Lora Taylor. "'Winners of the West': A Personal Reminiscence of Lauren Winfield Aldrich." *Journal of the West* 33 (January 1994): 96–100.

Green, Rayna. "The Indian in Popular American Culture." In *Handbook of North American Indians,* ed. Wilcomb E. Washburn, 4:587–606. Washington, D.C.: Smithsonian Institution, 1988.

———. "The Pocahontas Perplex: The Image of Indian Women in American Culture." *Massachusetts Review* 16 (Autumn 1975): 698–714.

Greene, Jerome. *Indian War Veterans: Memories of Army Life and Campaigns in the West, 1864–1898.* New York: Savas Beatie, 2007.

Grover, La Fayette. *Report of Governor Grover to General Schofield on the Modoc War.* Salem, Ore.: Brown, 1874.

Halbwachs, Maurice. *On Collective Memory*. Chicago: University of Chicago Press, 1992.

Hall, Roger A. *Performing the American Frontier, 1870–1906*. Cambridge University Press, 2001.

Hamilton, John H. "In the Lava Beds: The Scene of the Canby Massacre Revisited." *Overland Monthly and Out West Magazine*, July 1894, 97–100.

Hardinge, Seth. *Modoc Jack; or, The Lion of the Lava Beds*. New York: Champion, 1873.

Harrison, Jonathan Baxter. *The Latest Studies on Indian Reservations*. Philadelphia: Indian Rights Association, 1887.

Hauptman, Laurence. *The Iroquois in the Civil War*. Syracuse: Syracuse University Press, 1993.

Hidy, Ralph W., Frank Ernest Hill, and Allen Nevins. *Timber and Men: The Weyerhaeuser Story*. New York: Macmillan, 1963.

Horner, John B. *Oregon: Her History, Her Great Men, Her Literature*. Corvallis, Ore.: Press of the Gazette-Times, 1919.

Hong, Grace. *Ruptures of American Capital: Women of Color Feminism and the Culture of Immigrant Labor*. Minneapolis: University of Minnesota Press, 2006.

Howard, Charles. *The Squaw Spy; or, The Ranger of the Lava-Beds*. New York: Beadle and Adams, 1873.

Huhndorf, Shari. *Going Native: Indians in the American Cultural Imagination*. Ithaca: Cornell University Press, 2001.

Hurtado, Albert A. "The Modocs and the Jones Family Indian Ring: Quaker Administration of the Quapaw Agency, 1873–1879." In *Oklahoma's Forgotten Indians*, ed. Robert E. Smith, 86–107. Oklahoma City: Oklahoma Historical Society, 1981.

Isenberg, Andrew C. *Mining California: An Ecological History*. New York: Hill and Wang, 2006.

Jacobson, Matthew Frye. *Roots Too: White Ethnic Revival in Post–Civil Rights America*. Cambridge: Harvard University Press, 2006.

Jacoby, Karl. *Shadows at Dawn: A Borderlands Massacre and the Violence of History*. New York: Penguin, 2008.

Jaffer, Jameel, and Amrit Singh. *Administration of Torture: A Documentary Record from Washington to Abu Ghraib and Beyond*. New York: Columbia University Press, 2009.

James, Cheewa. *Modoc: The Tribe That Wouldn't Die*. Happy Camp, Calif.: Naturegraph, 2008.

Jefferson, Thomas. *The Papers of Thomas Jefferson: Retirement Series*. Ed. J. Jefferson Looney. Vol. 1. Princeton: Princeton University Press, 2004.

Kammen, Michael. *Mystic Chords of Memory: The Transformation of Tradition in American Culture*. New York: Knopf, 1991.

Keith, LeeAnna. *The Colfax Massacre: The Untold Story of Black Power, White Terror, and the Death of Reconstruction*. New York: Oxford University Press, 2008.

Klamath Chamber of Commerce. *Klamath County, Oregon*. San Francisco: Janssen, 1911.

Klamath County: Its Resources and Advantages, Its Present and Future: The Land of Great Pines, Hardy Cattle, Wonderful Lakes, and Temperate Climate. Klamath Falls, Ore.: Klamath Falls Express, 1900.

Klamath County Board of Immigration. *The Great Klamath Basin of Southern Oregon: Fertile Lands and Happy Homes.* Oakland, Calif.: Pacific, 1885.

Klamath Development Company. *Klamath Falls, Oregon: The Distributing Point for a Vast Timber, Live Stock, and Agricultural Empire.* San Francisco: Sunset, 1909.

Klein, Kerwin Lee. *From History to Theory.* Berkeley: University of California Press, 2011.

——. *Frontiers of Historical Imagination: Narrating the European Conquest of Native America, 1890–1990.* Berkeley: University of California Press, 1999.

Klein, Milton M. "Everyman His Own Historian: Carl Becker as Historiographer." *History Teacher* 19 (November 1985): 101–9.

Klima, Alan. *The Funeral Casino: Meditation, Massacre, and Exchange with the Dead in Thailand.* Princeton: Princeton University Press, 2002.

Konkle, Maureen. *Writing Indian Nations: Native Intellectuals and the Politics of Historiography, 1827–1863.* Chapel Hill: University of North Carolina Press, 2004.

Kroeber, Alfred. *Handbook of the Indians of California.* New York: Dover, 1976.

Kropp, Phoebe. *California Vieja: Culture and Memory in a Modern American Place.* Berkeley: University of California Press, 2006.

Lass, Andrew. "Romantic Documents and Political Monuments: The Meaning-Fulfillment of History in Nineteenth-Century Czech Nationalism." *American Ethnologist* 15 (August 1988): 456–71.

Lawson, Benjamin S. "Joaquin Miller (Cincinnatus Hiner)." In *Encyclopedia of American Poetry: The Nineteenth Century,* ed. Eric L. Haralson and John Hollander, 301–2. Chicago: Fitzroy Dearborn, 1998.

Leavitt, A. L. "Reflections and Recollections of Circuit Judge A. L. Leavitt, an Address to the Daughters of the American Revolution, September 17, 1925." *Klamath Echoes* 13 (1975): 55.

Lemann, Nicholas. *Redemption: The Last Battle of the Civil War.* New York: Farrar, Straus and Giroux, 2006.

Libby, O. G. "Review of *The Indian History of the Modoc War and the Causes That Led to It* by Jeff C. Riddle, the Son of Winema." *Mississippi Valley Historical Review* 2 (June 1915): 136.

Limerick, Patricia Nelson. *The Legacy of Conquest: The Unbroken Past of the American West.* New York: Norton, 1987.

Lindsay, Brendan C. *Murder State: California's Native American Genocide, 1846–1873.* Lincoln: University of Nebraska Press, 2012.

MacConnell, Stuart. *Glorious Contentment: The Grand Army of the Republic, 1865–1900.* Chapel Hill: University of North Carolina Press, 1992.

Mardock, Robert. *The Reformers and the American Indian.* Columbia: University of Missouri Press, 1971.

Markovitz, Jonathan. *Legacies of Lynching: Racial Violence and Memory.* Minneapolis: University of Minnesota Press, 2004.

Marriott, Alice, and Carol K. Rachlin, eds. *American Indian Mythology*. New York: Crowell, 1968.

Marx, Karl. "Eighteenth Brumaire of Louis Bonaparte." In *The Marx-Engels Reader*, ed. Robert C. Tucker, 594–617. New York: Norton, 1978.

McGerr, Michael. *The Decline of Popular Politics: The American North, 1865–1928*. New York: Oxford University Press, 1986.

McKivigan, John. *Forgotten Firebrand: James Redpath and the Making of Nineteenth-Century America*. Ithaca: Cornell University Press, 2008.

Meacham, Alfred B. *Wigwam and War-Path; or, The Royal Chief in Chains*. Boston: Dale, 1875.

——. *Wi-ne-ma (The Woman-Chief) and Her People*. Hartford, Conn.: American, 1876.

Meyer, Carter Jones, and Diana Royer, eds. *Selling the Indian: Commercializing and Appropriating American Indian Culture*. Tucson: University of Arizona Press, 2001.

Miller, Joaquin. *Life amongst the Modocs: Unwritten History*. 1873. Berkeley: Urion, 1996.

——. *My Life among the Indians*. Chicago: Belford-Clarke, 1892.

——. *My Own Story*. Chicago: Belford-Clarke, 1890.

——. *Paquita, the Indian Heroine*. Hartford, Conn.: American, 1881.

——. *Songs of the Sierras*. London: Longmans, Green, Reader, and Dyer, 1871.

——. *Unwritten History*. London: Bentley, 1874.

Moses, L. G. *Wild West Shows and the Images of American Indians, 1883–1933*. Albuquerque: University of New Mexico Press, 1999.

Most, Stephen. *River of Renewal: Myth and History in the Klamath Basin*. Seattle: University of Washington Press, 2006.

Murray, Keith A. *The Modocs and Their War*. Norman: University of Oklahoma Press, 1959.

Nash, Philleo. "The Place of Religious Revivalism in the Formation of the Intercultural Community on Klamath Reservation." In *Social Anthropology of North American Tribes*, ed. Fred Eggan, 377–449. Chicago: University of Chicago Press, 1955.

Nora, Pierre. *Realms of Memory: The Construction of the French Past*. New York: Columbia University Press, 1996.

O'Brien, Jean M. *Firsting and Lasting: Writing Indians Out of Existence in New England*. Minneapolis: University of Minnesota Press, 2010.

O'Callaghan, Jerry A. "Klamath Indians and the Wagon Road Grant." *Oregon Historical Quarterly* 53 (March 1952): 23–28.

Ostler, Jeffrey. *The Plains Sioux and U.S. Colonialism from Lewis and Clark to Wounded Knee*. New York: Cambridge University Press, 2004.

Palmquist, Peter. "Imagemakers of the Modoc War: Louis Heller and Eadweard Muybridge." *Journal of California Anthropology* 4 (Winter 1977): 206–21.

"Panel Discussion of the Modoc War by Descendants of Participants." *Journal of the Shaw Historical Library* 3 (Fall 1988): 45–52.

Parry, Jonathan. "The Gift, the Indian Gift, and the 'Indian Gift.'" *Man* 21 (September 1986): 453–73.

Peterson, Martin Severin. *Joaquin Miller: Literary Frontiersman*. Stanford: Stanford University Press, 1937.

Powers, Stephen. "The California Indians, No. VIII—The Modocs." *Overland Monthly*, June 1873, 535–45.

Quinn, Arthur. *Hell with the Fire Out: A History of the Modoc War*. Boston: Faber and Faber, 1997.

Rabasa, José. *Writing Violence on the Northern Frontier: The Historiography of Sixteenth Century New Mexico and Florida and the Legacy of Conquest*. Durham: Duke University Press, 2000.

Raibmon, Paige. *Authentic Indians: Episodes of Encounter from the Late-Nineteenth-Century Northwest Coast*. Durham: Duke University Press, 2005.

Reep, Diana. *The Rescue and Romance: Popular Novels before World War I*. Bowling Green, Ohio: Bowling Green State University Popular Press, 1982.

Riddle, Jeff C. *The Indian History of the Modoc War and the Causes That Led to It*. San Francisco: Marnell, 1914.

Robbins, William G. *Landscapes of Promise: The Oregon Story, 1800–1940*. Seattle: University of Washington Press, 1997.

Sayre, Gordon Mitchell. *The Indian Chief as Tragic Hero: Native Resistance and the Literatures of America, From Moctezuma to Tecumseh*. Chapel Hill: University of North Carolina Press, 2005.

Scott, Harvey Whitefield, ed. *History of Portland, Oregon, with Illustrations and Biographical Sketches of Prominent Citizens and Pioneers*. Portland, Ore.: Mason, 1890.

Sedgwick, Catharine Maria. *Hope Leslie; or, Early Times in the Massachusetts*. Ed. Mary Kelley. New Brunswick: Rutgers University Press, 1987.

Shaver, F. A., et al. *An Illustrated History of Central Oregon*. Spokane: Western Historical, 1905.

Silva, Noenoe. *Aloha Betrayed: Native Hawaiian Resistance to American Colonialism*. Durham: Duke University Press, 2004.

Sim, David. "The Peace Policy of Ulysses S. Grant." *American Nineteenth Century History* 9 (September 2008): 241–68.

Simpson, William. *Meeting the Sun: A Journey All around the World through Egypt, China, Japan, and California*. London: Longmans, Green, Reader, and Dyer, 1874.

Skocpol, Theda. *Protecting Soldiers and Mothers: The Political Origins of Social Policy in the United States*. Cambridge: Belknap Press of Harvard University Press, 1992.

Skogen, Larry. *Indian Depredation Claims, 1796–1920*. Norman: University of Oklahoma Press, 1996.

Slotkin, Richard. *The Fatal Environment: The Myth of the Frontier in the Age of Industrialization*. Norman: University of Oklahoma Press, 1998.

———. *Gunfighter Nation: The Myth of the Frontier in Twentieth-Century America*. New York: Atheneum, 1992.

Smith, Jean Edward. *Grant*. New York City: Simon and Schuster, 2001.

Smith, Linda Tuhiwai. *Decolonizing Methodologies: Research and Indigenous Peoples*. London: Zed, 1999.

Solnit, Rebecca. *River of Shadows: Eadweard Muybridge and the Technological Wild West.* New York: Penguin, 2004.

Southern, May H. "The Hard Winter of 1889–1890." In *The Covered Wagon,* 9–11. Redding, Calif.: Shasta Historical Society, 1966.

Spier, Leslie. *Klamath Ethnography.* Berkeley: University of California Press, 1930.

Starr, Paul. *The Creation of the Media: The Political Origins of Modern Communication.* New York: Basic Books, 2004.

Steele, Rufus. "The Cave of Captain Jack." *Sunset Magazine,* January 1913, 565–68.

Stern, Steve. *Remembering Pinochet's Chile: On the Eve of London 1998.* Durham: Duke University Press, 2004.

Stern, Theodore. "Klamath and Modoc." In *Handbook of North American Indians,* 12:446–66. Washington, D.C.: Smithsonian Institution, 1998.

——. "The Klamath Indians and the Treaty of 1864." *Oregon Historical Quarterly* 57 (December 1956): 229–73.

——. *The Klamath Tribe: A People and Their Reservation.* Seattle: University of Washington Press, 1965.

Stone, Buena. *Fort Klamath: Frontier Post in Oregon, 1863–1890.* Dallas: Royal, 1964.

Strahorn, Robert E. *Where Rolls the Oregon.* Denver: Denver Times, 1882.

Sturken, Marita. *Tangled Memories: The Vietnam War, the AIDS Epidemic, and the Politics of Remembering.* Berkeley: University of California Press, 1997.

——. *Tourists of History: Memory, Kitsch, and Consumerism from Oklahoma City to Ground Zero.* Durham: Duke University Press, 2007.

Taussig, Michael. "The Sun Gives without Receiving: An Old Story." *Comparative Studies in Society and History* 37 (April 1995): 368–98.

Thompson, Erwin N. *The Modoc War: Its Military History and Topography.* Sacramento: Argus, 1971.

Thompson, William. *Reminiscences of a Pioneer.* San Francisco: n.p., 1912.

Tilton, Robert S. *Pocahontas: The Evolution of an American Narrative.* New York: Cambridge University Press, 1994.

Trouillot, Michel-Rolph. *Silencing the Past: Power and the Production of History.* Boston: Beacon, 1995.

Turner, Stan. *The Years of Harvest: A History of the Tule Lake Basin.* Eugene, Ore.: Spencer Creek, 2002.

Twain, Mark. *The Complete Works of Mark Twain.* Vol. 24, *Mark Twain's Speeches.* New York: Harper, 1923.

Utley, Robert. *The Indian Frontier of the American West, 1846–1890.* Albuquerque: University of New Mexico Press, 1984.

Warren, Louis. *Buffalo Bill's America: William Cody and the Wild West Show.* New York: Knopf, 2005.

Warrior, Robert. *The People and the Word: Reading Native Nonfiction.* Minneapolis: University of Minnesota Press, 2005.

Wells, Harry. *History of Siskiyou County, California.* Oakland, Calif.: Stewart, 1881.

——. "The Massacre of the Peace Commissioners." *Cosmopolitan,* October 1891, 724.

Werner, Herman. *On the Western Frontier with the United States Cavalry Fifty Years Ago.* Akron, Ohio: Werner, 1934.

West, Elliott. *The Last Indian War: The Nez Perce Story*. New York: Oxford University Press, 2009.

———. "Reconstructing Race." *Western Historical Quarterly* 34 (Spring 2003): 7–26.

Whaley, Gray. *Oregon and the Collapse of Illahee: U.S. Empire and the Transformation of an Indigenous World, 1792–1859*. Chapel Hill: University of North Carolina Press, 2010.

Wilkinson, Charles. *Blood Struggle: The Rise of Modern Indian Nations*. New York: Norton, 2005.

Williams, James. *Life and Adventures of James Williams, a Fugitive Slave, with a Full Description of the Underground Railroad*. 4th ed. San Francisco: Women's Union Book and Job, 1873.

———. *Life and Adventures of James Williams, a Fugitive Slave, with a Full Description of the Underground Railroad*. 5th ed. Philadelphia: Sickler, 1875.

Wilson, Hugh R. *The Causes and Significance of the Modoc War*. Klamath Falls, Ore.: Guide Print, 1953.

Witt, John Fabian. *Lincoln's Code: The Laws of War in American History*. New York: Free Press, 2013.

Wolfe, Patrick. "Settler Colonialism and the Elimination of the Native." *Journal of Genocide Research* 8 (December 2006): 387–409.

Wrobel, David. *Promised Lands: Promotion, Memory, and the Creation of the American West*. Lawrence: University Press of Kansas, 2002.

Yoneyama, Lisa. *Hiroshima Traces: Time, Space, and the Dialectic of Memory*. Berkeley: University of California Press, 1999.

Young, Harvey. "The Black Body and Souvenir in American Lynching." *Theatre Journal* 57 (December 2005): 639–57.

DISSERTATIONS AND PAPERS

Blee, Lisa. "Framing Chief Leshi: Narratives and the Politics of Historical Justice in the South Puget Sound." Ph.D. diss., University of Minnesota, 2008.

Fossum, Embert A. "Newsmen on the Warpath: A Study of the Newspaper Coverage of the Modoc, Nez Perce, and Bannock-Paiute Indian Wars of the 1870s." Master's thesis, University of Oregon, 1973.

Laugesen, Amanda Pia Krarup. "Making Western Pasts: Historical Societies of Kansas, Wisconsin, and Oregon, 1870–1920." Ph.D. diss., Australian National University, 2000.

Madley, Benjamin. "American Genocide: The California Indian Catastrophe, 1846–1873." Ph.D. diss., Yale University, 2009.

Norrgard, Chantal M. "Seasons of Change: Treaty Rights, Labor, and the Historical Memory of Work among Lake Superior Ojibwe, 1870–1942." Ph.D. diss., University of Minnesota, 2008.

Phinney, Edward Serle. "Alfred B. Meacham, Promoter of Indian Reform." Ph.D. diss., University of Oregon, 1963.

Zakoji, Hiroto. "Klamath Culture Change." Master's thesis, University of Oregon, 1953.

Acknowledgments

This book has come about through the support of my family, friends, and colleagues. I thank James F. Brooks, Robin Einhorn, Carolyn Knapp, Robert Middlekauff, and Jen Spear for nurturing my interest in history and historiography during my undergraduate years at the University of California, Berkeley. Kevin Murphy and Jeani O'Brien have been both mentors and friends as they provided encouragement, insight, and unerring guidance through my doctoral training at the University of Minnesota and beyond. I owe an additional debt of gratitude to Jean Langford for expanding my horizons, Tracey Deutsch for grounding them in political economy, and Patrick McNamara for his insights into performance and Latin American studies and for suggesting that I get a basketball. Many others at the University of Minnesota have influenced this book. Sarah Chambers, David Chang, Kirsten Fischer, Chris Isett, Regina Kunzel, Rus Menard, Jeffrey Pilcher, Ajay Skaria, and Barbara Welke enriched this project and helped me think about the production of historical knowledge in new ways. For their helpful feedback on early drafts of this book, I thank the participants in the American Indian Studies Workshop; the Workshop for the Comparative History of Women, Gender, and Sexuality; and the Graduate Workshop on Modern History at the University of Minnesota. Special thanks go to Justin Biel, Lisa Blee, Demetri Debe, Tracey Deutsch, Jill Doerfler, Seth Epstein, Alan Fujishin, Rob Gilmer, Sheryl Lightfoot, Kevin Murphy, Chantal Norrgard, Jeani O'Brien, Andy Paul, Heidi Kiiwetinepinesiik Stark, Jimmy Sweet, Laurie Richmond, Kate Williams, Mike Wise, and Liz Zanoni.

This book simply would not have been possible if not for a series of grants and fellowships that funded my research and introduced me to vibrant intellectual communities. I received early support from the following institutions at the University of Minnesota: the Center for Early Modern History; the College of Liberal Arts in the form of a Graduate Research Partnership Program; the American Indian Studies Workshop; and the Department of History in the form of an A. Beebe White Fellowship. I also received support from the Newberry Library's D'Arcy McNickle Center for American Indian and Indigenous Studies in the form of a Newberry Consortium in American Indian Studies Fellowship and from Yale University and the Howard R. Lamar Center for the Study of Frontiers and Borders, where I held the inaugural Henry Roe Cloud Dissertation Writing Fellowship in American Indian and Indigenous Studies.

More recently, I have been welcomed with open arms into the Department of History at York University in Toronto. Completing this book would have been unimaginable without the generous support, caring guidance, and valuable advice of my colleagues. Thank you to Bettina Bradbury, Jonathan Edmondson, Marc Egnal, Sakis Gekas, Aitana Guia, Craig Heron, Ben Kelly, Sean Kheraj, Janice Kim, David Koffman, Rachel Koopmans, Molly Ladd-Taylor, Marcel Martel, Kate McPherson, Jaclyn Neel, Deb Neill, Carolyn Podruchny, Nick Rogers, Anne Rubenstein, Myra Rutherdale, Marlene Shore, Adrian Shubert, Marc Stein, Jessica van Horssen, and Bill Wicken. From the York–U of T Indigenous History Writing Group, I thank Carl Benn, James Cullingham, Erin Dolmage, Victoria Freeman, Brittany Luby, Stacy Nation-Knapper, Alison Norman, Melissa Otis, Émilie Pigeon, Carolyn Podruchny, and Dan Rueck. I would also like to thank York University's Faculty of Liberal Arts and Professional Studies for its generous support.

This book has benefited greatly from the wisdom, generosity, and patience of my editors as well as publishing and archival professionals. Special thanks go to Mark Simpson-Vos, Caitlin Bell-Butterfield, Zachary Read, and the whole staff at the University of North Carolina Press. Thank you to Natasha Varner for her work with the First Peoples initiative. And I especially thank Coll Thrush and Ari Kelman for their careful and thought-provoking comments on the manuscript and for their encouragement and support throughout this process. I also thank Dave Kruse and David Larson at Lava Beds National Monument; Todd Kepple and the entire staff at the Klamath County Museum; Ileana Maestas at the California Indian Heritage Center; Geoff Wexler at the Oregon Historical Society; David Farrell, Peter Hanff, and David Kessler at the Bancroft Library; John Aubrey, Diane Dillon, and Scott Manning Stevens at the Newberry Library; and George Miles and Morgan Swan at the Beinecke Rare Book and Manuscript Library.

The field of Modoc War studies and Klamath Basin Indian history is an intimate one, and I have been welcomed into it. Ryan Bartholomew, Doris Omundson Bowan, Fred Brown, Anne Hiller Clark, Mark Clark, Barbara Ditman, Craig Dorman, Kevin Fields, Lee Juillerat, Todd Kepple, Stephen Mark, and John William Quinn all shared their knowledge of the basin with me. Modoc War enthusiast Daniel Woodhead helped me figure out many things and put me back on the right track more than once. A special thanks go to the members of the Klamath Tribes and the descendants of those connected to the Modoc War who shared their thoughts, experiences, and stories with me, particularly Christine Allen, Tom Ball, Raefield Benson, Perry Chocktoot, Taylor David, Clay Dumont, Shawn Dumont, Debbie Herrera, Cheewa James, Gerald Skelton, and Lynn Schonchin.

I cannot imagine having written this book without the support of numerous friends. Frequent discussions with Lisa Blee, Demetri Debe, Seth Epstein, Joe Genetin-Pilawa, Rob Gilmer, Andy Paul, and Mike Wise have deepened my understanding of memory, American history, and culture criticism. Ned Blackhawk, Alyssa Mt. Pleasant, Josh Reid, and Ted Van Alst welcomed me to Yale University with hospitality, friendship, and humor. Marcel Garcia, Ryan Hall, Todd Holmes,

Khili Johnson, Andrew Offenburger, and Ashley Riley Sousa welcomed me into the Westerners' community, and Johnny Mack Faragher, Jay Gitlin, and Edith Rotkopf hosted me at the Howard R. Lamar Center for the Study of Frontiers and Borders. My transition to York University and my introduction to Canadian life have been made all the richer for the warm friendship of Sakis Gekas, Craig Heron, Sean Kheraj, Janice Kim, Molly Ladd-Taylor, Jaclyn Neel, Deb Neill, Anne Rubenstein, and Marc Stein. And a special thanks go to Adrian Shubert for showing me the ropes, to Jennifer Polk for being my first Canadian friend, and to Rachel Koopmans for always being there and for welcoming me to Toronto. Finally, this project benefited from conversations with Damon Akins, Kent Blansett, James Brooks, Kevin Bruyneel, Cathleen Cahill, Jessica Cattelino, Christine Delucia, Joe Genetin-Pilawa, David Grua, Angela Pulley Hudson, J. Kēhaulani Kauanui, Ari Kelman, Jeffrey Means, Jeff Ostler, Juliana Hu Pegues, Renya Ramirez, Scott Manning Stevens, Coll Thrush, Natasha Varner, Nat Zappia, and many, many others.

Above all, I thank my family. My father, Boyd, has nurtured my love for history since I was a young boy, and in many ways I have written this book with him always in my mind. My sisters, Emiko, Angela, and Suzanne; my nieces, Alora, Emily, and Willow; and my mother, Mary, have brought joy to my heart and meaning to my life. My in-laws, Peter and Donna Thomas, have been enthusiastic supporters of my work and model scholars in their own right. But ultimately none of this would have been possible if not for the love, support, and encouragement of my partner and best friend, Tanya Cothran. She has been this book's most enthusiastic supporter and keenest editor. And so I dedicate it to her with all my heart.

Index

Page numbers in italics refer to illustrations.

Afghanistan, 76

Agriculture: fruit industry, 117, 130; irrigation, 127–28, 131; ranching, 8, 25, 32, 37, 42, 115, 117, 119–20, 122, 123, 124, 126, 130, 132, 139, 153, 162, 172; sheep industry, 122, 171–72, 174–75

Alcatraz Island, 9, 72

Allen, Christine, 108

Allotments, 115, 122, 125, 126–27, 130, 132, 137, 154, 157

Alsea Indian Reservation, 39

Alturas Plain-Dealer, 163, 177, 178, 179, 180

American Colonization Society, 65

American Historical Association, 6

American Indian Aid Association, 68, 71

American innocence. *See* Innocence: American

American West: colonization of, 15–16, 20, 109, 187; and historical memory, 21, 23, 157, 185; promotion of, 116, 123; violence in, 12, 19, 34, 53, 109, 145, 187

Antowine, 151

Applegate, Ivan D., 114, *167*

Applegate, Jesse, 39, 40

Applegate, Oliver: as captain of Oregon Militia, 152; and commemoration, 135, 162, 174; and Indian war veterans organizations, 143, 152; as member of Alfred B. Meacham Lecture Company, 88; and promotional activities, 124; as superintendent of Klamath Reservation, 85, 88, 121, 135

Army and Navy Journal, 49, 59

Ashland, Ore., 8, 125

Assimilation, 94, 125, 154, 191

Babcock, O. L., 152

Baker, Fred, 156

Bancroft, Hubert Howe, 3

Barncho, 9, 68, 71, 72, 73

Baxter, Lenox, 146

Beatty, Joseph L., 158

Becker, Carl, 6

Bend, Ore., 106

Ben-John, Nancy, 158, 159

Bennett, Etta, 159

Bennett, James Gordon, Jr., 30, 31, 41

Ben Wright Massacre, 18, 42, 46, 56

Black Jim, 68, 71; execution of, 9, 15

Board of Indian Commissioners, 39

Bogus Charley, 64, 69, 73, 118

Boosterism, 25, 116, 117, 131, 139; and promotional literature, 14, 116, 122, 131–32

Booth, Newton, 35

Boston Charley, 68, 71, 73; execution of, 9, 15, 73

Boston Evening Journal, 29

Boston Evening Transcript, 56, 138

Boston Globe, 70

Boston Herald, 121

Boutelle, Frazier A., 33

Brown, Dee, 82

Brown, Dick, 159

Brown, Frederick, 174

Brown, Harrison, 155, 159

Brown, Henry, 150, 158, 159

Brown, Kate, 159

Brown, Sargent, 153, 159, 160

"Buffalo Bill" (William Cody), 20, 21, 85, 88, 133

Bureau of Indian Affairs, 59, 107, 190

Bureau of Pensions, 142, 143, 149, 152, 153, 154, 155, 156, 157, 158, 161, 207 (n. 1)
Butler, Robert R., 153
Byrd, Jodi A., 77, 206 (n. 3)

California, 10, 37, 146, 164, 176, 181
California and Oregon Land Company, 119, 126, 127
California Diamond Jubilee, 180–81, 183
California Indian Heritage Center, 10, 200 (n. 10)
California Society of Pioneers, 10
Camp Grant, Ariz., 34
Camp Yainax, 32
Canby, Edward R. S., 3; death of, 4, 9, 18, 48–50, 53, 59, 69, 73, 134, 166; and peace commission, 39, 40, 48–50, 59, 68; representations of, 4–5, 24, 26, 29, 32, 50–53, 51, 83, 95, 132, 162, 164, 165–66, 168, 172, 183, 184, 185; responses to death of, 54, 58, 62, 66, 74
Canby's Cross, 4–6, 5, 7, 166, 167, 168, 169, 172
Captain Jack: appropriations of, 118, 132, 133, 172, 192; and commemoration, 177, 190, 192; display of body, 11, 93, 201; execution of, 9–11, 15, 72–73, 81, 168, 173; media representations of, 33, 41, 43, 44, 49, 51–52, 54, 56, 62, 63, 74–75, 98–99, 170; memorabilia of, 10, 12, 14; and Modoc relocation, 32, 35, 43, 45, 193; and peace negotiations, 41, 44, 47; and St. Valentine Day's Treaty, 37; status among Modoc, 63, 71, 155; surrender of, 4–5, 7, 40, 44, 62, 64; theatrical representations of, 84, 95, 98; and Toby Riddle, 105, 108, 137–38; trial of, 64, 68, 71, 73
Captain Jack's Stronghold, 1, 2, 4, 5, 48, 53, 55, 59, 61, 168, 169, 172, 174, 175
Carlisle Indian School, 159
Carson, Kit, 133, 134
Case, Samuel, 39, 45
Cayuse War, 18
Chapman, Thomas, 151

Checaskane, Cinda, 159–60
Checaskane, Eli "Walter," 159–60
Chemult, Ore., 106
Cherokee Nation v. Georgia, 78
Cheyenne people, 146
Chicago Daily Inter Ocean, 8, 56
Chicago Daily Tribune, 50, 56
Chicago Journal, 56
Chicago Times, 56
Chǐkclǐkam-Lupalkuelátko, 33, 60. See also Scarface Charley
Chiloquin, 87, 135
Chiloquin, George, 157
Chiloquin, Mary, 156, 158, 159
Chiloquin, Ore., 17, 129, 156
Cholah, Peter, 152, 153, 155, 159
Christian martyrdom, 5, 19, 24, 52, 183
Civil War, 5, 11, 30, 31, 34, 36, 62, 67, 116, 144, 146. See also Reconstruction
Cleveland, Grover, 120
Colonialism. See Settler colonialism: and colonialism
Columbia River, 117, 170, 191
Colwell-Chanthaphonh, Chip, 195
Congress, U.S.: and Indian policy, 34, 38–39, 47; land grants, 119, 127; and legislation, 74, 115, 190; and parks, 176, 178, 217 (n. 57); and pensions, 81–82, 103, 142, 143, 150, 153, 155, 159; treaties, 126–27, 193. See also Indian depredation claims system
Constitution, U.S., 76
Cookingham, R. T., 152, 155
Copperfield, Jim, 153, 159
Copperfield, Mary Ann, 153, 158
Corruption: and Gilded Age press, 37–38, 40, 41; accusations of in Indian affairs, 34, 37–38, 39, 40, 43, 86
Council Grove, 46. See also Treaty of 1864
Crater Lake National Park, 176
Crawford, Wade, 158
Crosby Expedition, 18
Curtin, Jeremiah, 3, 4, 120
Curtis, H. P., 66, 68, 72
Cusick, Cornelius C., 152

Custer, George Armstrong, 3, 21, 167, 175, 184, 185
Cutter, Barbara, 167

Daily Alta California, 33, 75
Daily Colorado Miner, 54
Daily Evening Bulletin, 169
Daily Oregon Herald, 35, 202 (n. 24)
Dakota War of 1862, 9, 56
Dancing, 4, 35, 106, 113, 180
Daughters of the American Revolution, 106, 162, 209 (n. 1)
David, Allen, 69, 87, 88
Davis, Jefferson C., 62, 64
Davis, Jefferson F., 74
Dawes Act. *See* General Allotment Act
Delano, Columbus, 39, 45, 71, 86
Delaware people, 146
Deloria, Philip, 108, 170, 181
Deloria, Vine, Jr., 108
Democratic Party, 26, 67
Department of Agriculture, U.S., 106, 191
Dime novels, 14, 82, 98, 99, 101, 165
Disease, 15, 16, 86, 196
Donation Land Claim Act of 1850, 47
Drannan, William, 132–34, 136
Dred Scott v. Sanford, 65
Dry Lake, Battle of, 63, 179
Dufur, Edmund, 152, 153
Dyar, Leroy S., 45, 48, 87, 119

Elliott, Stuart H., 152
Empire, 15, 19, 77, 78, 116, 122–23, 166, 176. *See also* Settler colonialism: and empire
Enemy combatants, 66, 76–78
É-ukskni, 16. *See also* Klamath people
Executions: Indigenous memory of, 194; and media, 8, 12, 67, 72, 74; and memorabilia, 10–11, 12, 14; of Modoc men, 9, 10, 15, 52, 64, 72, 93; as spectacle, 14, 168
Extermination, 1, 3, 4, 18, 48, 52, 56, 61–62, 65, 100, 117, 164; discourses of, 61–62, 65

Fairchild, James, 64, 65
Fairchild, John, 41, 44, 45, 64, 71, 166
Faithful, Charley, 153, 159
Fisher, Elihu, 146
Flores, Richard, 182
Foote, Kenneth E., 182
Fort Klamath, 8, 9, 17, 32, 68, 72, 75, 113, 118, 120, 121, 123, 168, 193
Franco-Prussian War, 34, 46, 50
Frank Leslie's Illustrated Newspaper, 12–13, 53–54, 57–58, 61
Frost, Linda, 57

Gardner, Washington, 149
General Allotment Act, 115, 125. *See also* Allotments
Genetin-Pilawa, C. Joseph, 39
Geneva Convention, 76
Gerishe, Peter, 146
Gilded Age, 14, 20, 24, 30–31, 35, 37, 38, 43, 52, 73, 74, 75, 78, 144, 194
Gillem, Alvan C., 59, 62, 168
Gillem's Bluff. *See* Sheepy Ridge
Global War on Terror, 76, 77–78
Gmukamps, 4, 45
Golden Bear Monument, 162–63, 164, 178, 179, 180
Gold Hill News, 34
Good, Rachel Applegate, 154
Grand Army of the Republic, 11, 144, 151–52
Grant, Ulysses S., 9, 18, 31, 34–35, 46, 47, 54, 55, 57, 62, 65, 67, 71, 72, 87–88, 90, 91, 151. *See also* Peace Policy
Greasy Grass, Battle of, 3, 167
Grover, LaFayette, 35–36, 39, 40, 53

Hamilton, John, 169–70
Hamilton, Oliver, 146
Hardinge, Seth, 98–99, 101; *Modoc Jack; or, The Lion of the Lava Beds*, 98–99
Harper's Weekly, 12, 50–51, 53, 55, 56, 60, 61–62, 75, 165
Hartford Daily Courant, 33

Hawley, Willis C., 153, 159
Heller, Louis H., 12–13, 165
Herrera, Debra, 108, 201
Hill, David, 87–88, 90, 107, 126, 208
 (n. 19)
Himes, George H., 149
Historical justice, 26, 186, 189, 195
Historical reenactment, 14, 113, 114, 115,
 116
Hoge, George B., 9, 10
Holliquilla, Anna, 159
Holliquilla, Jerry, 159
Holliquilla, Tullux, 159
Homestead Act, 125, 126
Hood, Charles S., 159, 171
Hooker Jim, 64, 69, 70, 184, 185
Horner, John B., 82
Horse Mountain, 4
Hunter, Joseph, 152
Hyzer, Josephy H., 64

Illustrated London News, 50–51
Indianapolis Sentinel, 54
Indian Court of Claims, 127
Indian Depredation Act of 1891, 147
Indian depredation claims system,
 145–47
Indian policy, 31, 34, 35, 39, 56, 67, 86,
 88, 99. See also Peace Policy
Indian Robert, 151
Indian's Friend, 138
Indigenous criminality, 5, 7, 24, 36, 39,
 46, 47, 52, 53, 54, 75, 78, 166, 194
Indigenous naming practices, 153–54
Indigenous resistance, 11, 36, 52, 66,
 81–82, 98, 135, 164, 166, 185
Indigenous sovereignty, 15–16, 22, 34, 67,
 115, 116, 130, 136, 139, 192
Innocence: American, 15, 19, 20, 23–24,
 25–26, 31–32, 36, 38, 39, 47–48, 49,
 52, 62, 75, 77–78, 96, 109, 110, 114,
 116, 143, 151, 161, 163–64, 166, 168,
 174, 179, 182, 183, 185, 186, 187, 195,
 196–97; Christian, 5, 19; Indigenous,
 52; nature of, 6, 7, 19

Jack, John, 152, 154
Jack, Millie, 158
Jackson, Albert, 150, 152, 153, 159
Jackson, Drew, 153, 156, 159
Jackson, James, 32
Jacksonville, Ore., 3
Jacobson, Matthew, 189
Jacoby, Karl, 35
James, Cheewa, 1, 2–3, 7, 171
Jefferson, Thomas, 19, 166
John, Birdie, 153, 159

Kammen, Michael, 21
Katchia, Daniel, 155
Keating Measure, 141, 142, 149
Kepple, Todd, 1
Kingsbury, George W., 8, 9, 200 (n. 10)
Kintpuash, 1. See also Captain Jack
Klamath Basin, 2, 6, 8, 15, 16, 17, 18,
 23, 25, 26, 29, 34, 41, 45, 47, 54, 107,
 113, 115, 117, 118, 122, 124, 128, 129,
 130–32, 139, 168, 170, 185
Klamath County Board of Immigration,
 117
Klamath County Museum, 10, 107,
Klamath Development Company, 122
Klamath Falls, Ore. See Linkville, Ore.
Klamath Falls Evening Herald, 174, 175
Klamath Falls Express, 114, 131
Klamath Indian Reservation, 2, 3, 17, 32,
 37, 40, 43, 45, 46, 72, 87, 91, 92, 93,
 103, 106, 115, 119, 120–23, 126, 128,
 130–31, 135, 152–53, 155, 157, 159,
 171, 173, 193
Klamath Marsh, 17, 46, 119
Klamath Memorial Association, 190
Klamath people, 2, 4, 6, 16, 47, 59, 69,
 70, 87, 88, 91, 114, 119, 120, 121, 127,
 135, 152, 153, 160, 185, 190, 192, 193
Klamath Project, 128, 129
Klamath Republican, 130
Klamath Restoration Act, 189, 192
Klamath Termination Act, 186, 189,
 190–91, 194
Klamath terminology, 199 (n. 1)

Klamath Tribes, 87, 106, 127, 135, 171, 186, 190–91, 219 (n. 11)

Klima, Alan, 195

Knapp, Oliver, 37

Koalakaka, 4

Kóketat, 2, 32, 199. *See also* Lost River

Konkle, Maureen, 108, 139

Konoki, Ruben, 153

Koppos, Adeline, 158

Koppos, John, 159

Kropp, Phoebe, 177–78

Kuckup, Albert, 155, 159

Lalakes, Solomon, 153

Langell Valley, *17*, 64

Lass, Andrew, 182

Lava Beds landscape, 53–54, 165, 169, 171, 182

Lava Beds National Monument, 1, *5*, 7, 162, 171, 179, *180*, 183, 184, 187–90, 192, 196, 217 (n. 57)

Lewis, E. J., 68

Life amongst the Modocs, 99–101, 209 (n. 51). *See also* Miller, Joaquin

Lincoln, Abraham, 9, 37, 68

Linksuilex, Charles, 151

Linkville, Ore., 32, 118, 121, 123, 124, 128, 169; renaming of, 124, 202 (n. 8)

Little John, 65

London, Jack, 21

Los Angeles Times, 138, 190

Lost River, 2, 3, 32, 33, 42, 43, 64, 70, 71. *See also* Kóketat

Lost River, Battle of, 70, 137, 184

Lost River Valley, 35, 37, 39, 44, 45, 46, 47, 48, 118, 128, 132, 172

Lumber industry, 25, 106, 115, 118, 122, 123–25, 127, 128, 130, 131, 139, 191

Máklaks, 16

Malheur River Indian Reservation, 84, 141

Malin, Ore., *17*, 130, 184–85

Manifest Destiny. *See* Settler colonialism: Manifest Destiny

Marias Massacre, 34

Marketplaces: land development, 139; media, 49, 52–53, 82, 91, 107, 109; memory, 14–15, 20, 21, 22, 23, 24, 31, 43, 78, 87, 138, 150, 160, 186, 188, 189, 195, 196, 197; newspapers, 30, 31, 37, 74; of violence, 14, 22, 44, 160. *See also* Memory

McGowan, A. W., 141

McKay, Donald, 59, 62, 84–85, 104, 141, 151

McNary, Charles, 144, 153

Meacham, Alfred: and Alfred B. Meacham Lecture Company, 82, 83–93, *89*, 96, 98, 102, 107, 134; as member of peace commission, 3, 4, 39, 40, 41, 44, 48, 69, 81; and Toby Riddle, 95, 103; *Wigwam and War-path; or, The Royal Chief in Chains*, 85, 97

Medford, Ore., 8

Medicine Lake Highlands, 4

Memory: commemoration, 20, 21, 136, 162, 183, 188; forgetting, 26, 115, 139, 182, 188, 189, 194, 195, 196; historical, 3, 23, 31, 109, 164, 195; landscape, 171, 174, 175, 183, 187, 196; memori-als, *5*, 6, 21, 25, 26, 67, 139, 162–67, 179, 184–88, 189, 192, 194–96. *See also* Lava Beds landscape

Mercer Survey, 119–21

Mexico, 34, 58, 62, 177

Military Road. *See* Oregon Central Military Road

Miller, Joaquin, 99–103; *Life amongst the Modocs*, 99–101, 209 (n. 51); *Song of the Sierra*, 101; *The Tale of the Tall Alcalde*, 99

Minneapolis Morning Tribune, 138

Móatokni É-ush, 2, 16, 29. *See also* Tule Lake

Móatokni máklaks, 16. *See also* Modoc people

Modernity: claims to, 25, 114–15, 122, 131, 139, 183; constructions of,

114–15; Indians and, 75, 117, 137, 172, 181; naming and, 132

Modoc Expedition. *See* Crosby Expedition

Modoc peace commission, 3, 4, 24, 31, 38, 39–41, 42, 44, 45, 46, 48, 49, 50, 56, 57, 64, 71, 72, 81, 83, 86, 96, 100, 134, 165, 173

Modoc people, 2, 4, 6, 14, 16, 18, 33, 37, 42, 47, 52, 56, 67, 70, 71, 75, 78, 81, 87, 97, 99, 137, 171, 188, 190, 191, 192–94, 197; appropriations of, 118, 132; Cottonwood band, 63; Hot Creek band, 63; Lost River band, 63; representations of, 170, 182

Modoc territory, 1, 44

Modoc War: and American expansion, 3, 18, 130–32, 183, 187; Indigenous histories of, 2–3, 82, 87, 103, 107, 135, 137–38, 160, 161, 171, 173, 191–93; legal legacy of, 76–78; memorials to, 5–6, 26, 113–16, 162–64, 177, 178–79, 184, 186, 190; representations of, 4, 7, 14–15, 18, 23–25, 31, 34–35, 37, 38, 43, 46, 50, 52, 56–58, 61, 73–75, 82–85, 88, 95–96, 98–101, 107, 109, 134, 136, 139, 165, 181–82, 185, 186, 187, 194, 196; as spectacle, 8, 62, 168, 170, 172, 174; veterans of, 141–43, 150–57, 160–61

Montoya v. United States, 147

Mooch, 65

Mosenkosket, 121

Mott, Lucretia, 34

Mount Shasta, 4, *17*, 100

Muir, John, 169

Multicultural revisionism, 188, 189, 192

Murray, Keith, 70

Nation, 138

National Indian War Veterans, 25, 148, 151; collaboration with other organizations, 148

National Park Service, 2, 6, 7, 26, 178, 183, 187, 192

Native Daughters of the Golden West, 149, 162, *163*, 177–80

Newlands Reclamation Act, 127–28

New York Herald, 8, 30, 31, 41, 43, 44, 45, 54

New York Times, 8, 30, 34, 36, 37, 53, 56, 57, 69

New York Tribune, 30, 37, 67, 102

Norrgard, Chantal, 173

Northern Paiute people, 16. *See also* Yahooskin Paiute people

Odeneal, Thomas B.: as editor of *Portland Daily Bulletin*, 46–48; as superintendent of Indian affairs, 32, 46

Office of Indian Affairs, 38, 39, 40, 119, 120, 123, 143, 146, 147

Oklahoma, 2, 44, 87, 103, 137, 173, 194, 196, 209 (n. 62)

Oregon Central Military Road, 119, 122, 126, 127, 130

Oregon Historical Society, 149

Oregonian, 138

Oregon State Board of Immigration, 116

Oregon Statesmen, 36

Oregon Volunteers, 64, 65

Owhy, Ike, 155, 160, 215 (n. 84)

Paiute peoples, 6, 88, 89, 141, 170, 185, 191

Parker, Ely S., 34, 151

Patriotism, 113, 114, 144, 177

Peace commission. *See* Modoc peace commission

Peace Policy, 34, 35, 47, 54, 55, 56, 67. *See also* Indian policy

Pensions, 24, 81, 83, 96, 103, 141–45, 147–61, 207 (n. 1); and kinship, 159, 160

Phillips, Wendell, 34, 86

Pierce, Walter M., 153

Pitt, John, 159

Pitt River people, 4

Pocahontas: life of, 98; in media, 97, 98, 99; as savior, 81, 95, 101; and Toby

Riddle, 82, 93, 96–97, 102, 104, 107, 109

Pony, 65

Portland, Ore., 12, 36, 52, 84, 116, 125, 126, 149, 162

Portland Daily Bulletin, 46

Prater, John, 146

Quaker Policy. *See* Peace Policy

Quapaw Reservation, 86

Raibmon, Paige, 172

Railroads: California Northeastern Railway, 125; construction of, 25, 125, 130, 139; Klamath Lake Railroad, 125; promotion of, 115, 116, 122, 131, 168; Southern Pacific Railroad, 116, 122, 125, 179; Union Pacific Railroad, 125

Reconstruction, 15, 24, 57, 58, 118, 195, 206 (n. 2). *See also* Civil War

Redemptive violence. *See* Violence: redemptive

Redpath, James, 90, 92

Red Power movement, 191

Republican Party, 35, 36, 37, 50, 54, 124, 206 (n. 2); and pensions, 143, 150

Rickard, Clinton, 152

Riddle, Frank, 44, 68–69, 88, *89*, 92, 93, 94, 95, 134, 209 (n. 1)

Riddle, Jeff, 88, *89*, 92–93, 102, 134, *138*, 139; *The Indian History of the Modoc War*, 136, 138; as tour guide, 172

Riddle, Toby, 24, 44, 69, 73, *89*, 90, 92–93, 95–97, 99, 101, 103, 107, 108–9, 134, 209 (n. 1); as Winema, 82–84, 86, 88, 93, 95–96, 99, 102, 104, 107, 108, 110

Rogers, Graham, 146

Roork, John R., 119

Roosevelt, Theodore, 21, 127, 134

Rosborough, Alexander M., 40, 44, 46

Sacajawea, 82

Sacramento, Calif., 2, 10, 87, 88, 179, 200 (n. 10)

Sacramento Bee, 178

Sacramento Daily Union, 33

Sacramento Record, 69, 90

St. Valentine's Day Treaty, 37, 202 (n. 29)

Sand Butte, 59

Sand Creek Massacre, 3

San Francisco Call, 8, 128, 170

San Francisco Chronicle, 8, 29, 36, 37, 40, 44, 45, 50, 56, 63, 75, 98, 166, 170, 181, 182

San Francisco Examiner, 114

Scarface Charley, 33, 69, 87, 88, *89. See also* Chĭkclĭkam-Lupalkuelátko

Schofield, John McAlister, 48

Schonchin, Lynn, 191, 192, 195, 196

Schonchin, Peter, 172–73

Schonchin Butte, 4

Schonchin John, 10, 42, 68, 71, 96, 173, 192; execution of, 9, 15, 73, 194

Settler colonialism: and colonialism, 15, 18, 23, 25, 38, 75, 109, 136, 139, 145, 151, 161, 164–65, 170, 182, 185, 188–89, 196; and commodification of Indigenous cultures, 22, 95, 108; through consumption, 22, 110, 116, 168; definition of, 15–16; and empire, 15, 19, 77, 78, 116, 122–23, 166, 176; Manifest Destiny, 19, 44, 71, 75, 81, 139, 140, 163, 194

Shacknasty Jim, 3, 64, 69, 87, 88–89, *89*

Shaler, W. H., 146

Shasta people, 4, 170

Shawnee people, 146

Sheepy Ridge, 4, 5

Sherman, William Tecumseh, 48, 62, 64

Shkeitko, 3. *See also* Shacknasty Jim

Shore, Julia, 152

Siemens, John, 113

Sinnott, Nicholas J., 150, 153

Sioux, 9, 92

Siskiyou News, 177

Siwash John, 151

Skellock, Thomas, 152, 153, 159, 160

Skogen, Larry C., 145, 146

Slolux, 9, 68, 72, 73

Slotkin, Richard, 31
Smiley, Kate, 150, 152
Smith, Edward, 65, 90
Smithsonian Institute, 11, 201 (n. 14)
Solomon, Sam, 153, 159
Stanley, Henry Morton, 31, 42, 43
Steamboat Frank, 63, 64, 69, 73, 87, 88, *89*
Steamboats, 104, 105, 128, 131, 132
Steele, Elijah, 37–38, 40, 44–45, 68
Steiwer, Frederick, 153, 155, 159
Stern, Theodore, 135, 157
Stronghold. *See* Captain Jack's
    Stronghold
Sturken, Marita, 20
Supreme Court, U.S., 66, 126, 127, 147
Sutter's Fort, 10
Sycan Valley, 119, 120, 121

Tahee Jack, 65
*Thirty-One Years on the Plains and in
    the Mountains*, 133, 134, 136. *See also*
    Drannan, William
Thomas, Eleazer, 4, 9, 45, 48–50, 52–54,
    59, 66, 69, 74, 77, 83, 165
Thomas, Jacob, 156, 159, 160
Timber. *See* Lumber industry
Tourism: automobile, 25, 26, 174, 175,
    176, 177, 179, 184, 195; Indians and,
    168, 169, 172; mementos, 10, 11, 12,
    14, 200 (n. 10); souvenirs, 10, 12, 14,
    20, 131
Traveling Indian shows, 14, 20, 24,
    82–85, 87, 88, 96, 98, 101–4, 107, 194
Treaty of 1864, 2, 32, 47, 119, 193
Trenton Gazette, 43
Tule Lake, 2, 4, *17*, 29, 41, 44, 45, 48, 64,
    106, 126, 128, *129*, 130, 162, 168, 169,
    171. *See also* Móatokni É-ush
Turner, Frederick Jackson, 21, 134

U.S. Army, 1, 2, 3, 4, 5, 6, 10, 25, 29, 34,
    35, 39, 40, 42, 44, 48, 49, 59, 60, 62,
    63, 64, 66, 77, 95, 121, 132, 134, 140,
    141, 143, 150, 160, 165, 187, 188, 189,
    192, 193

U.S. Army Medical Museum, 11
U.S. Army military tribunal, 52, 77, 78
University of California Museum of
    Anthropology, 10

Violence: atonement for, 189, 195, 196;
    as criminal, 51–53, 77–78, 117, 135,
    184–86; of equivalence, 195–96, 197;
    and genocide, 18; history of, 3, 6, 7,
    142, 143, 145, 186; and innocence,
    19–20, 38, 52, 62, 75, 109, 139, 195;
    legacies of, 23–26, 172, 173, 174, 188;
    and museums, 10; narratives of, 24,
    83, 96, 97, 109, 116, 117, 118, 131,
    132, 135, 136, 137, 139, 161–70, 177,
    182–89, 195; racial, 24, 32, 47–48,
    57, 74; redemptive, 15, 23, 166, 182;
    reenactments of, 114–15; and settler
    colonialism, 15–16, 25, 38, 109, 143,
    151; U.S.-Indian, 3, 7, 23–26, 33,
    35, 41, 43–44, 49, 51, 53–54, 56, 70,
    77–78, 100, 119, 132, 187, 188, 192,
    193; vigilante, 12, 14, 16, 65, 137, 189;
    and writing history, 18–19

Walker, Ruben, 153, 159
Walpapis people, 16
Wama Louie, 141, 155, 160
War Crimes Act of 1996, 76
War Department, U.S., 59, 143, 146, 149
Warm Springs Indian Agency, 152
Warm Springs Indians, 4, 6, 59, 60, 62,
    63, 84, 85, 104, 151, 154, 160, 179,
    180
Warrior, Robert, 139
Washump, David, 159
Webb, George, 145, 151
Wells, Harry, 117
West, Elliott, 58
West, Walter, 152
Wheaton, Frank, 9, 11, 29, 59, 134
Whistler, Ursula, 153, 156, 157, 159
White, George A., 150
White, Stewart Edward, 21
Whitman, Marcus and Narcissa, 16

Williams, George H., 66, 77, 206 (nn. 2, 3)
Williams, James, 74
Willow Creek, 5, 64
Wilson, Alex, 159
Winema. *See* Riddle, Toby
Winema National Forest, 106
Winners of the West, 145, 151
Winneshet, James, 159
Wounded Knee, Massacre at, 3, 82
Wright, Ben, 18, 42, 46, 56

Yahooskin, Nancy John, 152, 157
Yahooskin Paiute people, 2, 193. *See also*
    Northern Paiute people
Yoo, John C., 76–78
Yreka, Calif., 8, 10, 12, 29, 33, 37, 46, 88,
    137
Yreka Journal, 10, 50, 63, 67
Yreka Union, 43, 67
Yulalóna, 32, 202 (n. 8). *See also*
    Linkville, Ore.